NOV 2 4 2014
12-15 Ø
10.18 (4)

Ordinary

by Rob Williams & D'Israeli

Ordinary
by Rob Williams & D'Israeli

ORDINARY
ISBN: 9781782760092

Published by Titan Comics
A division of Titan Publishing Group Ltd.
144 Southwark St.
London
SE1 0UP

A CIP catalogue record for this title is available from the British Library.

First edition: December 2014.

10 9 8 7 6 5 4 3 2 1

Printed in China.
Titan Comics. TC0061

Previously printed in Judge Dredd Megazine #340-345

Rob would like to thank: Matt Brooker, Steve White and all at Titan, Matt Smith and all at Rebellion, Scott Agostoni, Laurence Campbell, JV Chamary, James Harren, Edmund Bagwell, Ben Oliver, Brian Ching, Michael Atiyeh, Simon Gurr, Brendan McCarthy, Neil Googe, Dom Reardon, Henry Flint, Alison Sampson, Ruth Redmond, Ale Aragon, Mark Buckingham, Warren Ellis, Garth Ennis, Al Ewing, Paul Cornell, Rick Remender.

Matt would like to thank Lynn: right back at you, *mutatis mutandis.*

Rob: For Sam, Elliott and Edie. "I had this dream."

Matt & Rob: To Matt Smith: with heartfelt thanks for your patience and support, without which *Ordinary* would never have been completed.

TITAN COMICS

EDITOR Steve White **DESIGNER** Russ Seal

TITAN COMICS EDITORIAL Andrew James, Gabriela Houston, Tom Williams
PRODUCTION SUPERVISORS Jackie Flook, Peter James
PRODUCTION CONTROLLER Obi Onuora
ART DIRECTOR Oz Browne
STUDIO MANAGER Emma Smith
CIRCULATION MANAGER Steve Tothill
SENIOR MARKETING & PRESS OFFICER Owen Johnson
MARKETING MANAGER Ricky Claydon
ADVERTISING MANAGER Michelle Fairlamb
PUBLISHING MANAGER Darryl Tothill
PUBLISHING DIRECTOR Chris Teather
OPERATIONS DIRECTOR Leigh Baulch
EXECUTIVE DIRECTOR Vivian Cheung
PUBLISHER Nick Landau

DISTRIBUTION: Direct Sales Diamond Comic Distributors

WWW.TITAN-COMICS.COM
Become a fan on Facebook.com/comicstitan
Follow us on Twitter @ComicsTitan

For information on advertising, contact:
adinfo@titanemail.com
or call +44 20 7620 0200

TITAN
COMICS

What did you think of this book? We love to hear from our readers. Please email us at: readercomments@titanemail.com, or write to us at the above address.

To receive news, competitions, and exclusive offers online, please sign up for the Titan Comics newsletter on our website: www.titan-comics.com

AN INTRODUCTION

It's an ordinary story. We've seen it done a few times before. A world in which everyone becomes special except our protagonist. It's often said that there are a limited number of stories to be told. What makes them worth our attention is *how* they're told. *Ordinary* is not ordinary. The sheer human wonder of its execution elevates it to best-in-class.

I've known and worked with D'Israeli for, god, half my adult life now. I am continually shocked and delighted at how he seems to keep growing with each new work. It's like there's no end to his gift. The miracles of his storytelling, the sheer beauty of his line and colors, and, yes, the worsening insanity that allows him to apply hilariously real body language to a giant black bear.

This is my first experience of Rob Williams' work, I'm sad to say, and I was immediately struck by how unafraid it is. It's an extremely delicate operation, to portray a "loser" protagonist and give real, grim texture to the depth of his human failure and still have him come out as somehow sympathetic. Williams doesn't soften any aspect of the guy's loserdom. A lesser writer would have lost the reader or had the reader relish the protagonist's discomfort.

Together, they produce a visually dazzling, emotionally complex piece of work that I recommend to you as one of the best short fictions of the year. I hope you have as much fun with it as I did.

Warren Ellis
England
June 2014

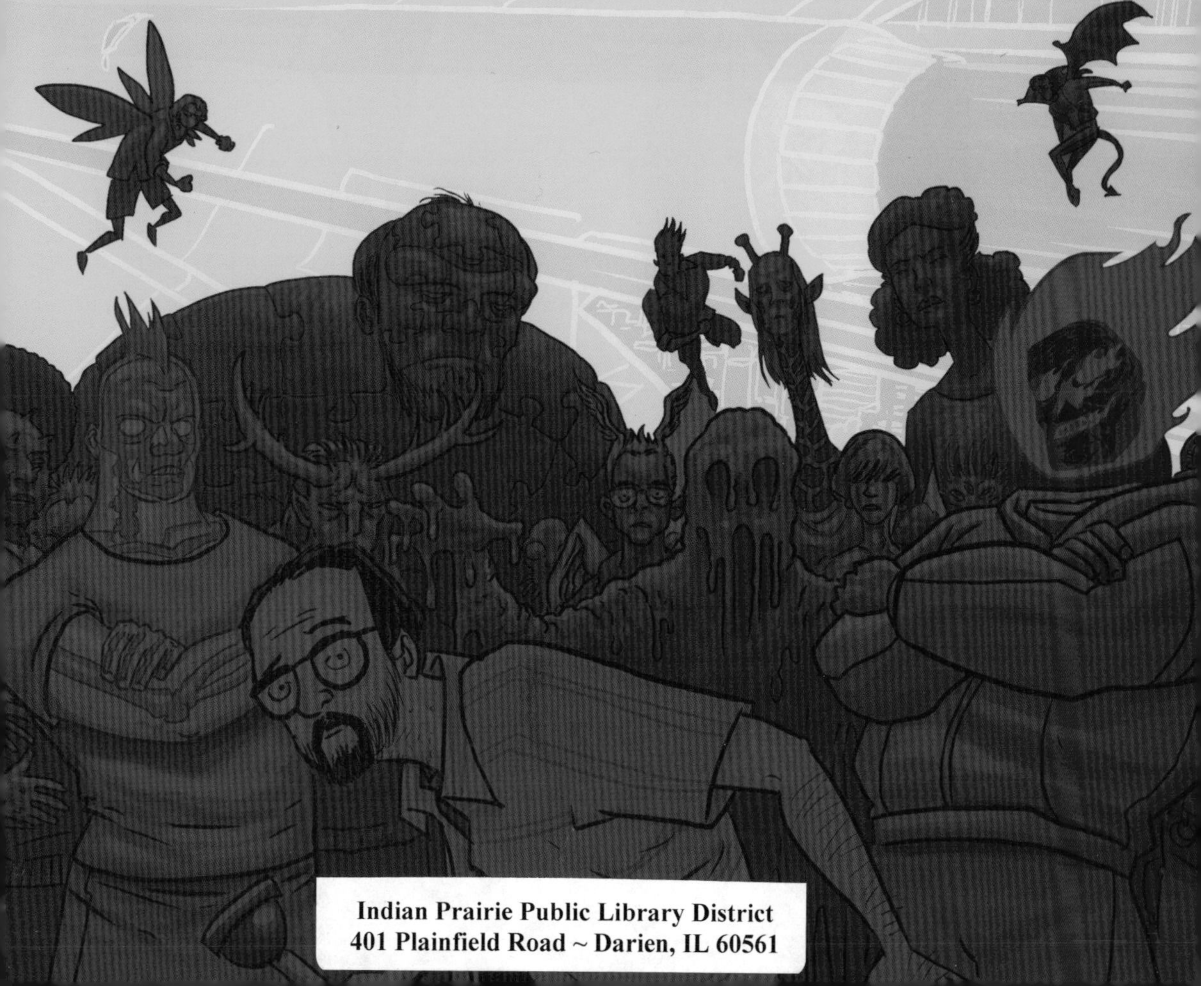

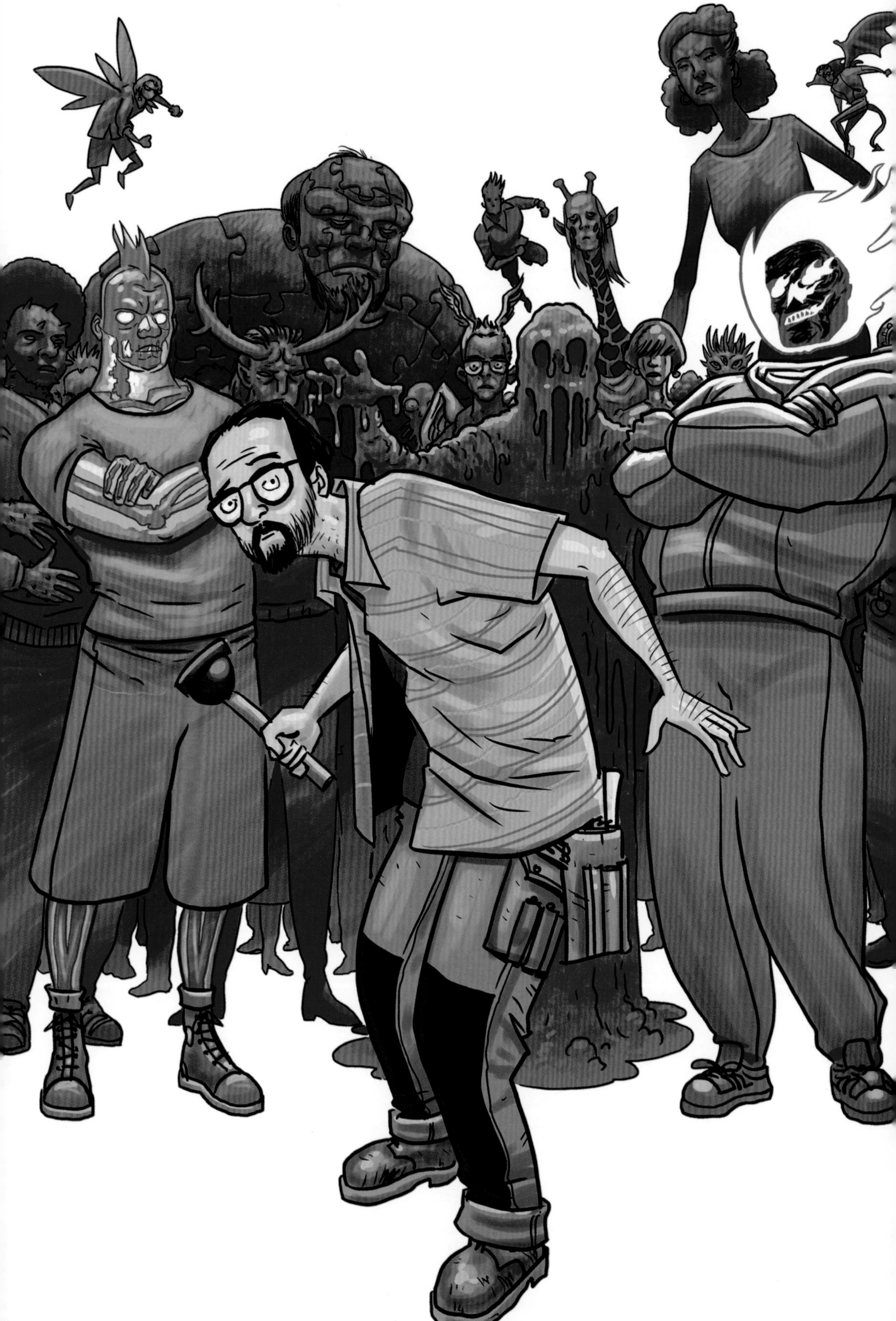

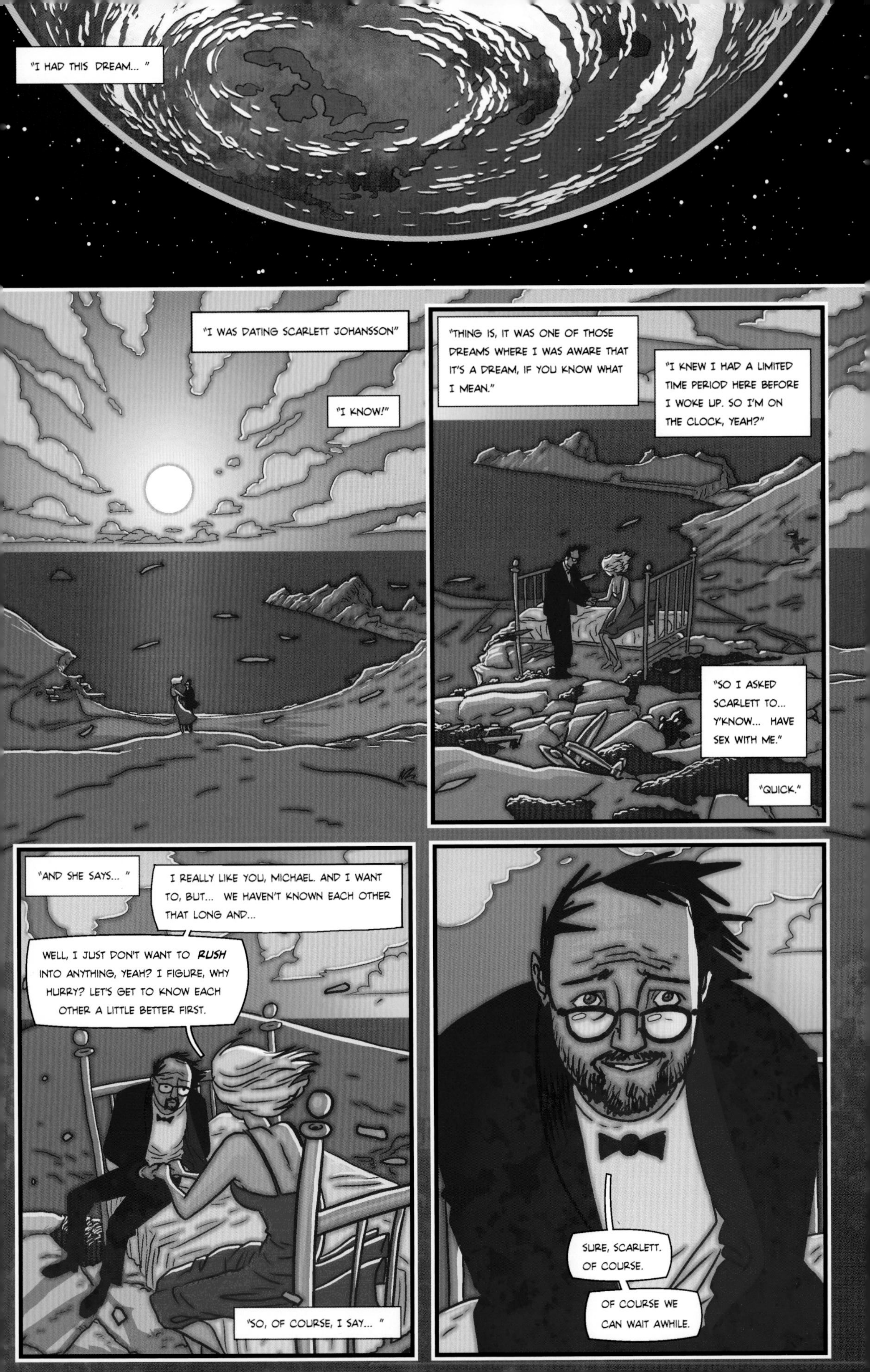
"I HAD THIS DREAM... "
"I WAS DATING SCARLETT JOHANSSON"
"I KNOW!"
"THING IS, IT WAS ONE OF THOSE DREAMS WHERE I WAS AWARE THAT IT'S A DREAM, IF YOU KNOW WHAT I MEAN."
"I KNEW I HAD A LIMITED TIME PERIOD HERE BEFORE I WOKE UP. SO I'M ON THE CLOCK, YEAH?"
"SO I ASKED SCARLETT TO... Y'KNOW... HAVE SEX WITH ME."
"QUICK."
"AND SHE SAYS... "
I REALLY LIKE YOU, MICHAEL. AND I WANT TO, BUT... WE HAVEN'T KNOWN EACH OTHER THAT LONG AND...
WELL, I JUST DON'T WANT TO RUSH INTO ANYTHING, YEAH? I FIGURE, WHY HURRY? LET'S GET TO KNOW EACH OTHER A LITTLE BETTER FIRST.
"SO, OF COURSE, I SAY... "
SURE, SCARLETT. OF COURSE.
OF COURSE WE CAN WAIT AWHILE.

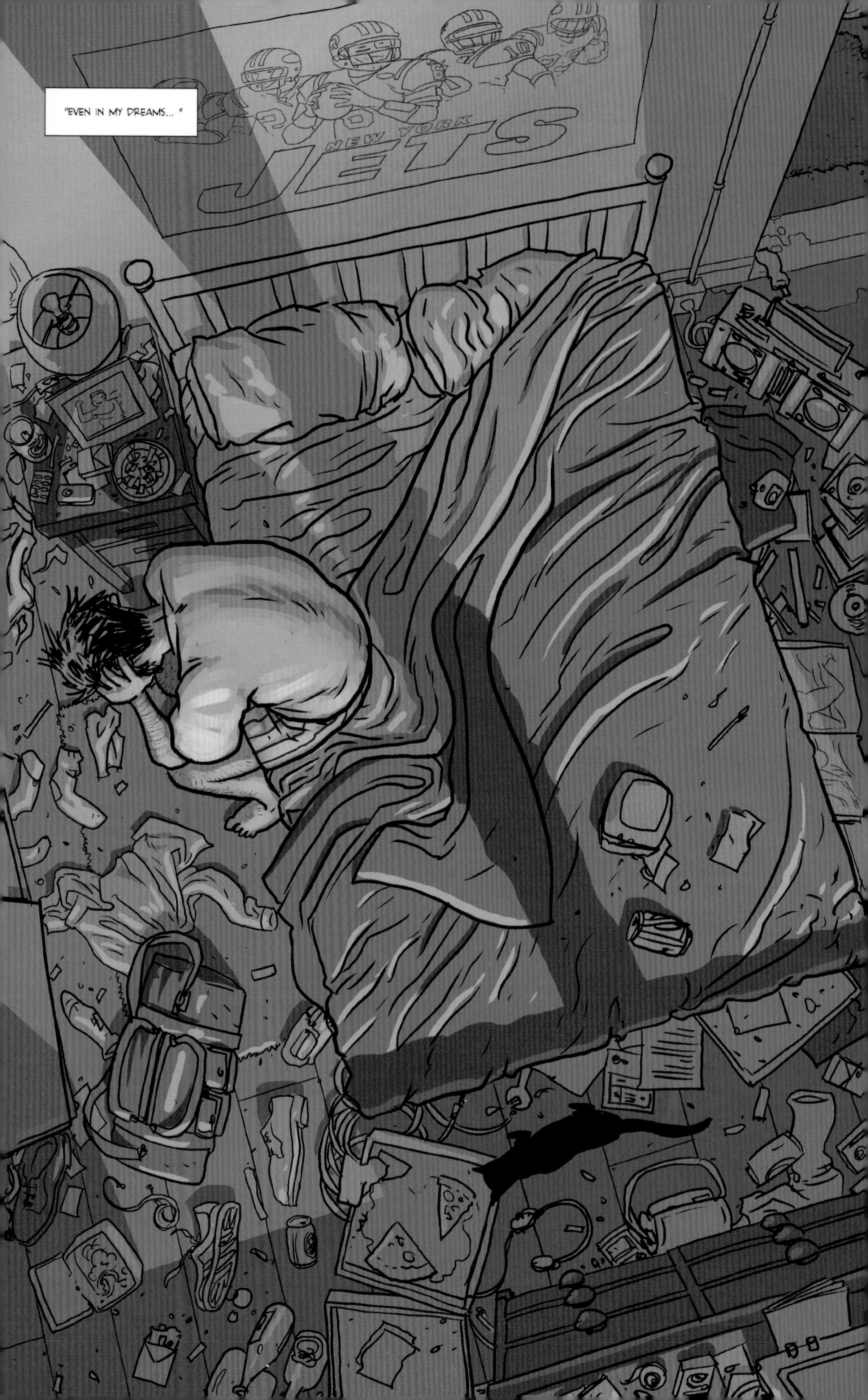
"EVEN IN MY DREAMS... "
NEW YORK
JETS

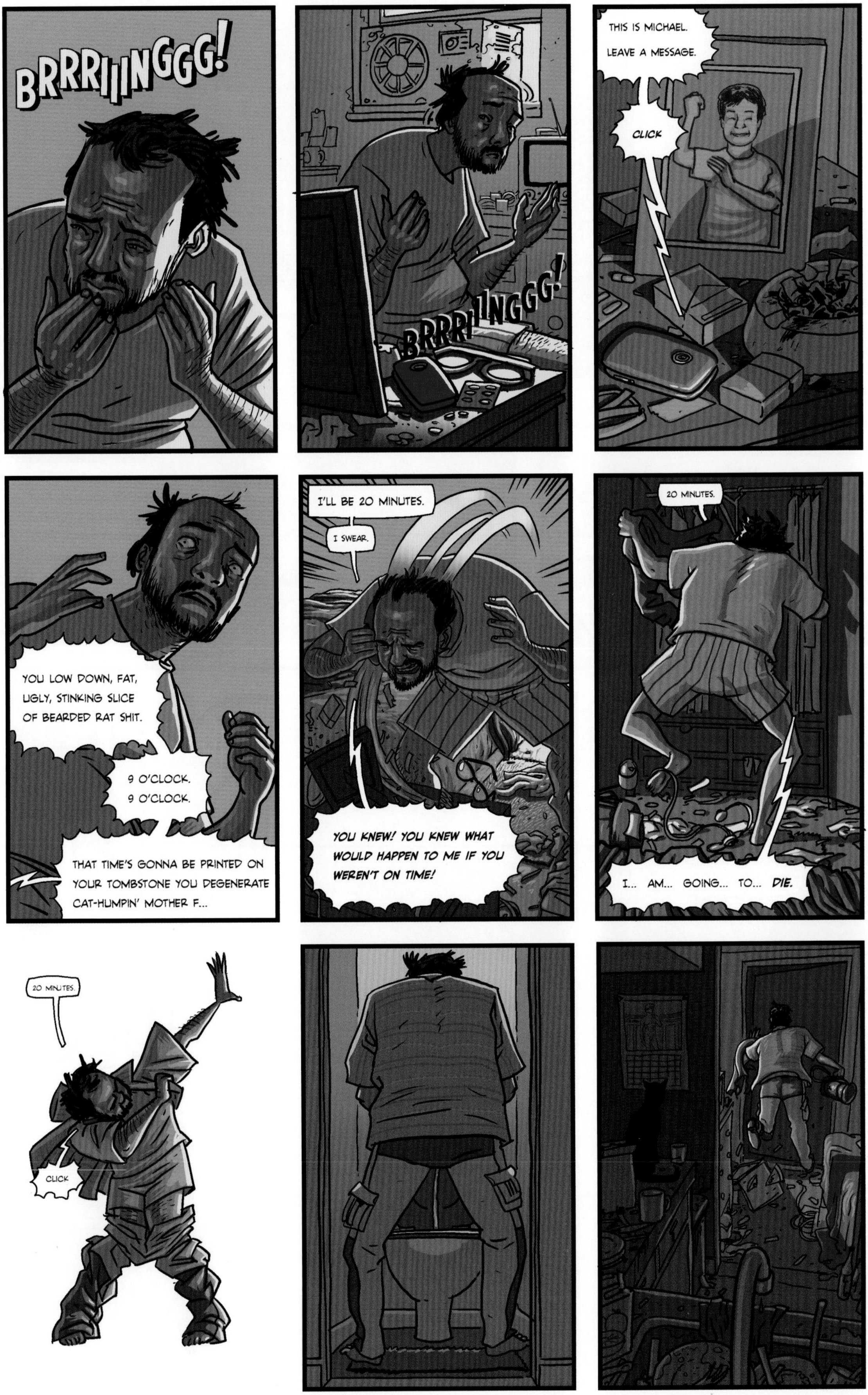
BRRRIIIINGGG!
BRRRIIINGGG!
THIS IS MICHAEL.
LEAVE A MESSAGE.
CLICK
YOU LOW DOWN, FAT, UGLY, STINKING SLICE OF BEARDED RAT SHIT.
9 O'CLOCK.
9 O'CLOCK.
THAT TIME'S GONNA BE PRINTED ON YOUR TOMBSTONE YOU DEGENERATE CAT-HUMPIN' MOTHER F...
I'LL BE 20 MINUTES.
I SWEAR.
YOU KNEW! YOU KNEW WHAT WOULD HAPPEN TO ME IF YOU WEREN'T ON TIME!
20 MINUTES.
I... AM... GOING... TO... DIE.
20 MINUTES.
CLICK

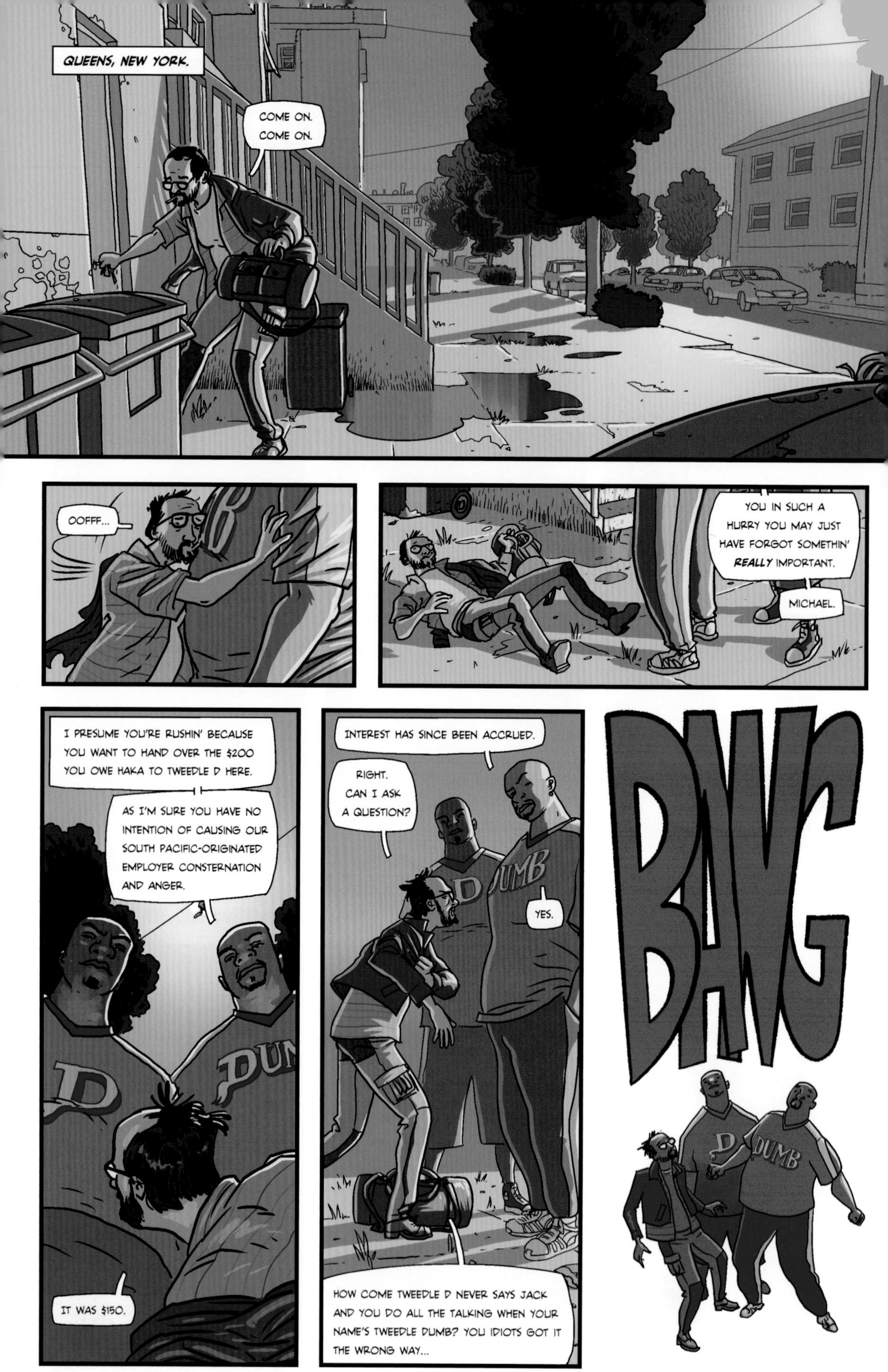
QUEENS, NEW YORK.
COME ON. COME ON.
OOFFF...
YOU IN SUCH A HURRY YOU MAY JUST HAVE FORGOT SOMETHIN' **REALLY** IMPORTANT.
MICHAEL.
I PRESUME YOU'RE RUSHIN' BECAUSE YOU WANT TO HAND OVER THE $200 YOU OWE HAKA TO TWEEDLE D HERE.
AS I'M SURE YOU HAVE NO INTENTION OF CAUSING OUR SOUTH PACIFIC-ORIGINATED EMPLOYER CONSTERNATION AND ANGER.
IT WAS $150.
INTEREST HAS SINCE BEEN ACCRUED.
RIGHT. CAN I ASK A QUESTION?
YES.
HOW COME TWEEDLE D NEVER SAYS JACK AND YOU DO ALL THE TALKING WHEN YOUR NAME'S TWEEDLE DUMB? YOU IDIOTS GOT IT THE WRONG WAY...
BANG

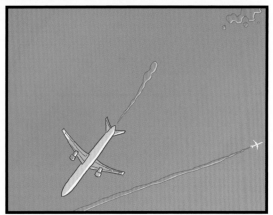

DID... DID YOU JUST SEE THAT SHIT?

THAT... THAT WAS SOME WEIRD -ASS SHI...

AH... HA!

YOU CAN TALK. I KNEW IT.

MICHAEL...

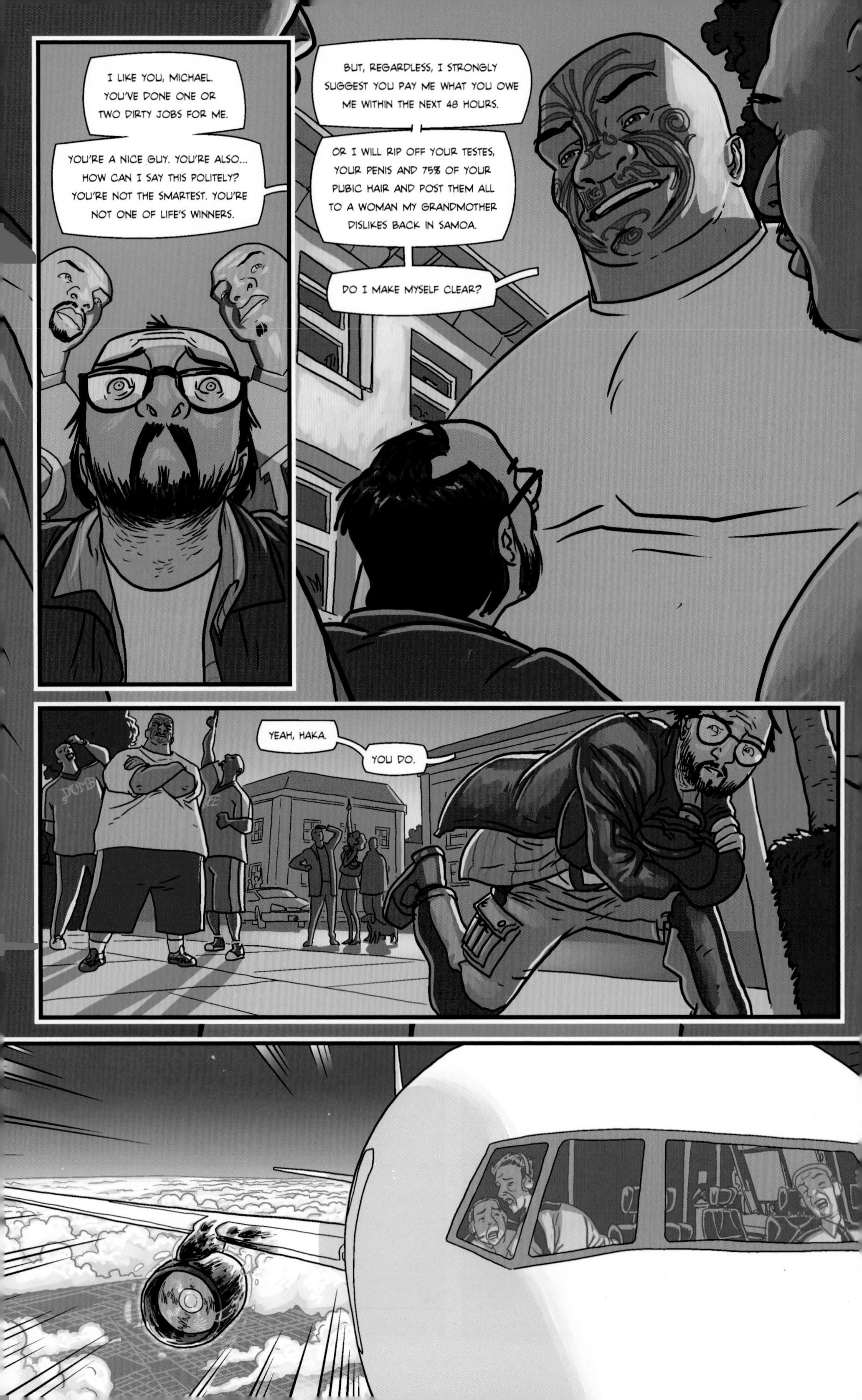
I LIKE YOU, MICHAEL. YOU'VE DONE ONE OR TWO DIRTY JOBS FOR ME.
YOU'RE A NICE GUY. YOU'RE ALSO... HOW CAN I SAY THIS POLITELY? YOU'RE NOT THE SMARTEST. YOU'RE NOT ONE OF LIFE'S WINNERS.
BUT, REGARDLESS, I STRONGLY SUGGEST YOU PAY ME WHAT YOU OWE ME WITHIN THE NEXT 48 HOURS.
OR I WILL RIP OFF YOUR TESTES, YOUR PENIS AND 75% OF YOUR PUBIC HAIR AND POST THEM ALL TO A WOMAN MY GRANDMOTHER DISLIKES BACK IN SAMOA.
DO I MAKE MYSELF CLEAR?
YEAH, HAKA.
YOU DO.
DUMB

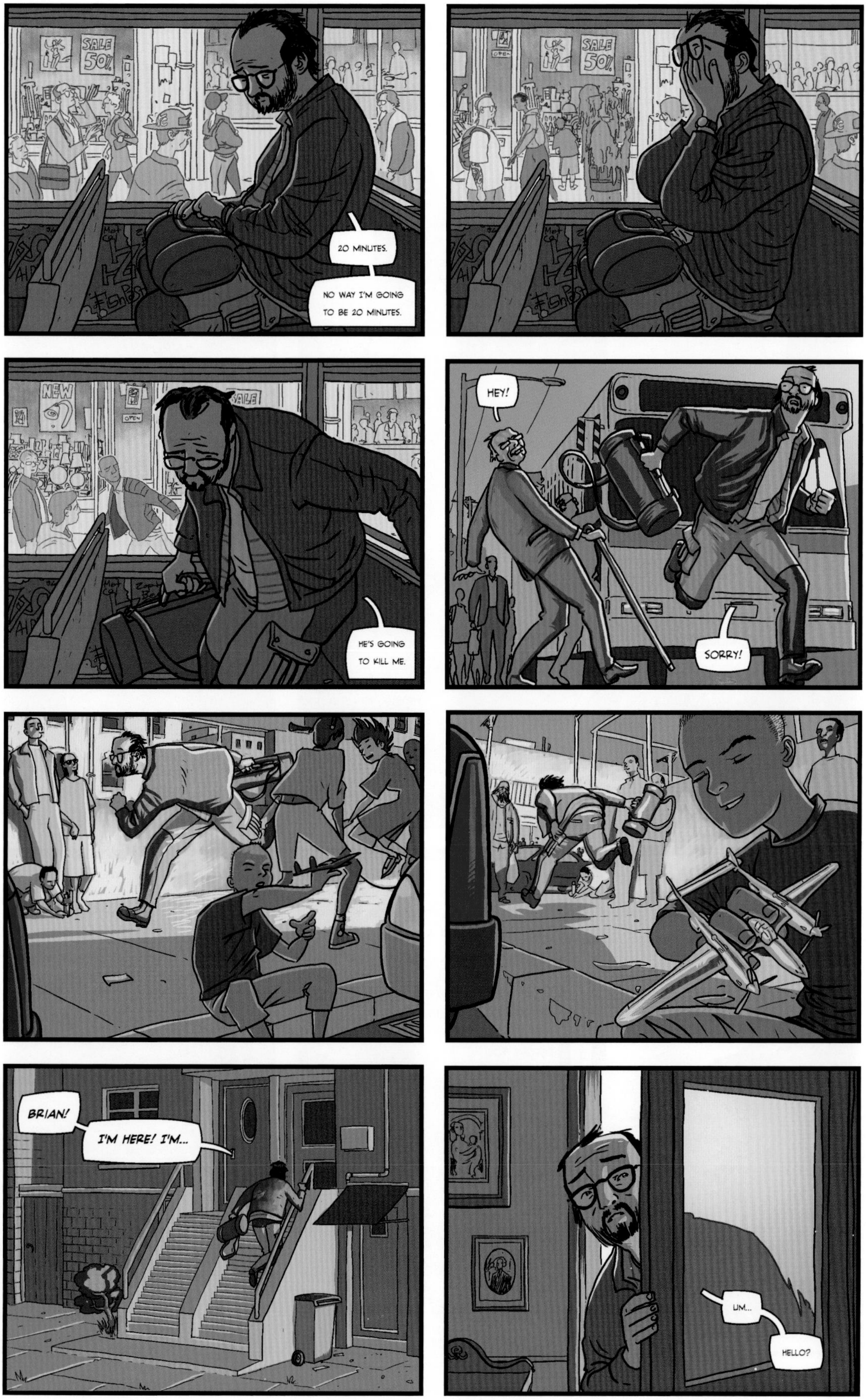

20 MINUTES.
NO WAY I'M GOING TO BE 20 MINUTES.
HE'S GOING TO KILL ME.
HEY!
SORRY!
BRIAN!
I'M HERE! I'M...
UM...
HELLO?

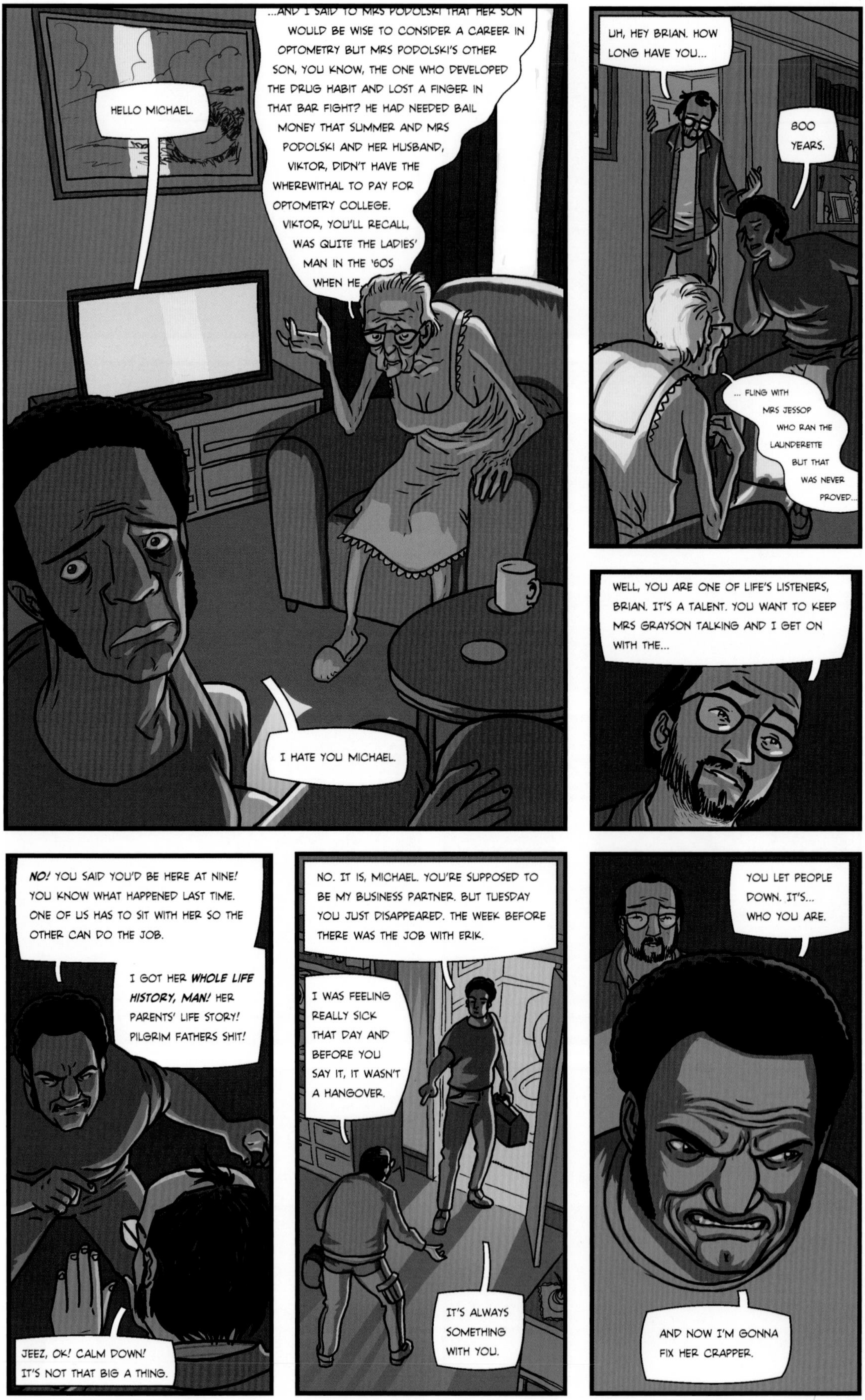
HELLO MICHAEL.
...AND I SAID TO MRS PODOLSKI THAT HER SON WOULD BE WISE TO CONSIDER A CAREER IN OPTOMETRY BUT MRS PODOLSKI'S OTHER SON, YOU KNOW, THE ONE WHO DEVELOPED THE DRUG HABIT AND LOST A FINGER IN THAT BAR FIGHT? HE HAD NEEDED BAIL MONEY THAT SUMMER AND MRS PODOLSKI AND HER HUSBAND, VIKTOR, DIDN'T HAVE THE WHEREWITHAL TO PAY FOR OPTOMETRY COLLEGE. VIKTOR, YOU'LL RECALL, WAS QUITE THE LADIES' MAN IN THE '60S WHEN HE...
I HATE YOU MICHAEL.
UH, HEY BRIAN. HOW LONG HAVE YOU...
800 YEARS.
... FLING WITH MRS JESSOP WHO RAN THE LAUNDERETTE BUT THAT WAS NEVER PROVED...
WELL, YOU ARE ONE OF LIFE'S LISTENERS, BRIAN. IT'S A TALENT. YOU WANT TO KEEP MRS GRAYSON TALKING AND I GET ON WITH THE...
NO! YOU SAID YOU'D BE HERE AT NINE! YOU KNOW WHAT HAPPENED LAST TIME. ONE OF US HAS TO SIT WITH HER SO THE OTHER CAN DO THE JOB.
I GOT HER WHOLE LIFE HISTORY, MAN! HER PARENTS' LIFE STORY! PILGRIM FATHERS SHIT!
JEEZ, OK! CALM DOWN! IT'S NOT THAT BIG A THING.
NO. IT IS, MICHAEL. YOU'RE SUPPOSED TO BE MY BUSINESS PARTNER. BUT TUESDAY YOU JUST DISAPPEARED. THE WEEK BEFORE THERE WAS THE JOB WITH ERIK.
I WAS FEELING REALLY SICK THAT DAY AND BEFORE YOU SAY IT, IT WASN'T A HANGOVER.
IT'S ALWAYS SOMETHING WITH YOU.
YOU LET PEOPLE DOWN. IT'S... WHO YOU ARE.
AND NOW I'M GONNA FIX HER CRAPPER.

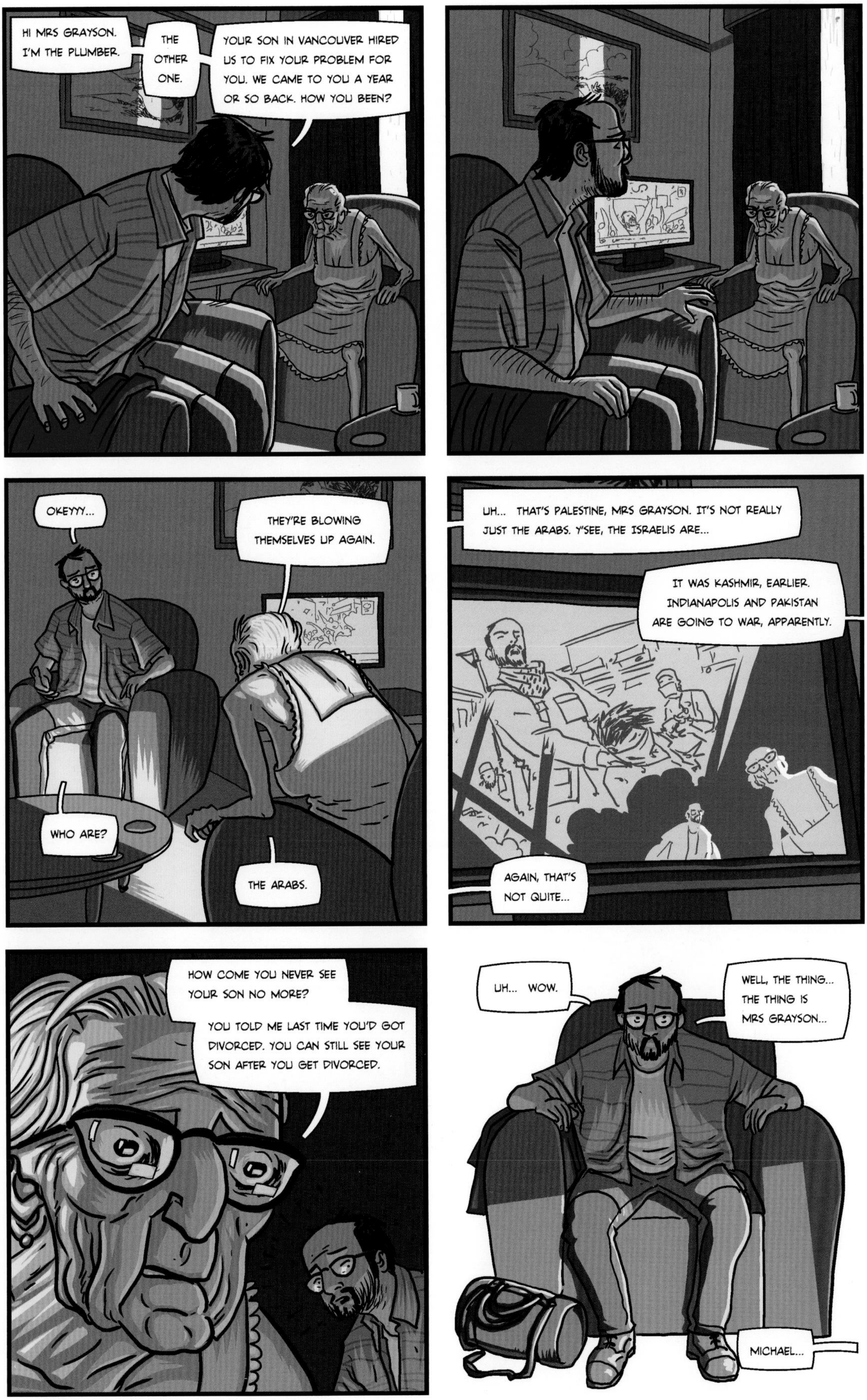
HI MRS GRAYSON. I'M THE PLUMBER.
THE OTHER ONE.
YOUR SON IN VANCOUVER HIRED US TO FIX YOUR PROBLEM FOR YOU. WE CAME TO YOU A YEAR OR SO BACK. HOW YOU BEEN?
OKEYYY...
THEY'RE BLOWING THEMSELVES UP AGAIN.
WHO ARE?
THE ARABS.
UH... THAT'S PALESTINE, MRS GRAYSON. IT'S NOT REALLY JUST THE ARABS. Y'SEE, THE ISRAELIS ARE...
IT WAS KASHMIR, EARLIER. INDIANAPOLIS AND PAKISTAN ARE GOING TO WAR, APPARENTLY.
AGAIN, THAT'S NOT QUITE...
HOW COME YOU NEVER SEE YOUR SON NO MORE?
YOU TOLD ME LAST TIME YOU'D GOT DIVORCED. YOU CAN STILL SEE YOUR SON AFTER YOU GET DIVORCED.
UH... WOW.
WELL, THE THING... THE THING IS MRS GRAYSON...
MICHAEL...

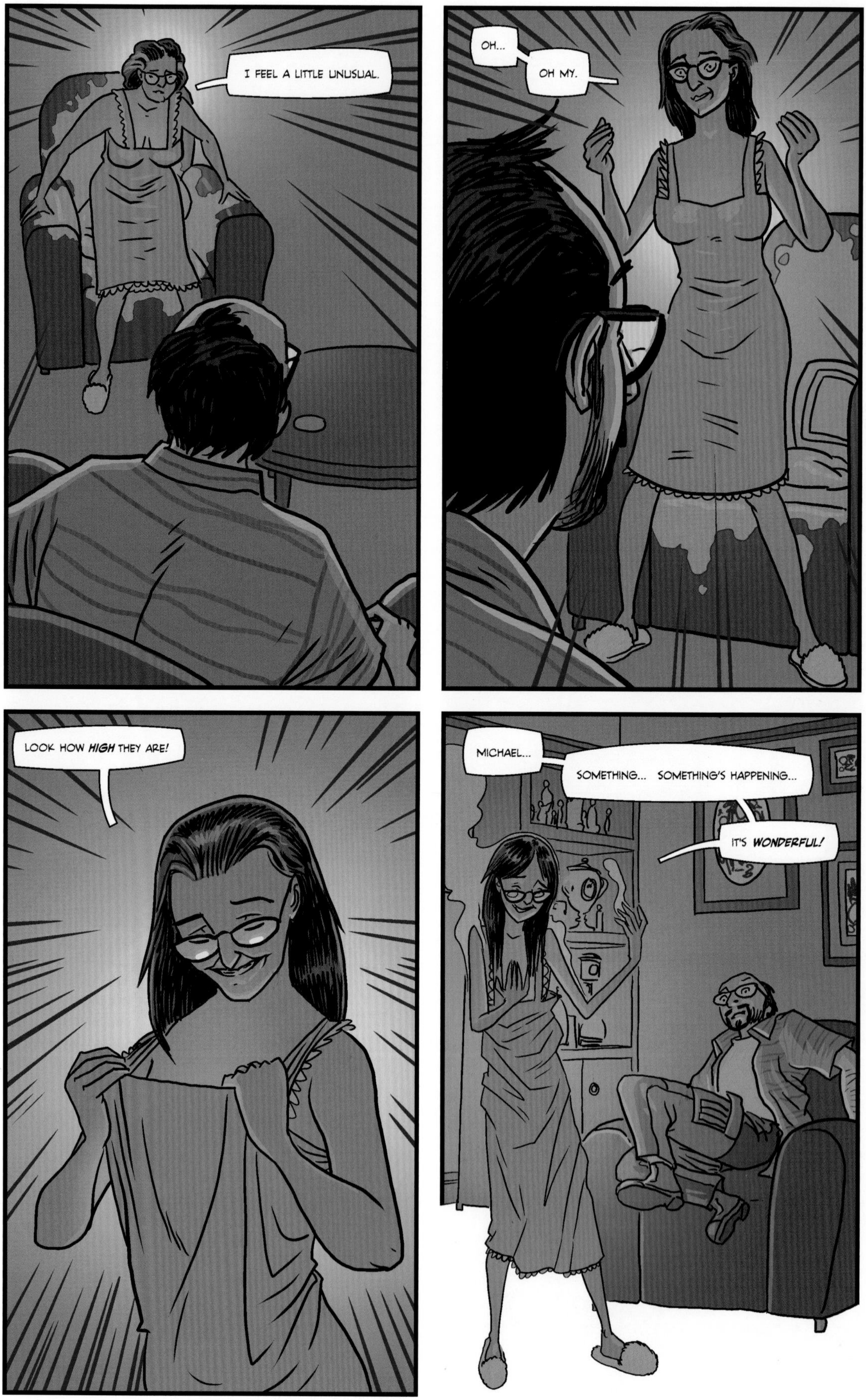
I FEEL A LITTLE UNUSUAL.
OH...
OH MY.
LOOK HOW HIGH THEY ARE!
MICHAEL...
SOMETHING... SOMETHING'S HAPPENING...
IT'S WONDERFUL!

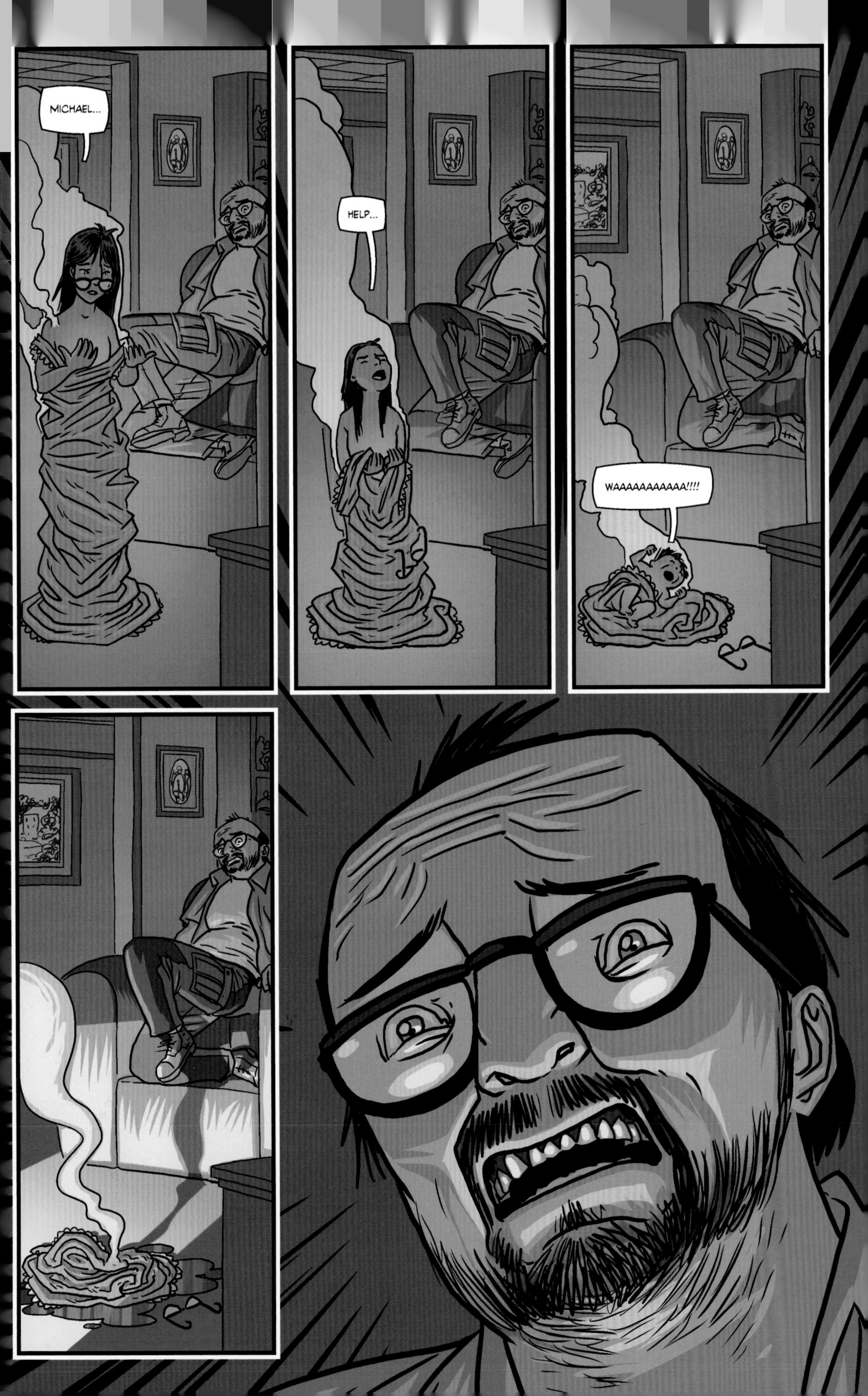
MICHAEL...
HELP...
WAAAAAAAAAAA!!!!

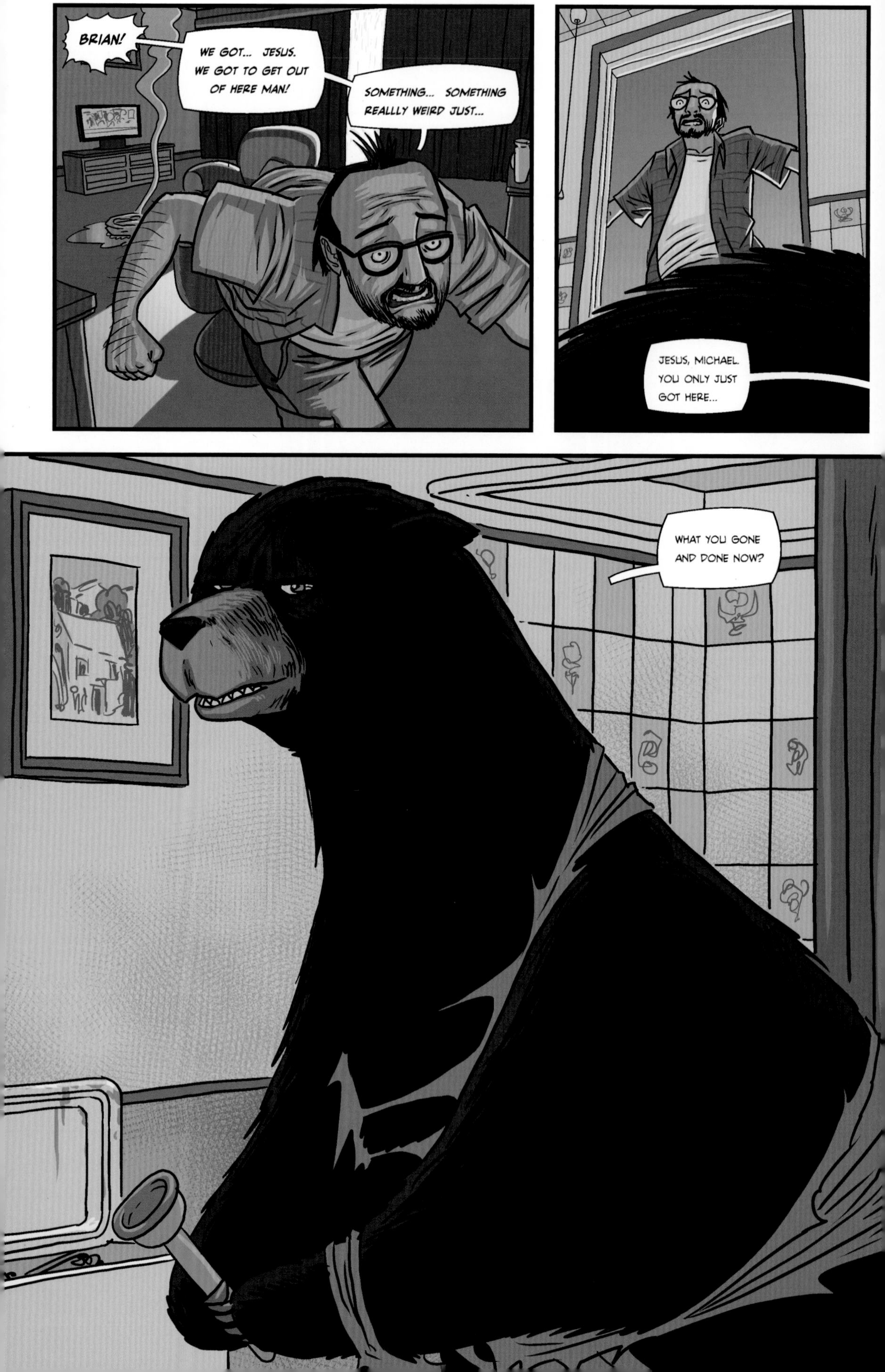
BRIAN!
WE GOT... JESUS. WE GOT TO GET OUT OF HERE MAN!
SOMETHING... SOMETHING REALLLY WEIRD JUST...
JESUS, MICHAEL. YOU ONLY JUST GOT HERE...
WHAT YOU GONE AND DONE NOW?

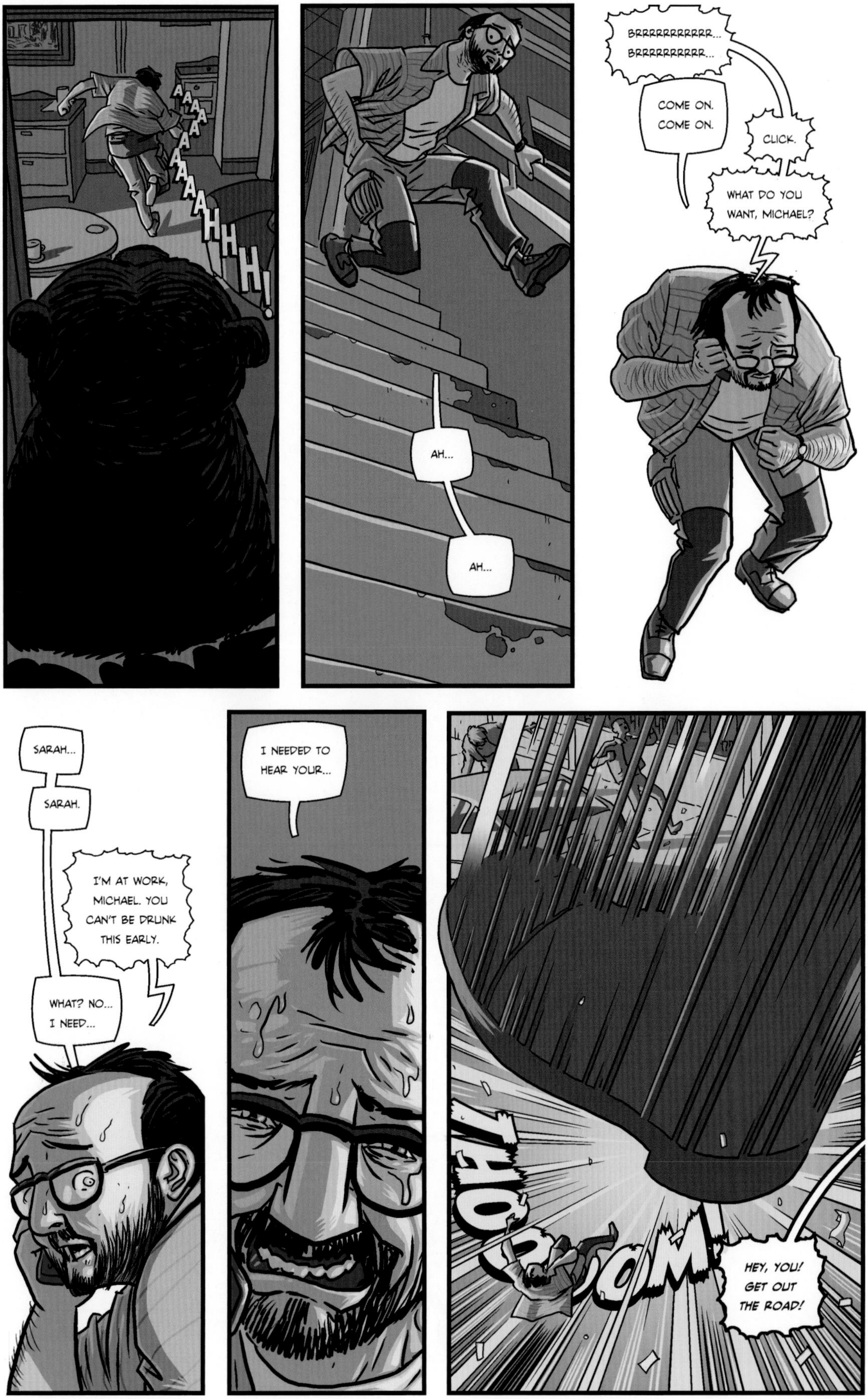
AAAAAAAAAAHHH!
AH...
AH...
BRRRRRRRRRRR...
BRRRRRRRRRR...
COME ON. COME ON.
CLICK.
WHAT DO YOU WANT, MICHAEL?
SARAH...
SARAH.
I'M AT WORK, MICHAEL. YOU CAN'T BE DRUNK THIS EARLY.
WHAT? NO... I NEED...
I NEEDED TO HEAR YOUR...
THOOOM!
HEY, YOU! GET OUT THE ROAD!

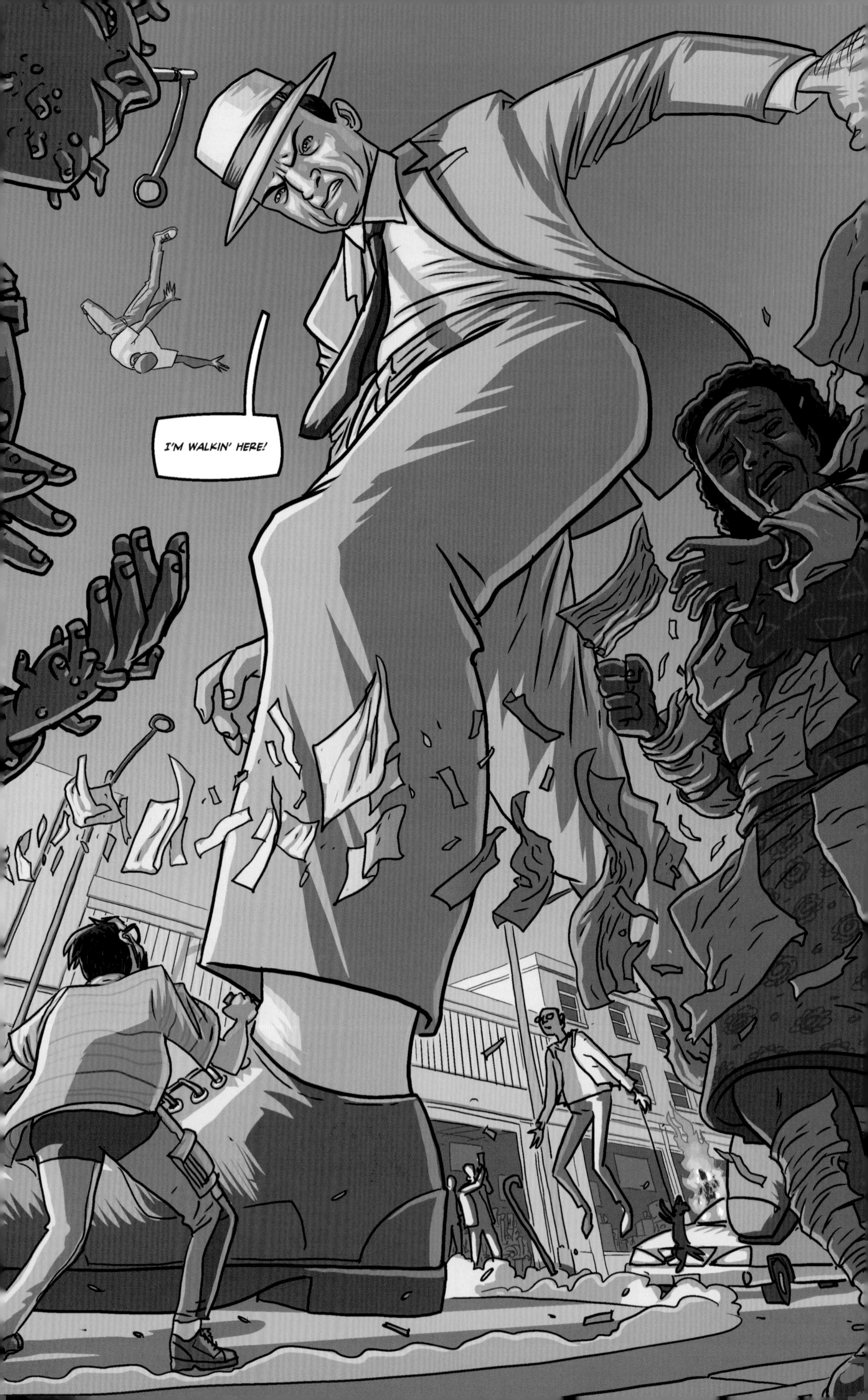
I'M WALKIN' HERE!

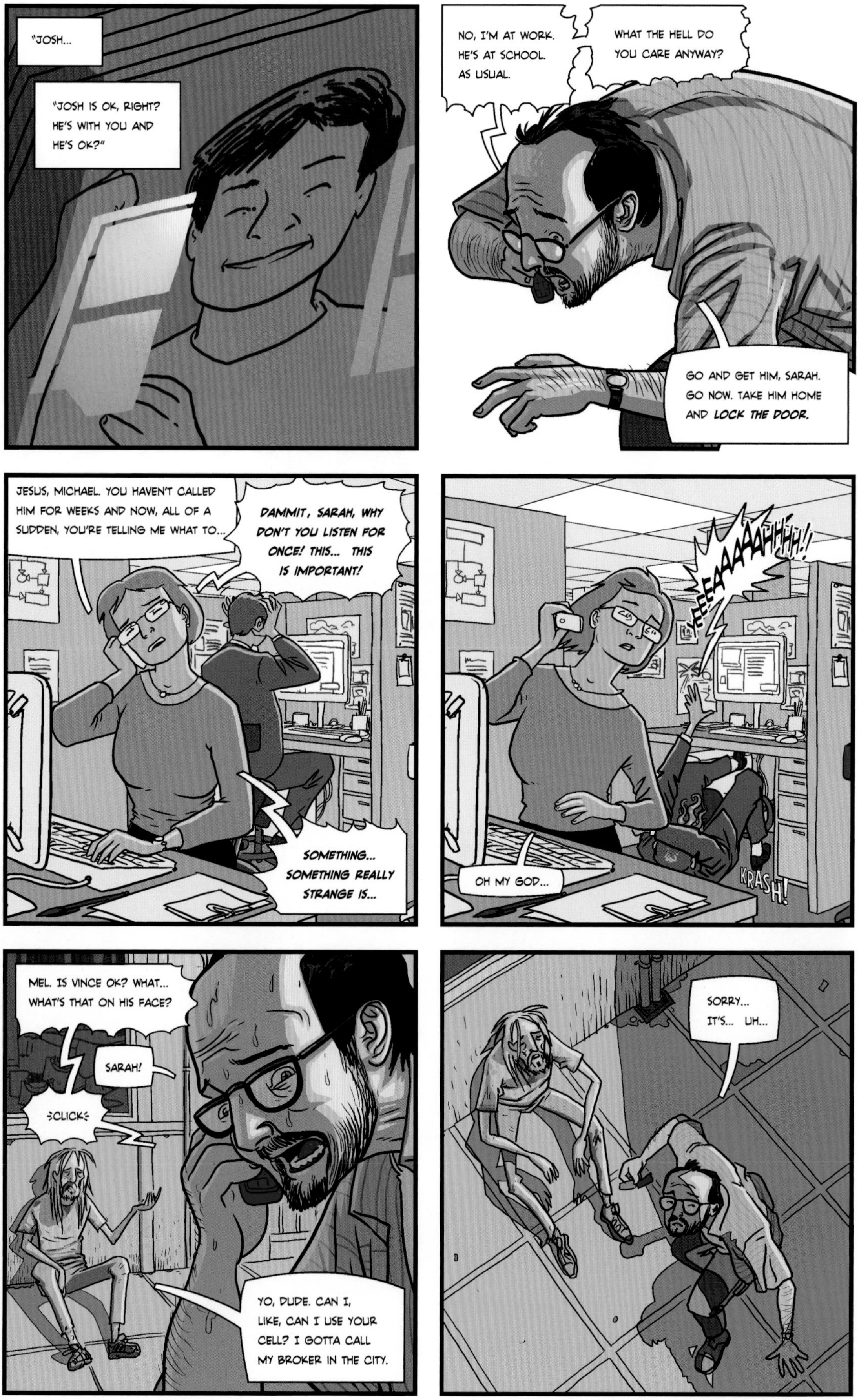
"JOSH...
"JOSH IS OK, RIGHT? HE'S WITH YOU AND HE'S OK?"
NO, I'M AT WORK. HE'S AT SCHOOL. AS USUAL.
WHAT THE HELL DO YOU CARE ANYWAY?
GO AND GET HIM, SARAH. GO NOW. TAKE HIM HOME AND LOCK THE DOOR.
JESUS, MICHAEL. YOU HAVEN'T CALLED HIM FOR WEEKS AND NOW, ALL OF A SUDDEN, YOU'RE TELLING ME WHAT TO...
DAMMIT, SARAH, WHY DON'T YOU LISTEN FOR ONCE! THIS... THIS IS IMPORTANT!
SOMETHING... SOMETHING REALLY STRANGE IS...
YEEEAAAAAHHHH!
OH MY GOD...
KRASH!
MEL. IS VINCE OK? WHAT... WHAT'S THAT ON HIS FACE?
SARAH!
CLICK
YO, DUDE. CAN I, LIKE, CAN I USE YOUR CELL? I GOTTA CALL MY BROKER IN THE CITY.
SORRY... IT'S... UH...

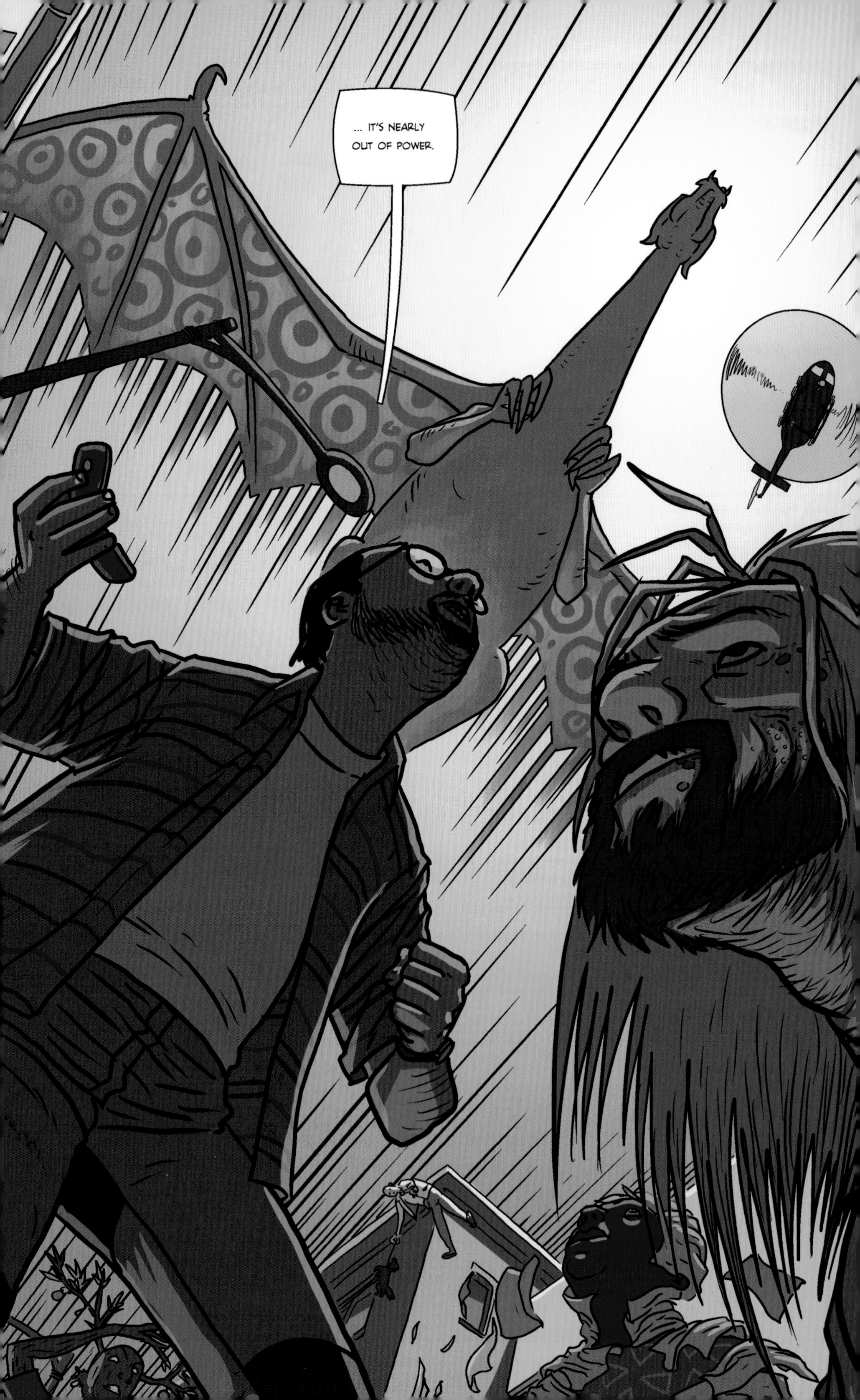
... IT'S NEARLY OUT OF POWER.

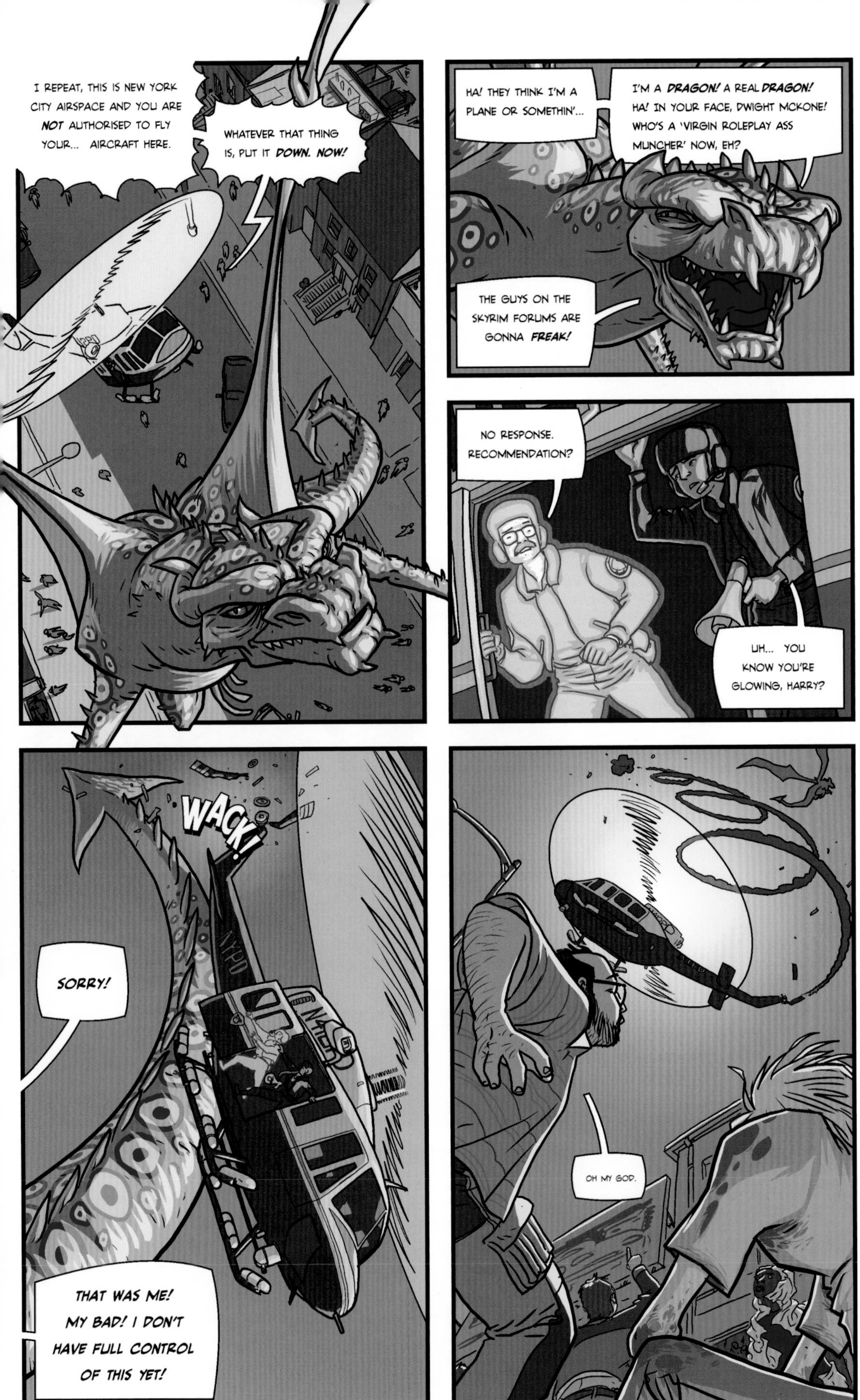
I REPEAT, THIS IS NEW YORK CITY AIRSPACE AND YOU ARE NOT AUTHORISED TO FLY YOUR... AIRCRAFT HERE.
WHATEVER THAT THING IS, PUT IT DOWN. NOW!
HA! THEY THINK I'M A PLANE OR SOMETHIN'...
I'M A DRAGON! A REAL DRAGON! HA! IN YOUR FACE, DWIGHT MCKONE! WHO'S A 'VIRGIN ROLEPLAY ASS MUNCHER' NOW, EH?
THE GUYS ON THE SKYRIM FORUMS ARE GONNA FREAK!
NO RESPONSE. RECOMMENDATION?
UH... YOU KNOW YOU'RE GLOWING, HARRY?
WACK!
NYPD
SORRY!
THAT WAS ME! MY BAD! I DON'T HAVE FULL CONTROL OF THIS YET!
OH MY GOD.

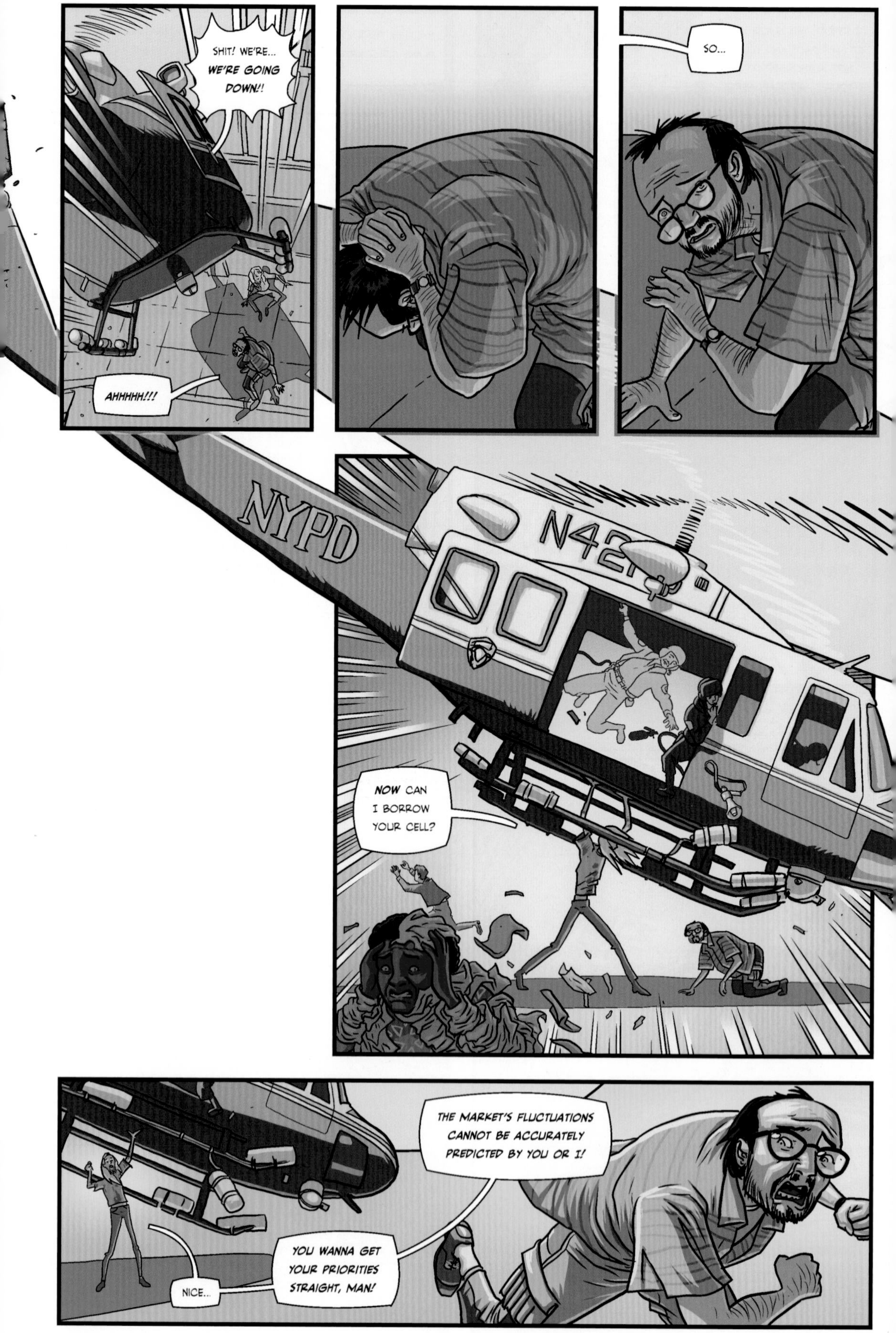
SHIT! WE'RE... WE'RE GOING DOWN!!
AHHHHH!!!
SO...
NYPD
N42
NOW CAN I BORROW YOUR CELL?
THE MARKET'S FLUCTUATIONS CANNOT BE ACCURATELY PREDICTED BY YOU OR I!
YOU WANNA GET YOUR PRIORITIES STRAIGHT, MAN!
NICE...

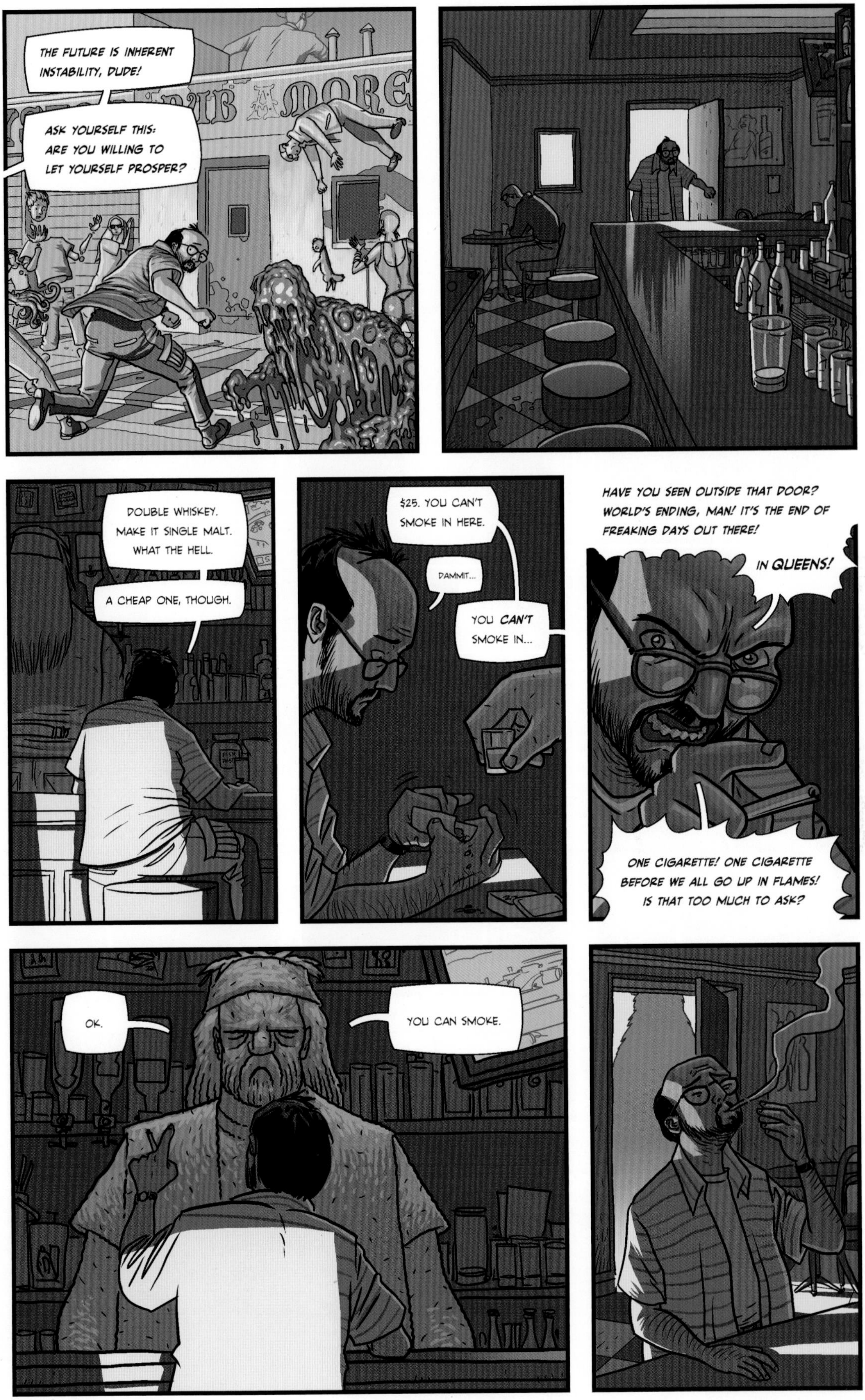
THE FUTURE IS INHERENT INSTABILITY, DUDE!
ASK YOURSELF THIS: ARE YOU WILLING TO LET YOURSELF PROSPER?
DOUBLE WHISKEY. MAKE IT SINGLE MALT. WHAT THE HELL.
A CHEAP ONE, THOUGH.
$25. YOU CAN'T SMOKE IN HERE.
DAMMIT...
YOU CAN'T SMOKE IN...
HAVE YOU SEEN OUTSIDE THAT DOOR? WORLD'S ENDING, MAN! IT'S THE END OF FREAKING DAYS OUT THERE!
IN QUEENS!
ONE CIGARETTE! ONE CIGARETTE BEFORE WE ALL GO UP IN FLAMES! IS THAT TOO MUCH TO ASK?
OK.
YOU CAN SMOKE.

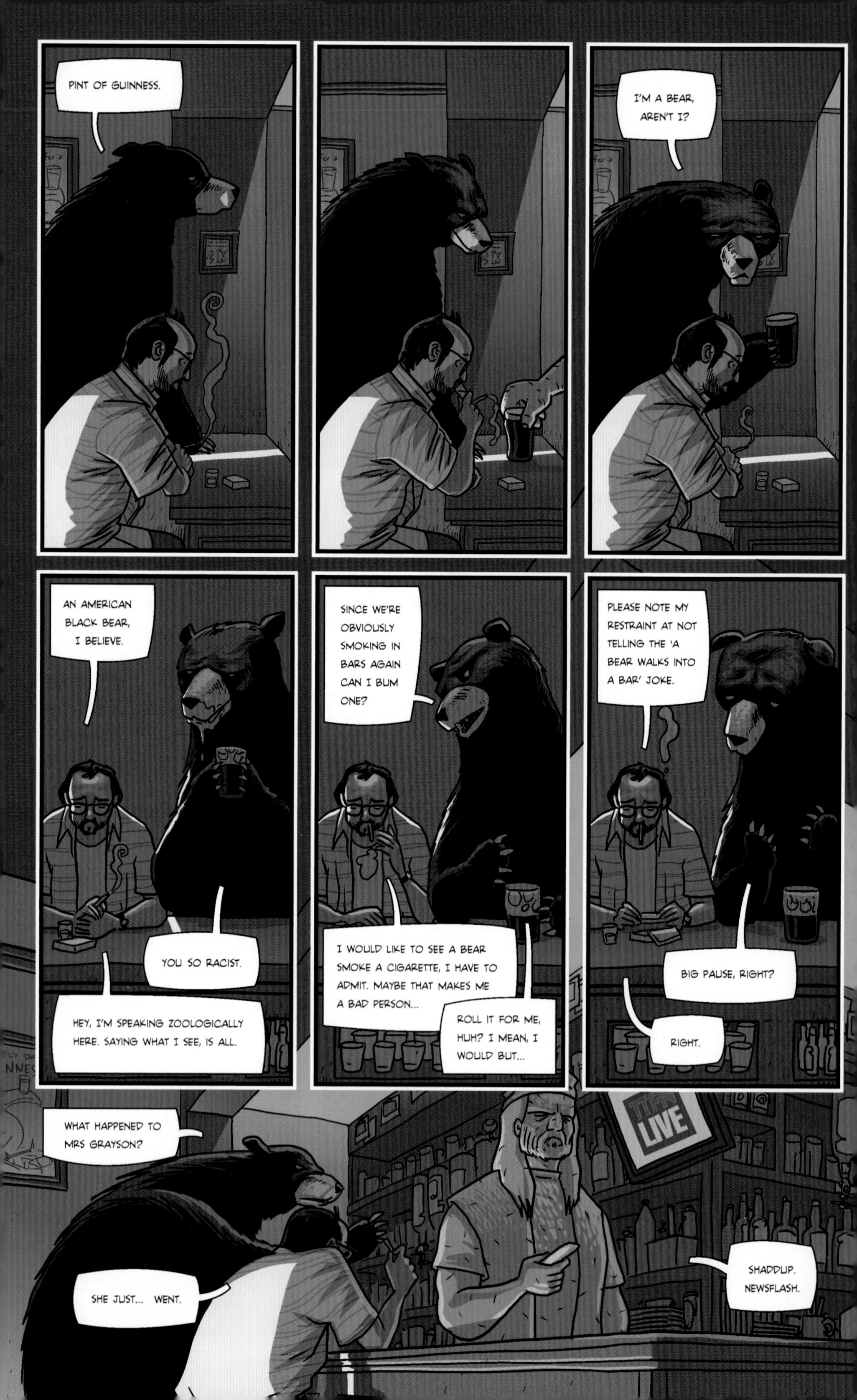
PINT OF GUINNESS.
I'M A BEAR, AREN'T I?
AN AMERICAN BLACK BEAR, I BELIEVE.
YOU SO RACIST.
HEY, I'M SPEAKING ZOOLOGICALLY HERE. SAYING WHAT I SEE, IS ALL.
SINCE WE'RE OBVIOUSLY SMOKING IN BARS AGAIN CAN I BUM ONE?
I WOULD LIKE TO SEE A BEAR SMOKE A CIGARETTE, I HAVE TO ADMIT. MAYBE THAT MAKES ME A BAD PERSON...
ROLL IT FOR ME, HUH? I MEAN, I WOULD BUT...
PLEASE NOTE MY RESTRAINT AT NOT TELLING THE 'A BEAR WALKS INTO A BAR' JOKE.
BIG PAUSE, RIGHT?
RIGHT.
WHAT HAPPENED TO MRS GRAYSON?
SHE JUST... WENT.
SHADDUP. NEWSFLASH.
LIVE

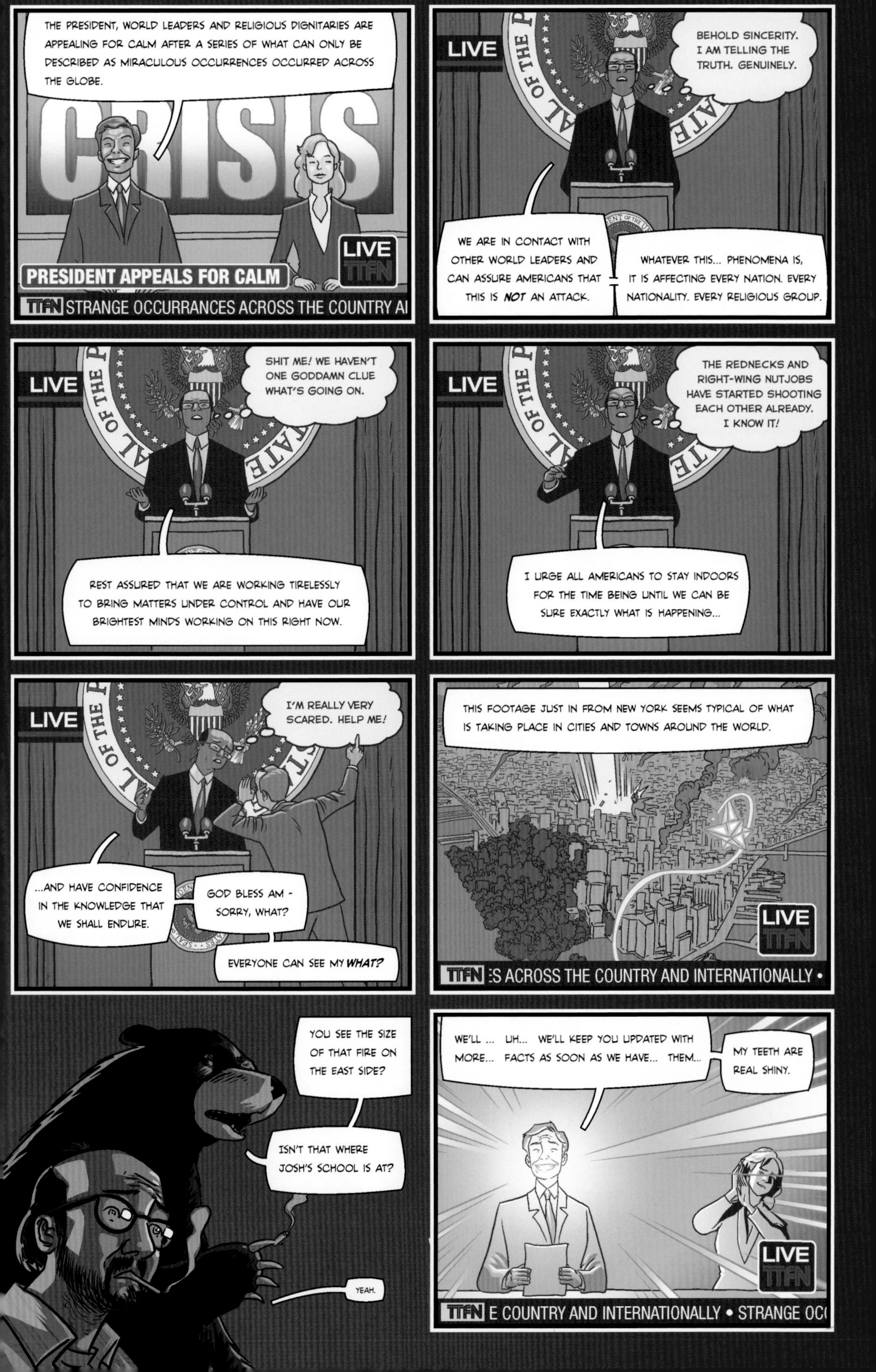
THE PRESIDENT, WORLD LEADERS AND RELIGIOUS DIGNITARIES ARE APPEALING FOR CALM AFTER A SERIES OF WHAT CAN ONLY BE DESCRIBED AS MIRACULOUS OCCURRENCES OCCURRED ACROSS THE GLOBE.
CRISIS
PRESIDENT APPEALS FOR CALM
LIVE TTFN
TTFN STRANGE OCCURRANCES ACROSS THE COUNTRY AI
LIVE
BEHOLD SINCERITY. I AM TELLING THE TRUTH. GENUINELY.
WE ARE IN CONTACT WITH OTHER WORLD LEADERS AND CAN ASSURE AMERICANS THAT THIS IS NOT AN ATTACK.
WHATEVER THIS... PHENOMENA IS, IT IS AFFECTING EVERY NATION. EVERY NATIONALITY. EVERY RELIGIOUS GROUP.
LIVE
SHIT ME! WE HAVEN'T ONE GODDAMN CLUE WHAT'S GOING ON.
REST ASSURED THAT WE ARE WORKING TIRELESSLY TO BRING MATTERS UNDER CONTROL AND HAVE OUR BRIGHTEST MINDS WORKING ON THIS RIGHT NOW.
LIVE
THE REDNECKS AND RIGHT-WING NUTJOBS HAVE STARTED SHOOTING EACH OTHER ALREADY. I KNOW IT!
I URGE ALL AMERICANS TO STAY INDOORS FOR THE TIME BEING UNTIL WE CAN BE SURE EXACTLY WHAT IS HAPPENING...
LIVE
I'M REALLY VERY SCARED. HELP ME!
...AND HAVE CONFIDENCE IN THE KNOWLEDGE THAT WE SHALL ENDURE.
GOD BLESS AM - SORRY, WHAT?
EVERYONE CAN SEE MY WHAT?
THIS FOOTAGE JUST IN FROM NEW YORK SEEMS TYPICAL OF WHAT IS TAKING PLACE IN CITIES AND TOWNS AROUND THE WORLD.
LIVE TTFN
TTFN :S ACROSS THE COUNTRY AND INTERNATIONALLY •
YOU SEE THE SIZE OF THAT FIRE ON THE EAST SIDE?
ISN'T THAT WHERE JOSH'S SCHOOL IS AT?
YEAH.
WE'LL ... UH... WE'LL KEEP YOU UPDATED WITH MORE... FACTS AS SOON AS WE HAVE... THEM...
MY TEETH ARE REAL SHINY.
LIVE TTFN
TTFN E COUNTRY AND INTERNATIONALLY • STRANGE OC(

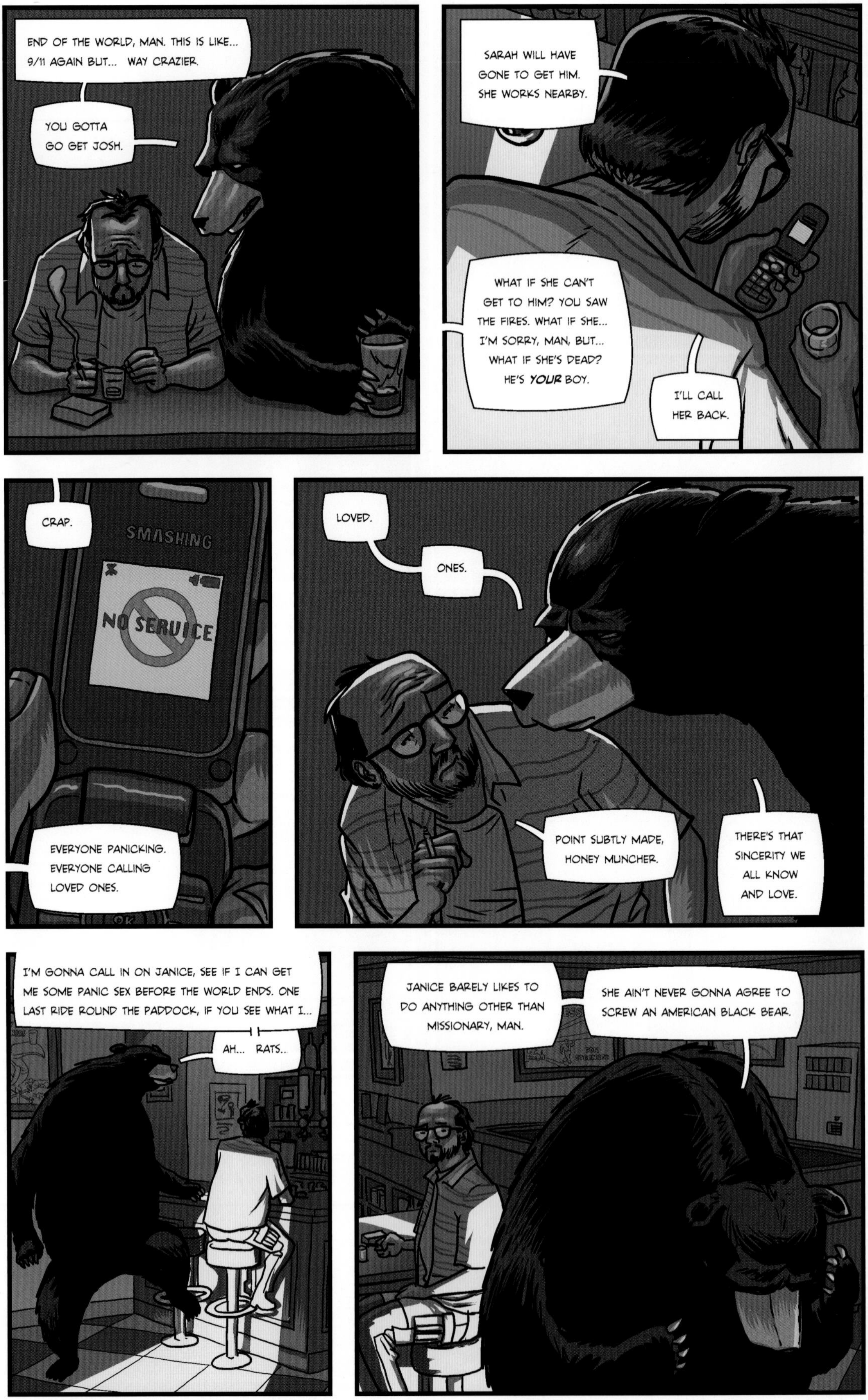
END OF THE WORLD, MAN. THIS IS LIKE... 9/11 AGAIN BUT... WAY CRAZIER.
YOU GOTTA GO GET JOSH.
SARAH WILL HAVE GONE TO GET HIM. SHE WORKS NEARBY.
WHAT IF SHE CAN'T GET TO HIM? YOU SAW THE FIRES. WHAT IF SHE... I'M SORRY, MAN, BUT... WHAT IF SHE'S DEAD? HE'S *YOUR* BOY.
I'LL CALL HER BACK.
CRAP.
SMASHING
NO SERVICE
EVERYONE PANICKING. EVERYONE CALLING LOVED ONES.
LOVED.
ONES.
POINT SUBTLY MADE, HONEY MUNCHER.
THERE'S THAT SINCERITY WE ALL KNOW AND LOVE.
I'M GONNA CALL IN ON JANICE, SEE IF I CAN GET ME SOME PANIC SEX BEFORE THE WORLD ENDS. ONE LAST RIDE ROUND THE PADDOCK, IF YOU SEE WHAT I...
AH... RATS..
JANICE BARELY LIKES TO DO ANYTHING OTHER THAN MISSIONARY, MAN.
SHE AIN'T NEVER GONNA AGREE TO SCREW AN AMERICAN BLACK BEAR.

"I CATCH MYSELF WONDERING IF THAT'S THE LAST TIME I'LL EVER SEEN BRIAN."

"IF THOSE ARE THE LAST WORDS I'LL EVER HEAR HIM SAY... "

"ALTHOUGH THEY MAKE ABOUT AS MUCH SENSE AS ANYTHING ELSE I'VE EVER HEARD COME OUT OF HIS MOUTH."

"BUT I KNOW HE'S RIGHT."

"JOSH... "

"I'M REALLY SCARED."

HEY!

HEY YOU, OLD GUY WITH THE GLASSES.

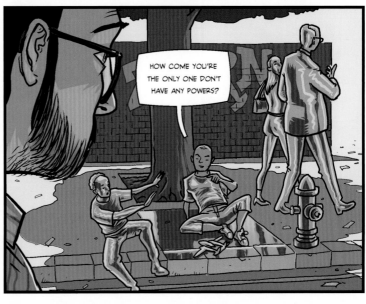

HOW COME YOU'RE THE ONLY ONE DON'T HAVE ANY POWERS?

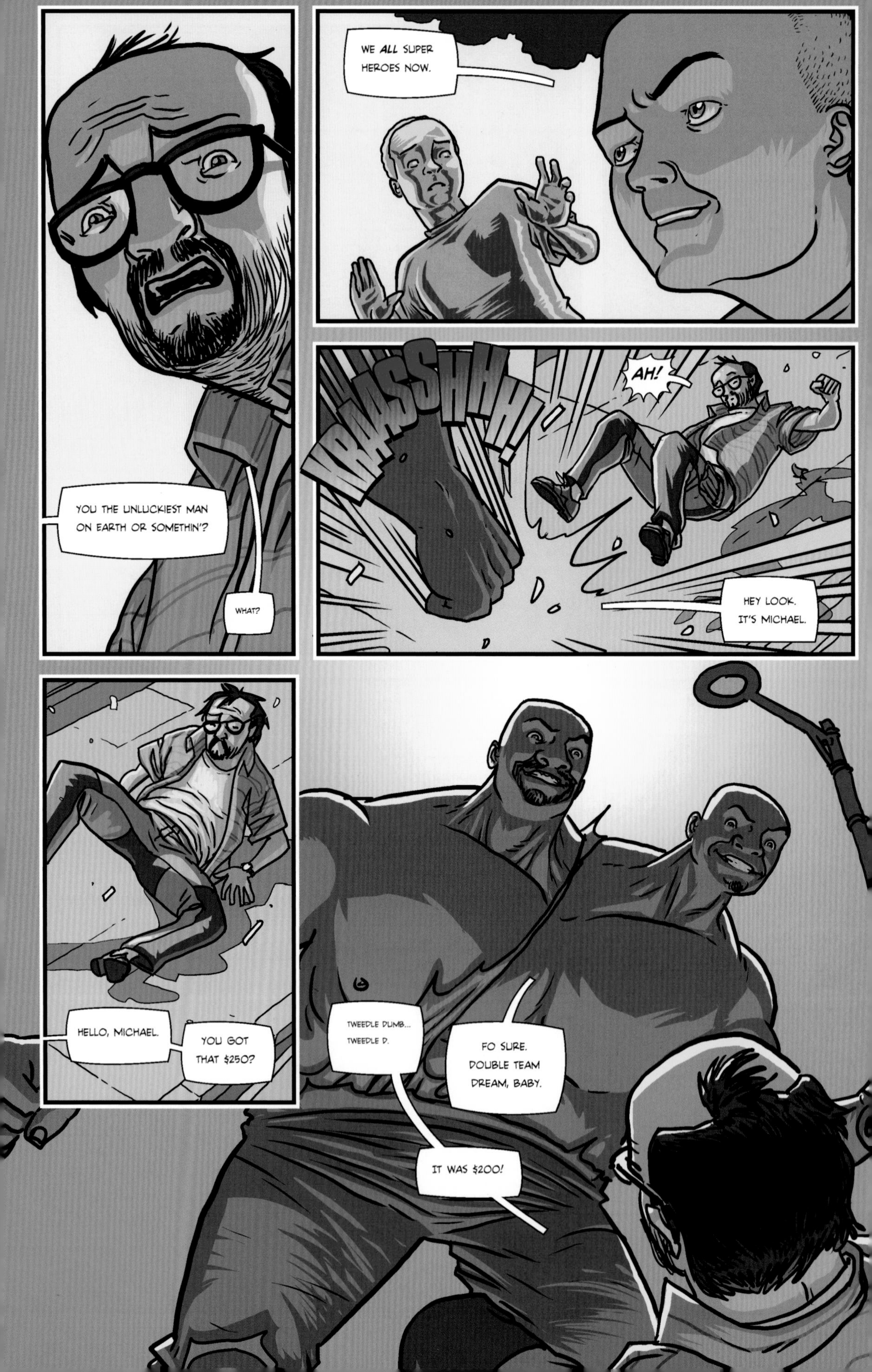
WE ALL SUPER HEROES NOW.
YOU THE UNLUCKIEST MAN ON EARTH OR SOMETHIN'?
WHAT?
KRASSHHH!
AH!
HEY LOOK. IT'S MICHAEL.
HELLO, MICHAEL.
YOU GOT THAT $250?
TWEEDLE DUMB... TWEEDLE D.
FO SURE. DOUBLE TEAM DREAM, BABY.
IT WAS $200!

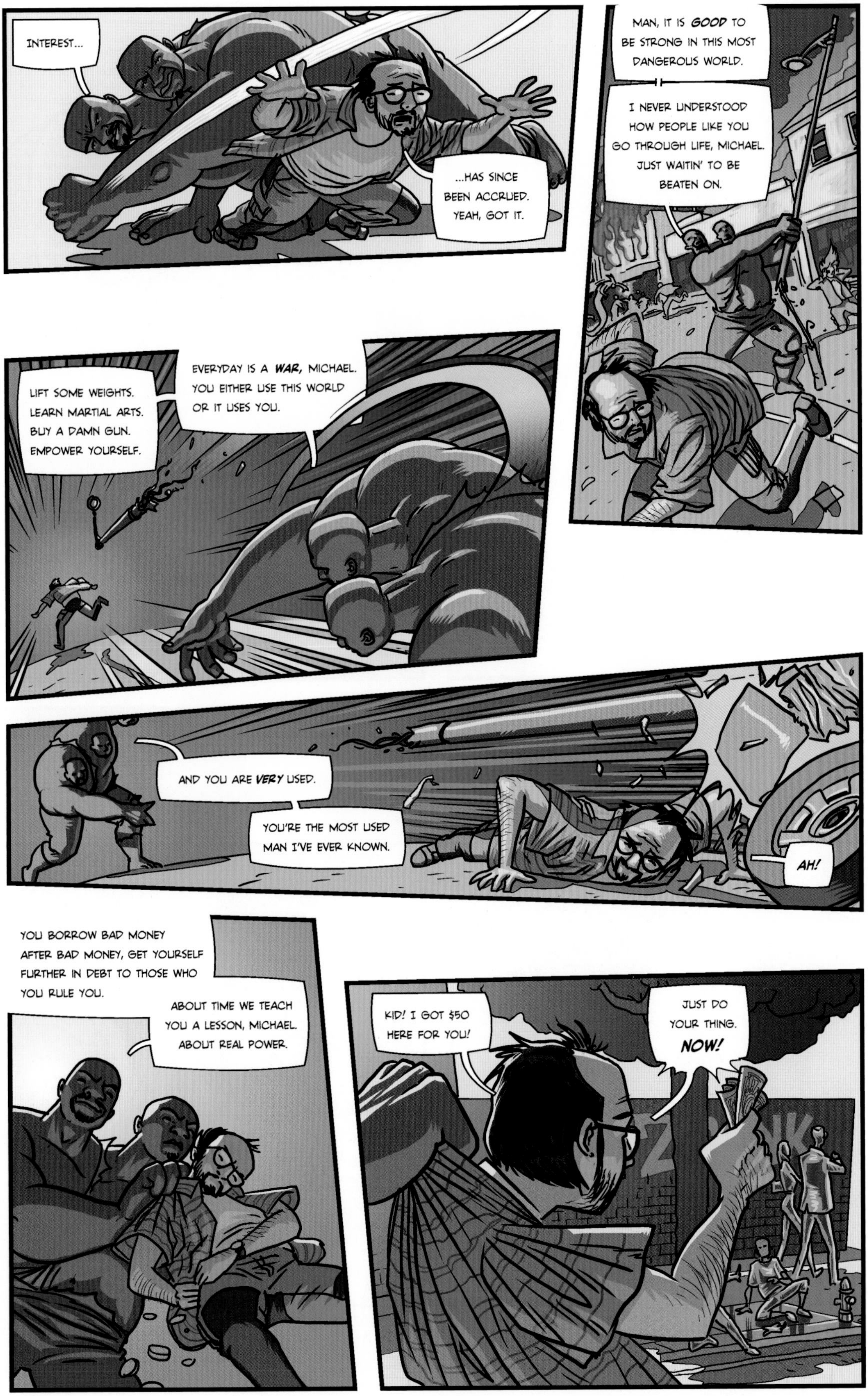
INTEREST...
...HAS SINCE BEEN ACCRUED. YEAH, GOT IT.
MAN, IT IS **GOOD** TO BE STRONG IN THIS MOST DANGEROUS WORLD.
I NEVER UNDERSTOOD HOW PEOPLE LIKE YOU GO THROUGH LIFE, MICHAEL. JUST WAITIN' TO BE BEATEN ON.
LIFT SOME WEIGHTS. LEARN MARTIAL ARTS. BUY A DAMN GUN. EMPOWER YOURSELF.
EVERYDAY IS A **WAR,** MICHAEL. YOU EITHER USE THIS WORLD OR IT USES YOU.
AND YOU ARE **VERY** USED.
YOU'RE THE MOST USED MAN I'VE EVER KNOWN.
AH!
YOU BORROW BAD MONEY AFTER BAD MONEY, GET YOURSELF FURTHER IN DEBT TO THOSE WHO YOU RULE YOU.
ABOUT TIME WE TEACH YOU A LESSON, MICHAEL. ABOUT REAL POWER.
KID! I GOT $50 HERE FOR YOU!
JUST DO YOUR THING. **NOW!**

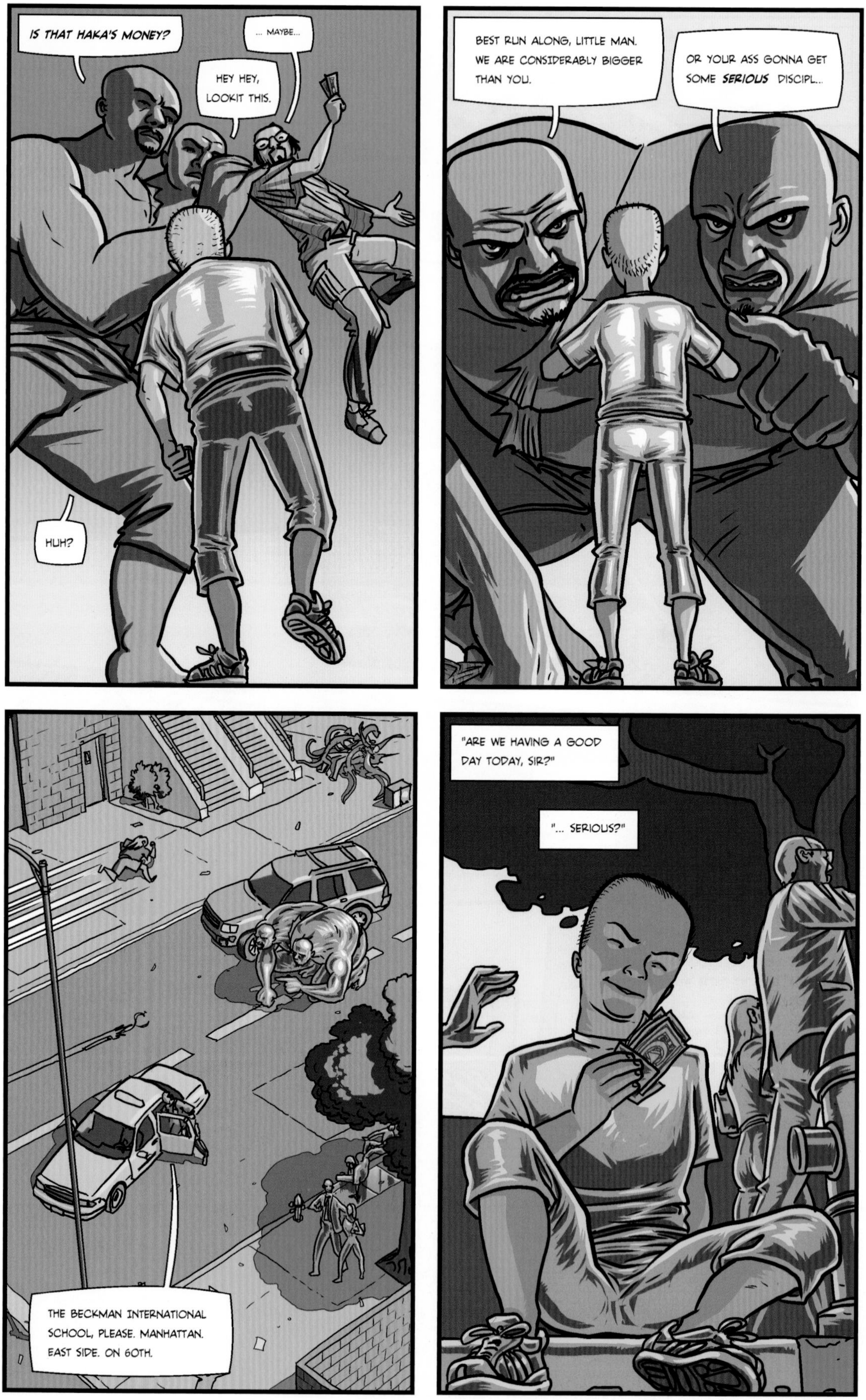
IS THAT HAKA'S MONEY?
... MAYBE...
HEY HEY, LOOKIT THIS.
HUH?
BEST RUN ALONG, LITTLE MAN. WE ARE CONSIDERABLY BIGGER THAN YOU.
OR YOUR ASS GONNA GET SOME SERIOUS DISCIPL...
THE BECKMAN INTERNATIONAL SCHOOL, PLEASE. MANHATTAN. EAST SIDE. ON 60TH.
"ARE WE HAVING A GOOD DAY TODAY, SIR?"
"... SERIOUS?"

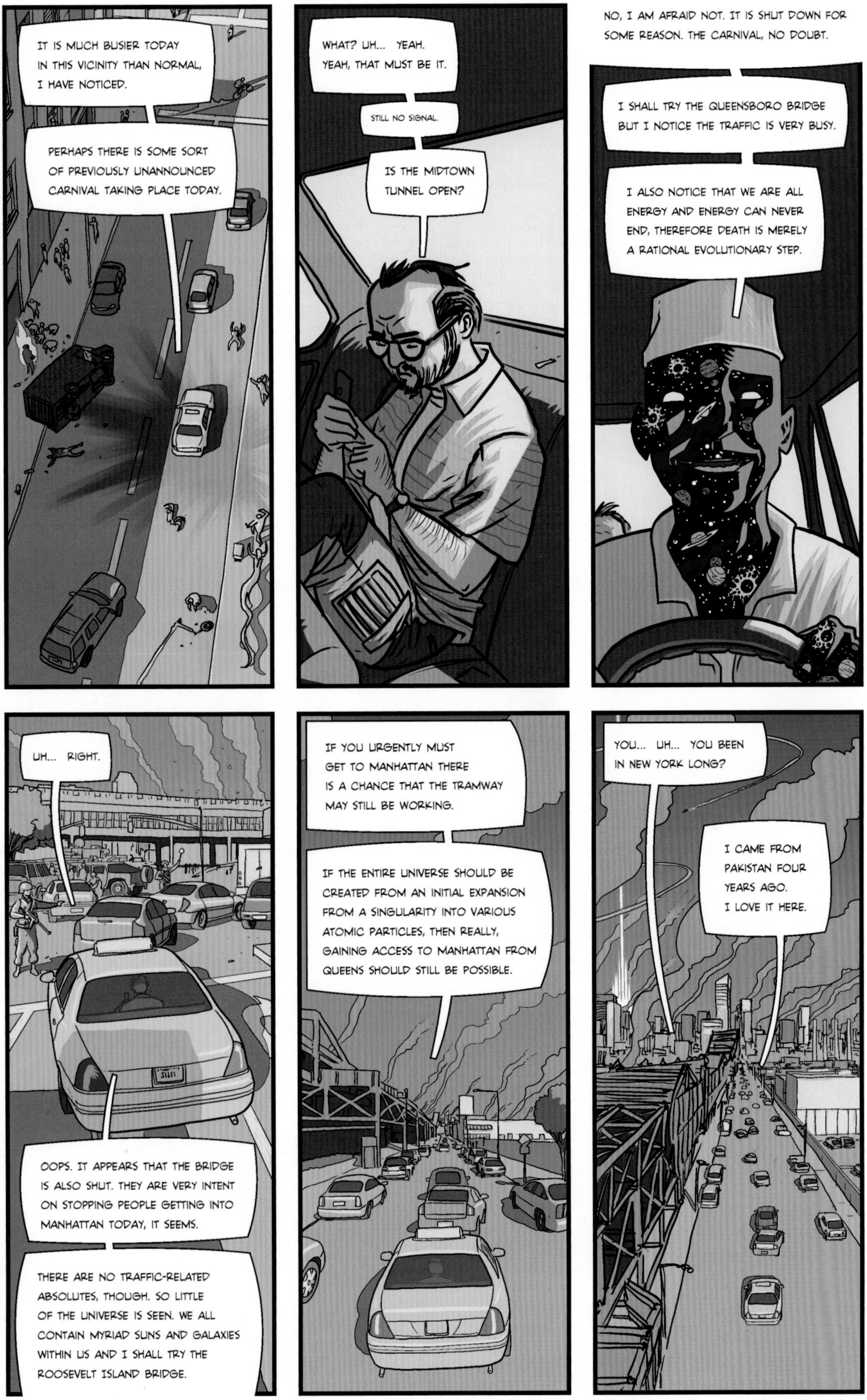
IT IS MUCH BUSIER TODAY IN THIS VICINITY THAN NORMAL, I HAVE NOTICED.
PERHAPS THERE IS SOME SORT OF PREVIOUSLY UNANNOUNCED CARNIVAL TAKING PLACE TODAY.
WHAT? UH... YEAH. YEAH, THAT MUST BE IT.
STILL NO SIGNAL.
IS THE MIDTOWN TUNNEL OPEN?
NO, I AM AFRAID NOT. IT IS SHUT DOWN FOR SOME REASON. THE CARNIVAL, NO DOUBT.
I SHALL TRY THE QUEENSBORO BRIDGE BUT I NOTICE THE TRAFFIC IS VERY BUSY.
I ALSO NOTICE THAT WE ARE ALL ENERGY AND ENERGY CAN NEVER END, THEREFORE DEATH IS MERELY A RATIONAL EVOLUTIONARY STEP.
UH... RIGHT.
OOPS. IT APPEARS THAT THE BRIDGE IS ALSO SHUT. THEY ARE VERY INTENT ON STOPPING PEOPLE GETTING INTO MANHATTAN TODAY, IT SEEMS.
THERE ARE NO TRAFFIC-RELATED ABSOLUTES, THOUGH. SO LITTLE OF THE UNIVERSE IS SEEN. WE ALL CONTAIN MYRIAD SUNS AND GALAXIES WITHIN US AND I SHALL TRY THE ROOSEVELT ISLAND BRIDGE.
IF YOU URGENTLY MUST GET TO MANHATTAN THERE IS A CHANCE THAT THE TRAMWAY MAY STILL BE WORKING.
IF THE ENTIRE UNIVERSE SHOULD BE CREATED FROM AN INITIAL EXPANSION FROM A SINGULARITY INTO VARIOUS ATOMIC PARTICLES, THEN REALLY, GAINING ACCESS TO MANHATTAN FROM QUEENS SHOULD STILL BE POSSIBLE.
YOU... UH... YOU BEEN IN NEW YORK LONG?
I CAME FROM PAKISTAN FOUR YEARS AGO. I LOVE IT HERE.

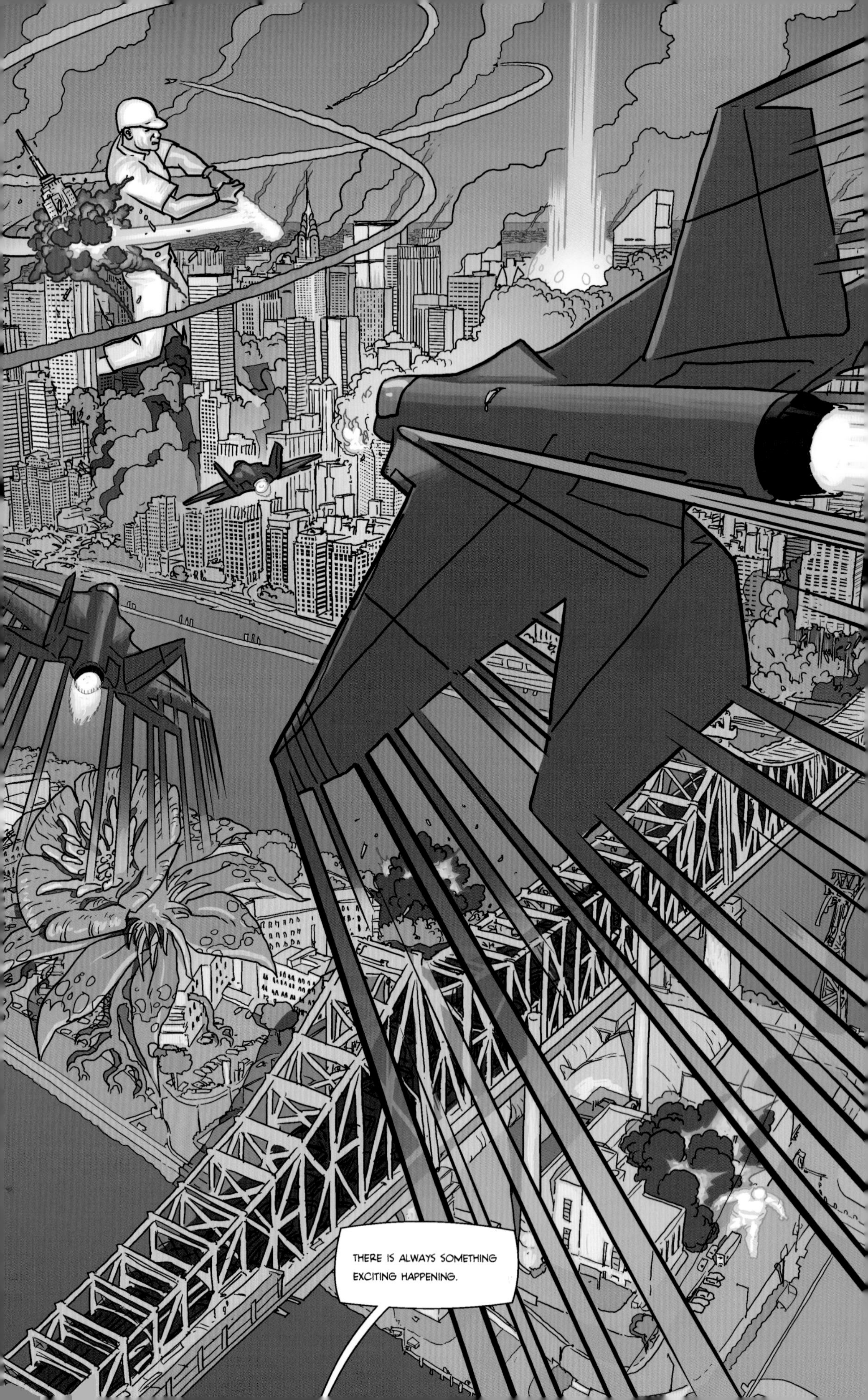
THERE IS ALWAYS SOMETHING EXCITING HAPPENING.

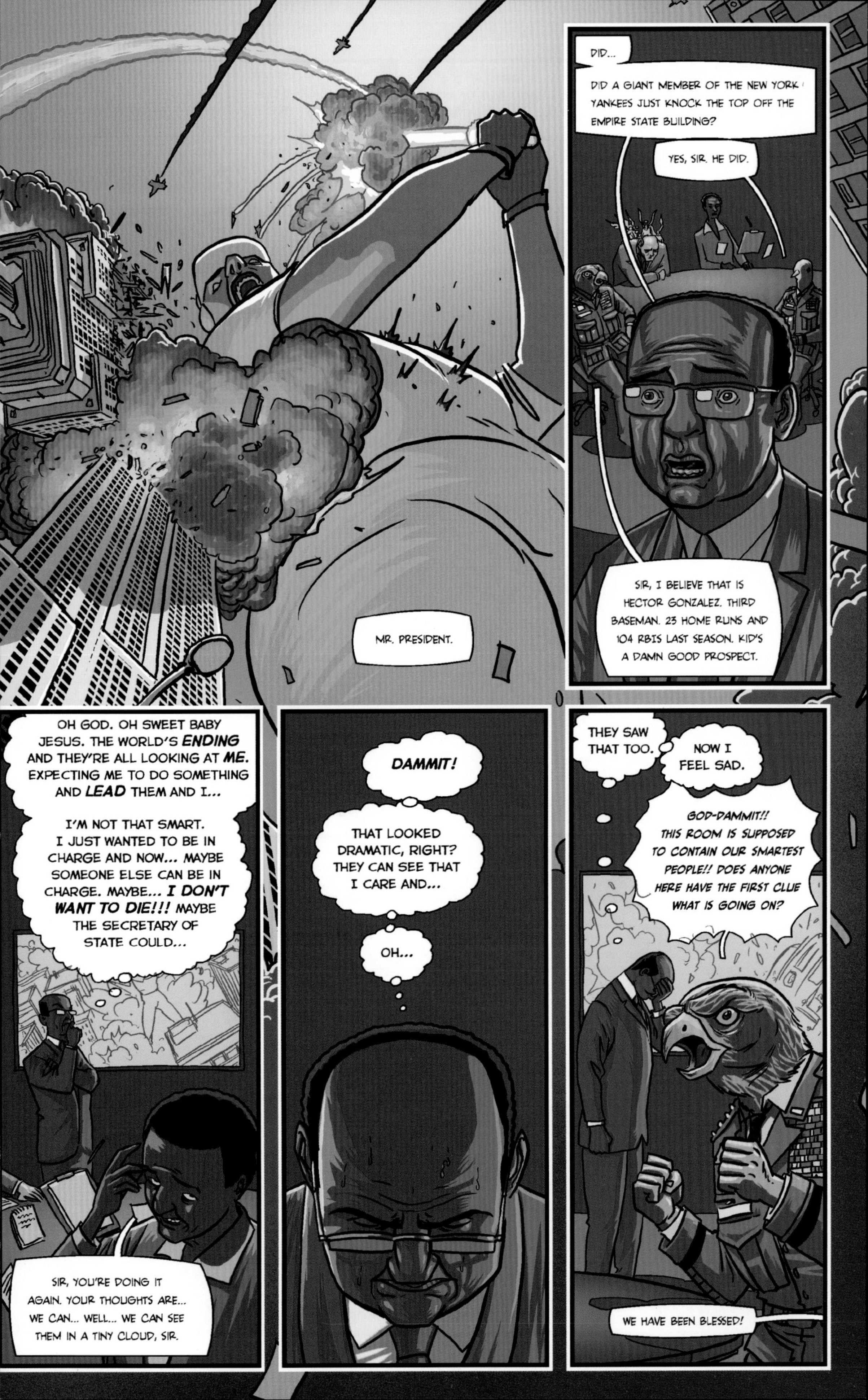
DID...
DID A GIANT MEMBER OF THE NEW YORK YANKEES JUST KNOCK THE TOP OFF THE EMPIRE STATE BUILDING?
YES, SIR. HE DID.
MR. PRESIDENT.
SIR, I BELIEVE THAT IS HECTOR GONZALEZ. THIRD BASEMAN. 23 HOME RUNS AND 104 RBIS LAST SEASON. KID'S A DAMN GOOD PROSPECT.
OH GOD. OH SWEET BABY JESUS. THE WORLD'S *ENDING* AND THEY'RE ALL LOOKING AT *ME*. EXPECTING ME TO DO SOMETHING AND *LEAD* THEM AND I...
I'M NOT THAT SMART. I JUST WANTED TO BE IN CHARGE AND NOW... MAYBE SOMEONE ELSE CAN BE IN CHARGE. MAYBE... *I DON'T WANT TO DIE!!!* MAYBE THE SECRETARY OF STATE COULD...
SIR, YOU'RE DOING IT AGAIN. YOUR THOUGHTS ARE... WE CAN... WELL... WE CAN SEE THEM IN A TINY CLOUD, SIR.
DAMMIT!
THAT LOOKED DRAMATIC, RIGHT? THEY CAN SEE THAT I CARE AND...
OH...
THEY SAW THAT TOO.
NOW I FEEL SAD.
GOD-DAMMIT!! THIS ROOM IS SUPPOSED TO CONTAIN OUR SMARTEST PEOPLE!! DOES ANYONE HERE HAVE THE FIRST CLUE WHAT IS GOING ON?
WE HAVE BEEN BLESSED!

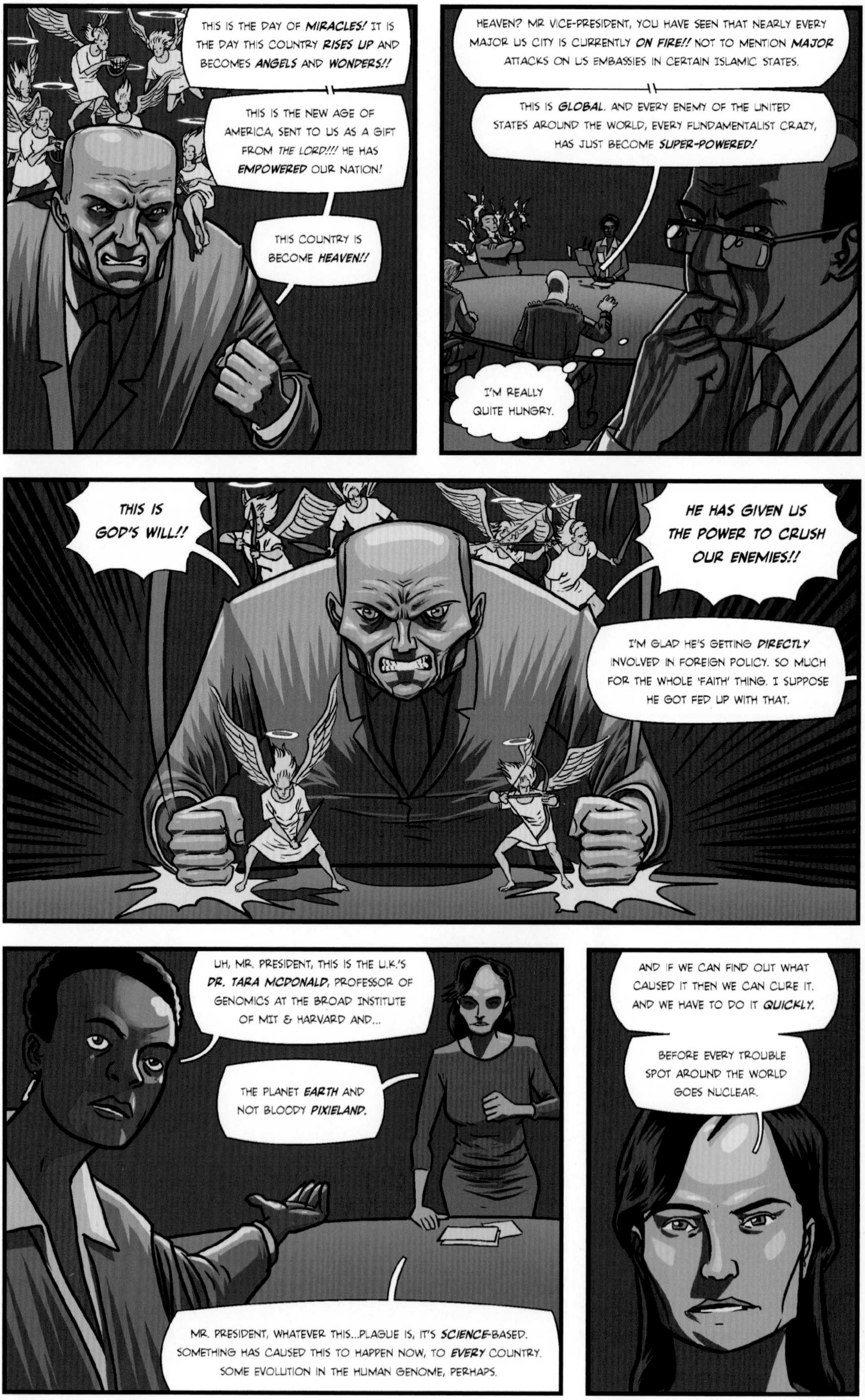
THIS IS THE DAY OF MIRACLES! IT IS THE DAY THIS COUNTRY RISES UP AND BECOMES ANGELS AND WONDERS!!
THIS IS THE NEW AGE OF AMERICA, SENT TO US AS A GIFT FROM THE LORD!!! HE HAS EMPOWERED OUR NATION!
THIS COUNTRY IS BECOME HEAVEN!!
HEAVEN? MR VICE-PRESIDENT, YOU HAVE SEEN THAT NEARLY EVERY MAJOR US CITY IS CURRENTLY ON FIRE!! NOT TO MENTION MAJOR ATTACKS ON US EMBASSIES IN CERTAIN ISLAMIC STATES.
THIS IS GLOBAL. AND EVERY ENEMY OF THE UNITED STATES AROUND THE WORLD, EVERY FUNDAMENTALIST CRAZY, HAS JUST BECOME SUPER-POWERED!
I'M REALLY QUITE HUNGRY.
THIS IS GOD'S WILL!!
HE HAS GIVEN US THE POWER TO CRUSH OUR ENEMIES!!
I'M GLAD HE'S GETTING DIRECTLY INVOLVED IN FOREIGN POLICY. SO MUCH FOR THE WHOLE 'FAITH' THING. I SUPPOSE HE GOT FED UP WITH THAT.
UH, MR. PRESIDENT, THIS IS THE U.K.'S DR. TARA MCDONALD, PROFESSOR OF GENOMICS AT THE BROAD INSTITUTE OF MIT & HARVARD AND...
THE PLANET EARTH AND NOT BLOODY PIXIELAND.
MR. PRESIDENT, WHATEVER THIS...PLAGUE IS, IT'S SCIENCE-BASED. SOMETHING HAS CAUSED THIS TO HAPPEN NOW, TO EVERY COUNTRY. SOME EVOLUTION IN THE HUMAN GENOME, PERHAPS.
AND IF WE CAN FIND OUT WHAT CAUSED IT THEN WE CAN CURE IT. AND WE HAVE TO DO IT QUICKLY.
BEFORE EVERY TROUBLE SPOT AROUND THE WORLD GOES NUCLEAR.

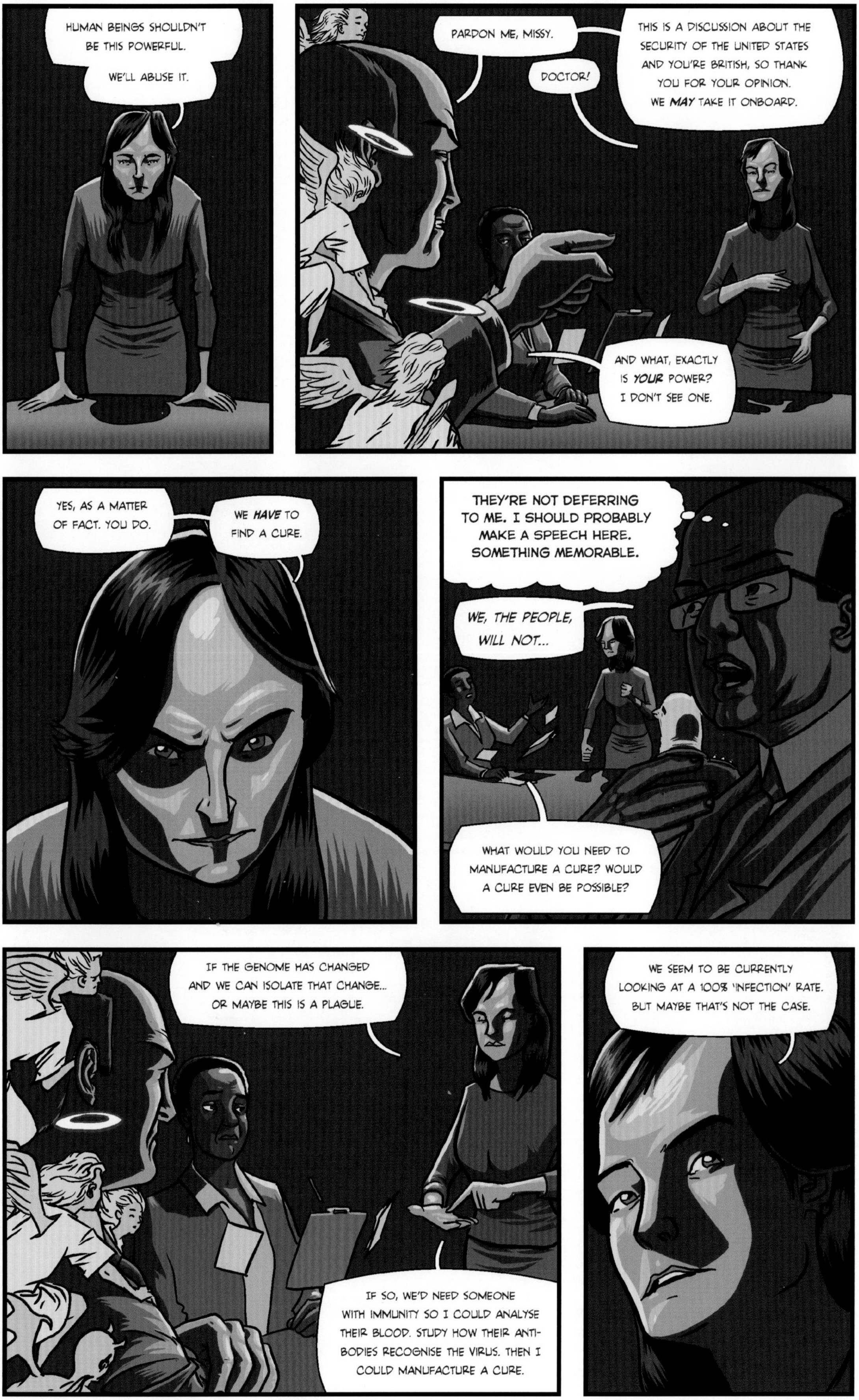
HUMAN BEINGS SHOULDN'T BE THIS POWERFUL.
WE'LL ABUSE IT.
PARDON ME, MISSY.
DOCTOR!
THIS IS A DISCUSSION ABOUT THE SECURITY OF THE UNITED STATES AND YOU'RE BRITISH, SO THANK YOU FOR YOUR OPINION. WE *MAY* TAKE IT ONBOARD.
AND WHAT, EXACTLY IS *YOUR* POWER? I DON'T SEE ONE.
YES, AS A MATTER OF FACT. YOU DO.
WE *HAVE* TO FIND A CURE.
THEY'RE NOT DEFERRING TO ME. I SHOULD PROBABLY MAKE A SPEECH HERE. SOMETHING MEMORABLE.
WE, THE PEOPLE, WILL NOT...
WHAT WOULD YOU NEED TO MANUFACTURE A CURE? WOULD A CURE EVEN BE POSSIBLE?
IF THE GENOME HAS CHANGED AND WE CAN ISOLATE THAT CHANGE... OR MAYBE THIS IS A PLAGUE.
IF SO, WE'D NEED SOMEONE WITH IMMUNITY SO I COULD ANALYSE THEIR BLOOD. STUDY HOW THEIR ANTI-BODIES RECOGNISE THE VIRUS. THEN I COULD MANUFACTURE A CURE.
WE SEEM TO BE CURRENTLY LOOKING AT A 100% 'INFECTION' RATE. BUT MAYBE THAT'S NOT THE CASE.

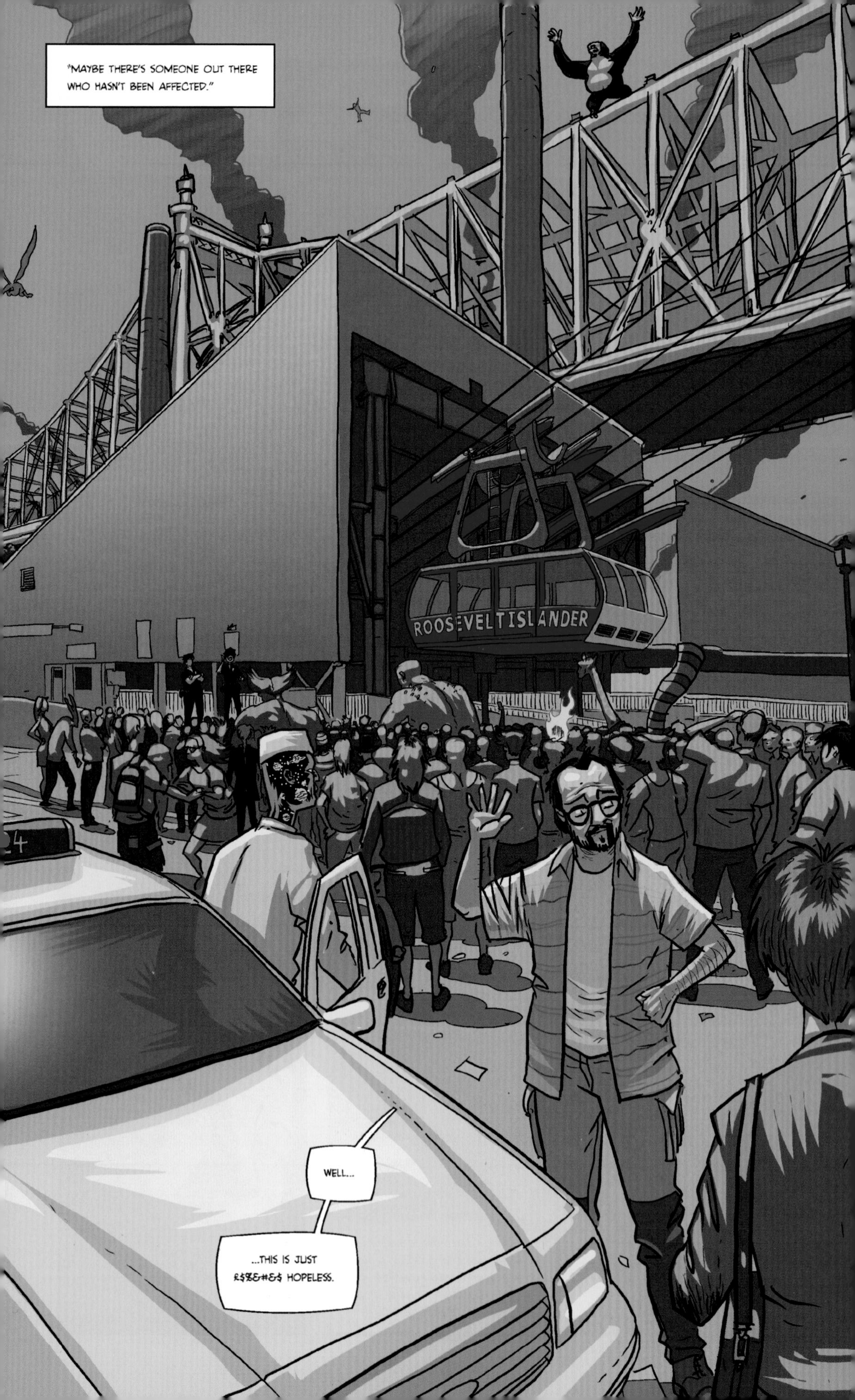
"MAYBE THERE'S SOMEONE OUT THERE WHO HASN'T BEEN AFFECTED."
ROOSEVELTISLANDER
WELL...
...THIS IS JUST £$%&#&$ HOPELESS.

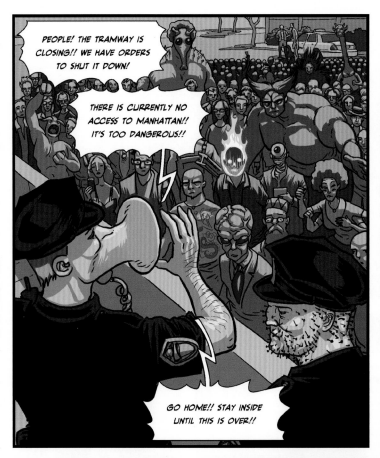

PEOPLE! THE TRAMWAY IS CLOSING!! WE HAVE ORDERS TO SHUT IT DOWN!

THERE IS CURRENTLY NO ACCESS TO MANHATTAN!! IT'S TOO DANGEROUS!!

GO HOME!! STAY INSIDE UNTIL THIS IS OVER!!

GO HOME? MY HOME'S IN MANHATTAN!! AND THE TUNNELS AND SUBWAY ARE SHUT!!

WHERE WE SUPPOSED TO GO?

THIS IS QUITE THE DISGRACE!

GREAT.

MANHATTAN'S BURNING, MY SON'S ON THE EAST SIDE AND I HAVE ABSOLUTELY NO WAY OF...

THE FACT THAT THIS EVER-EXPANDING UNIVERSE EMERGED FROM ONE SINGULARITY 13.75 BILLION YEARS AGO SHOULD REALLY SHOW THAT VERY LITTLE IS IMPOSSIBLE.

ALSO, YOU SHOULD REALLY STOP SMOKING. IT IS ENORMOUSLY BAD FOR YOU AND MAKES YOU SMELL LIKE AN ELEPHANT'S DUNG.

BOOOOOOOOOOM!!!!

JOSH.

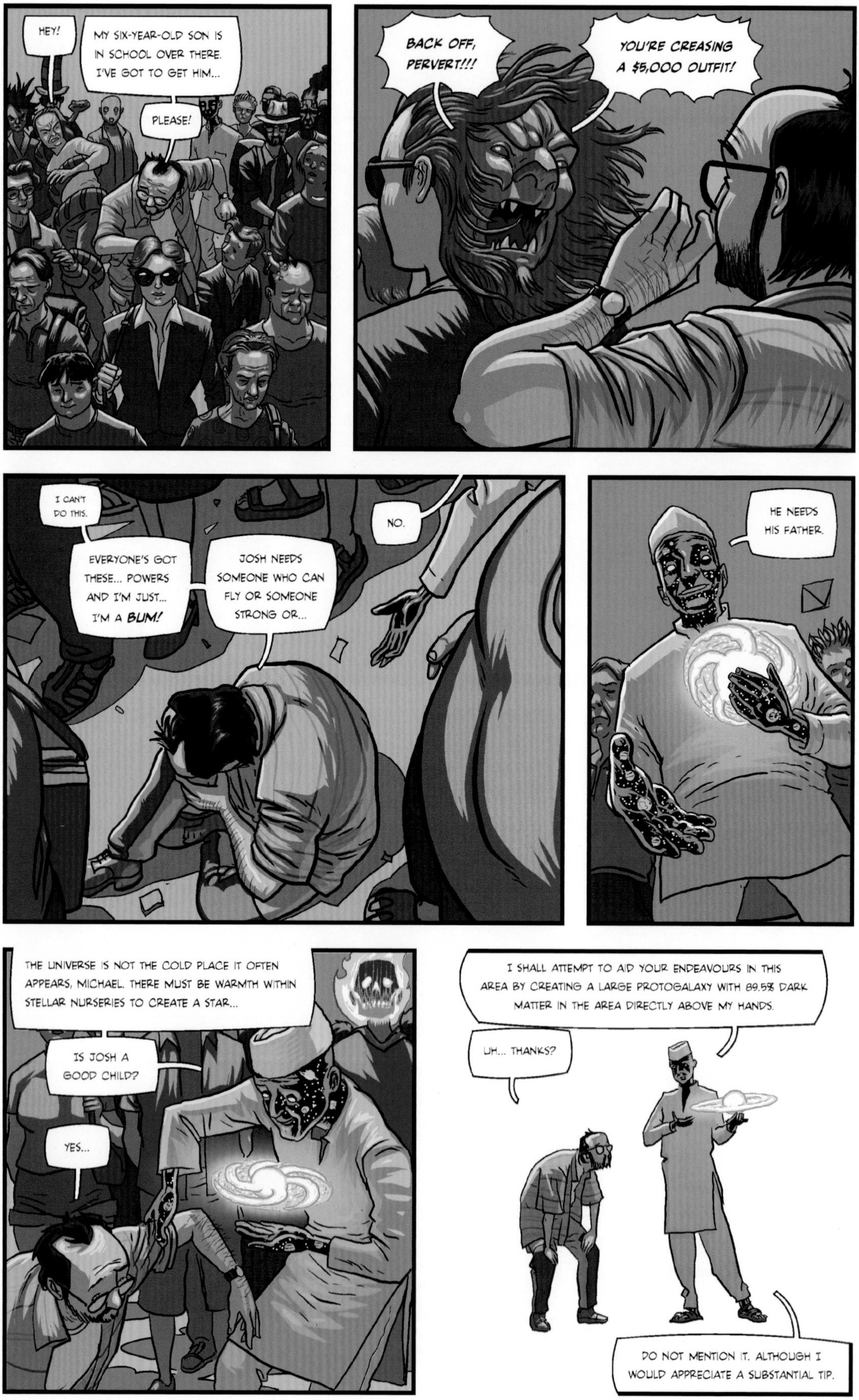
HEY!
MY SIX-YEAR-OLD SON IS IN SCHOOL OVER THERE. I'VE GOT TO GET HIM...
PLEASE!
BACK OFF, PERVERT!!!
YOU'RE CREASING A $5,000 OUTFIT!
I CAN'T DO THIS.
EVERYONE'S GOT THESE... POWERS AND I'M JUST... I'M A BUM!
JOSH NEEDS SOMEONE WHO CAN FLY OR SOMEONE STRONG OR...
NO.
HE NEEDS HIS FATHER.
THE UNIVERSE IS NOT THE COLD PLACE IT OFTEN APPEARS, MICHAEL. THERE MUST BE WARMTH WITHIN STELLAR NURSERIES TO CREATE A STAR...
IS JOSH A GOOD CHILD?
YES...
I SHALL ATTEMPT TO AID YOUR ENDEAVOURS IN THIS AREA BY CREATING A LARGE PROTOGALAXY WITH 89.5% DARK MATTER IN THE AREA DIRECTLY ABOVE MY HANDS.
UH... THANKS?
DO NOT MENTION IT. ALTHOUGH I WOULD APPRECIATE A SUBSTANTIAL TIP.

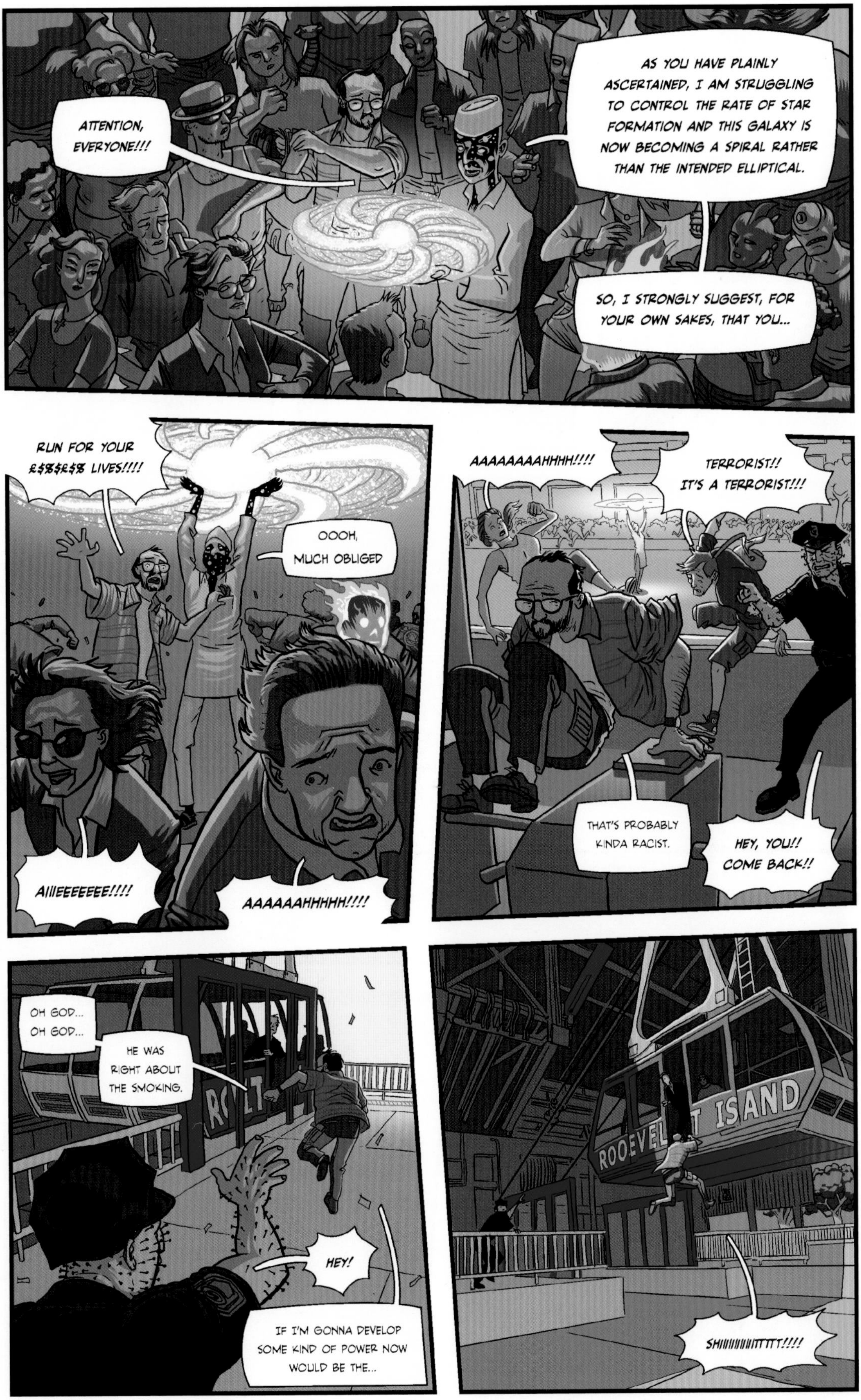
ATTENTION, EVERYONE!!!
AS YOU HAVE PLAINLY ASCERTAINED, I AM STRUGGLING TO CONTROL THE RATE OF STAR FORMATION AND THIS GALAXY IS NOW BECOMING A SPIRAL RATHER THAN THE INTENDED ELLIPTICAL.
SO, I STRONGLY SUGGEST, FOR YOUR OWN SAKES, THAT YOU...
RUN FOR YOUR £$%$£$% LIVES!!!!
OOOH, MUCH OBLIGED
AIIIEEEEEEE!!!!
AAAAAAHHHHH!!!!
AAAAAAAAHHHH!!!!
TERRORIST!! IT'S A TERRORIST!!!
THAT'S PROBABLY KINDA RACIST.
HEY, YOU!! COME BACK!!
OH GOD... OH GOD...
HE WAS RIGHT ABOUT THE SMOKING.
HEY!
IF I'M GONNA DEVELOP SOME KIND OF POWER NOW WOULD BE THE...
ROOEVEL T ISAND
SHIIIIIIIIIITTTTT!!!!

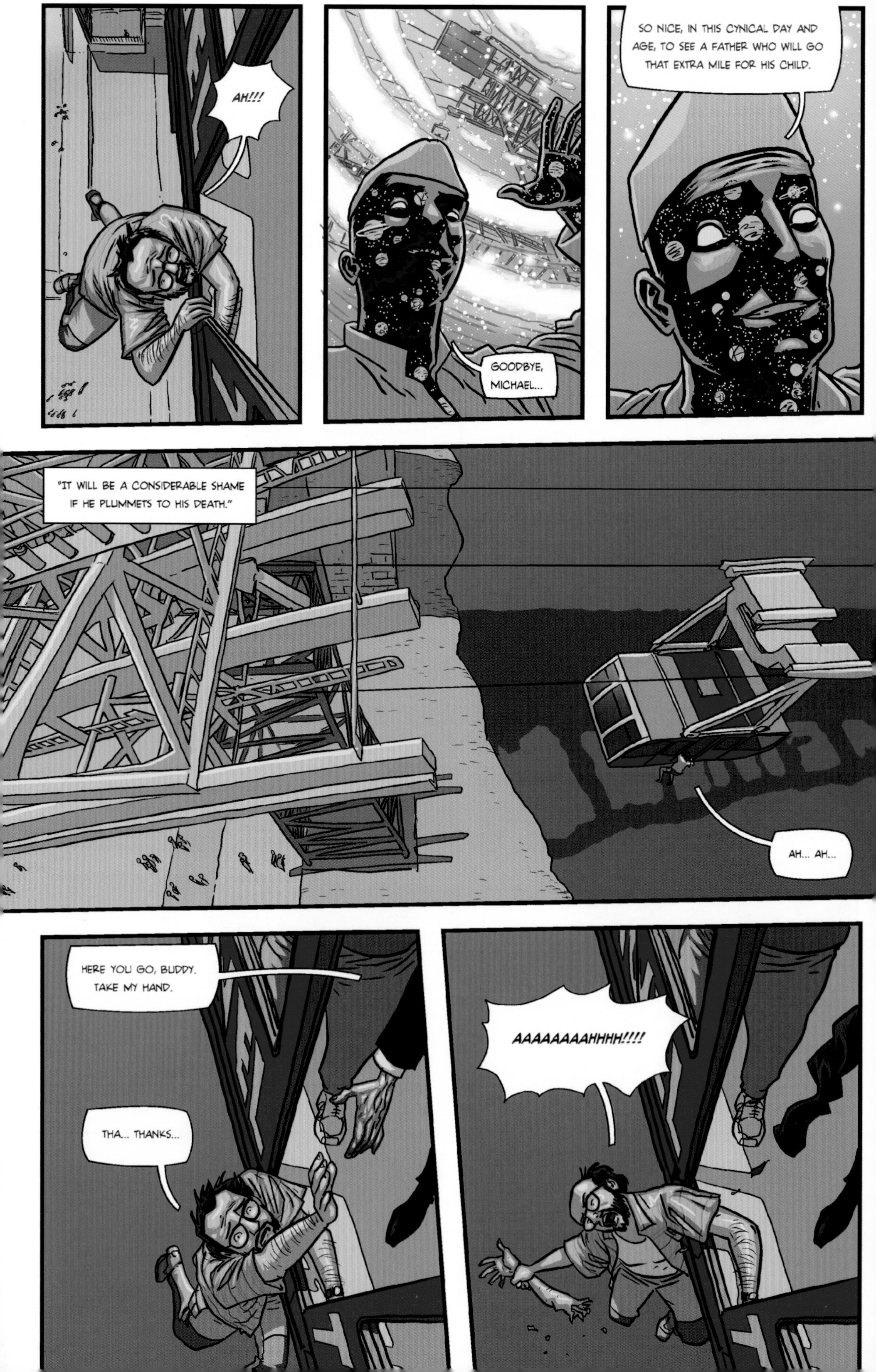
AH!!!
GOODBYE, MICHAEL...
SO NICE, IN THIS CYNICAL DAY AND AGE, TO SEE A FATHER WHO WILL GO THAT EXTRA MILE FOR HIS CHILD.
"IT WILL BE A CONSIDERABLE SHAME IF HE PLUMMETS TO HIS DEATH."
AH... AH...
HERE YOU GO, BUDDY. TAKE MY HAND.
THA... THANKS...
AAAAAAAAHHHH!!!!

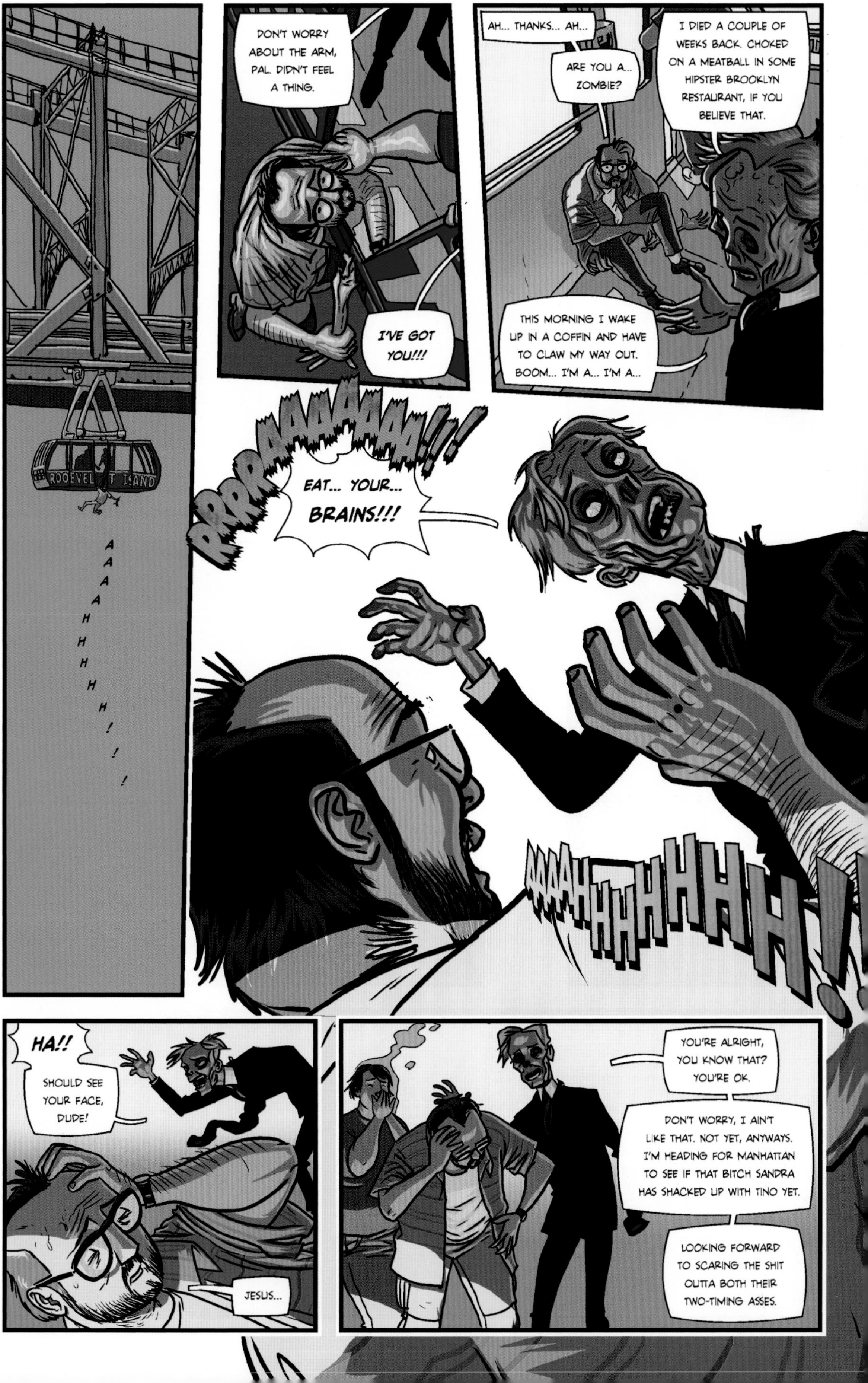
ROOSEVELT ISLAND
AAAAHHHHH!!!
DON'T WORRY ABOUT THE ARM, PAL. DIDN'T FEEL A THING.
I'VE GOT YOU!!!
AH... THANKS... AH...
ARE YOU A... ZOMBIE?
I DIED A COUPLE OF WEEKS BACK. CHOKED ON A MEATBALL IN SOME HIPSTER BROOKLYN RESTAURANT, IF YOU BELIEVE THAT.
THIS MORNING I WAKE UP IN A COFFIN AND HAVE TO CLAW MY WAY OUT. BOOM... I'M A... I'M A...
RRRRAAAAAAAAA!!!
EAT... YOUR... BRAINS!!!
AAAAHHHHHHHHH!!
HA!!
SHOULD SEE YOUR FACE, DUDE!
JESUS...
YOU'RE ALRIGHT, YOU KNOW THAT? YOU'RE OK.
DON'T WORRY, I AIN'T LIKE THAT. NOT YET, ANYWAYS. I'M HEADING FOR MANHATTAN TO SEE IF THAT BITCH SANDRA HAS SHACKED UP WITH TINO YET.
LOOKING FORWARD TO SCARING THE SHIT OUTTA BOTH THEIR TWO-TIMING ASSES.

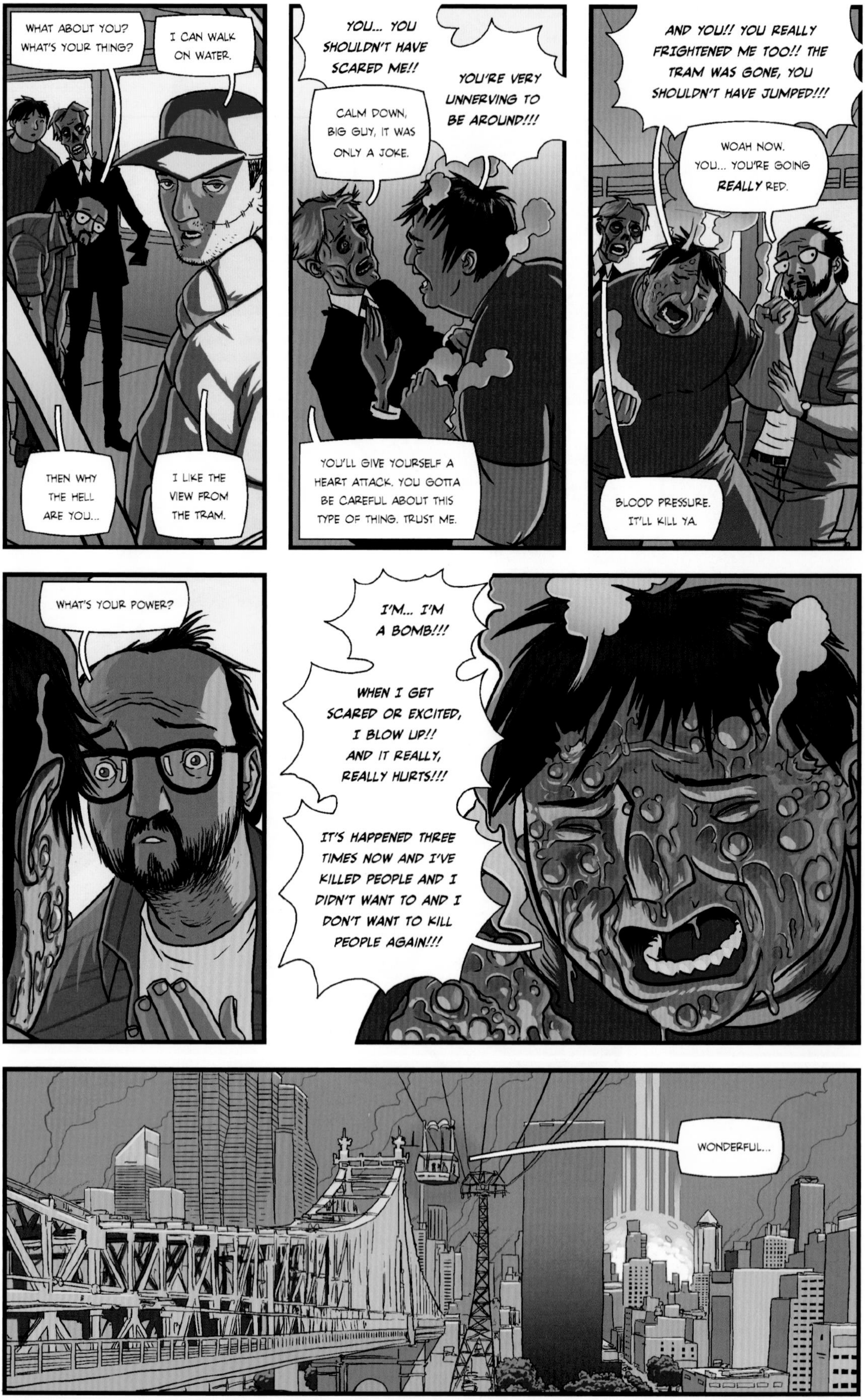
WHAT ABOUT YOU? WHAT'S YOUR THING?
I CAN WALK ON WATER.
THEN WHY THE HELL ARE YOU...
I LIKE THE VIEW FROM THE TRAM.
YOU... YOU SHOULDN'T HAVE SCARED ME!!
CALM DOWN, BIG GUY, IT WAS ONLY A JOKE.
YOU'RE VERY UNNERVING TO BE AROUND!!!
YOU'LL GIVE YOURSELF A HEART ATTACK. YOU GOTTA BE CAREFUL ABOUT THIS TYPE OF THING. TRUST ME.
AND YOU!! YOU REALLY FRIGHTENED ME TOO!! THE TRAM WAS GONE, YOU SHOULDN'T HAVE JUMPED!!!
WOAH NOW. YOU... YOU'RE GOING REALLY RED.
BLOOD PRESSURE. IT'LL KILL YA.
WHAT'S YOUR POWER?
I'M... I'M A BOMB!!!
WHEN I GET SCARED OR EXCITED, I BLOW UP!! AND IT REALLY, REALLY HURTS!!!
IT'S HAPPENED THREE TIMES NOW AND I'VE KILLED PEOPLE AND I DIDN'T WANT TO AND I DON'T WANT TO KILL PEOPLE AGAIN!!!
WONDERFUL...

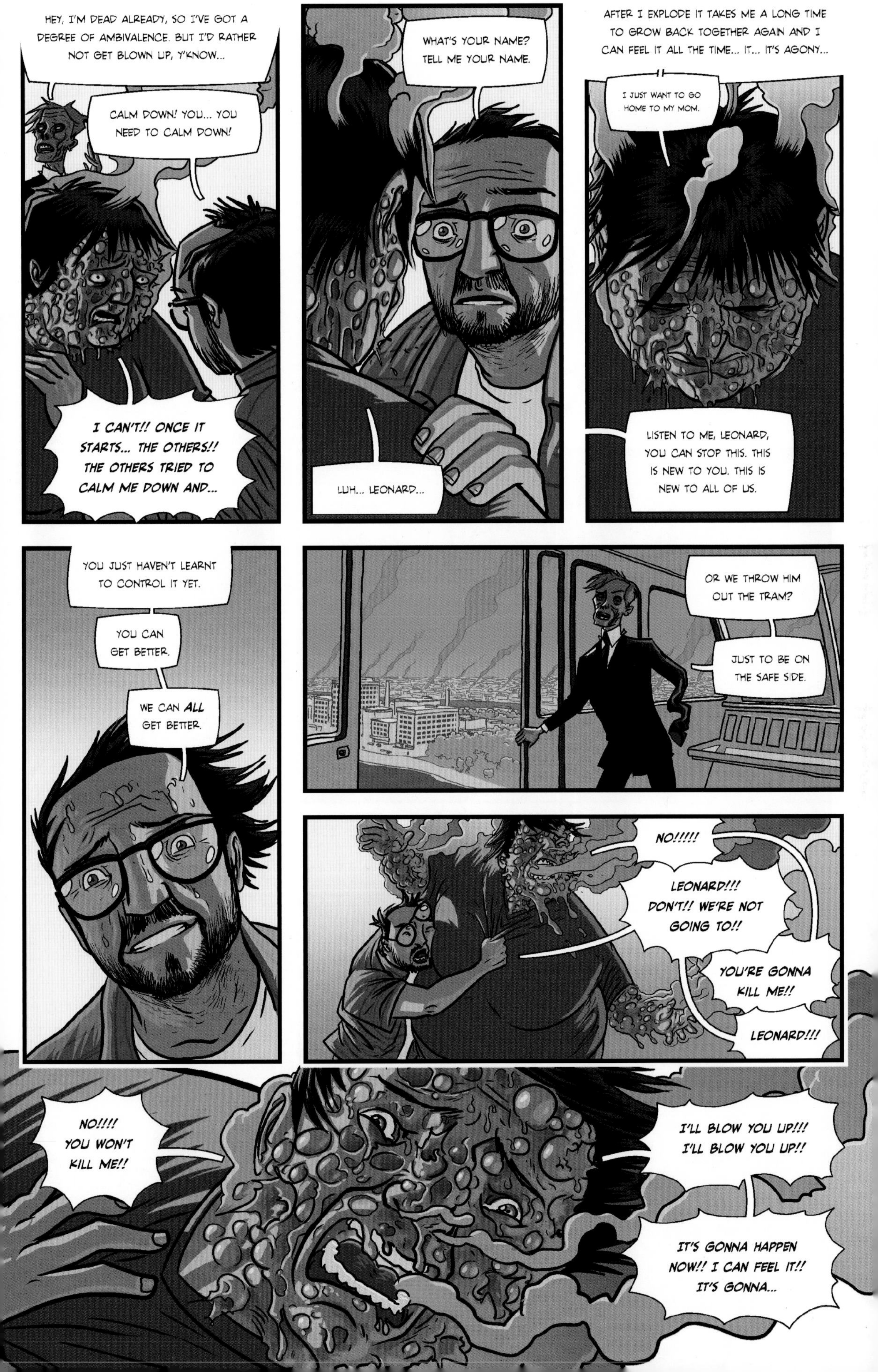
HEY, I'M DEAD ALREADY, SO I'VE GOT A DEGREE OF AMBIVALENCE. BUT I'D RATHER NOT GET BLOWN UP, Y'KNOW...
CALM DOWN! YOU... YOU NEED TO CALM DOWN!
I CAN'T!! ONCE IT STARTS... THE OTHERS!! THE OTHERS TRIED TO CALM ME DOWN AND...
WHAT'S YOUR NAME? TELL ME YOUR NAME.
LUH... LEONARD...
AFTER I EXPLODE IT TAKES ME A LONG TIME TO GROW BACK TOGETHER AGAIN AND I CAN FEEL IT ALL THE TIME... IT... IT'S AGONY...
I JUST WANT TO GO HOME TO MY MOM.
LISTEN TO ME, LEONARD, YOU CAN STOP THIS. THIS IS NEW TO YOU. THIS IS NEW TO ALL OF US.
YOU JUST HAVEN'T LEARNT TO CONTROL IT YET.
YOU CAN GET BETTER.
WE CAN ALL GET BETTER.
OR WE THROW HIM OUT THE TRAM?
JUST TO BE ON THE SAFE SIDE.
NO!!!!!
LEONARD!!! DON'T!! WE'RE NOT GOING TO!!
YOU'RE GONNA KILL ME!!
LEONARD!!!
NO!!!! YOU WON'T KILL ME!!
I'LL BLOW YOU UP!!! I'LL BLOW YOU UP!!
IT'S GONNA HAPPEN NOW!! I CAN FEEL IT!! IT'S GONNA...

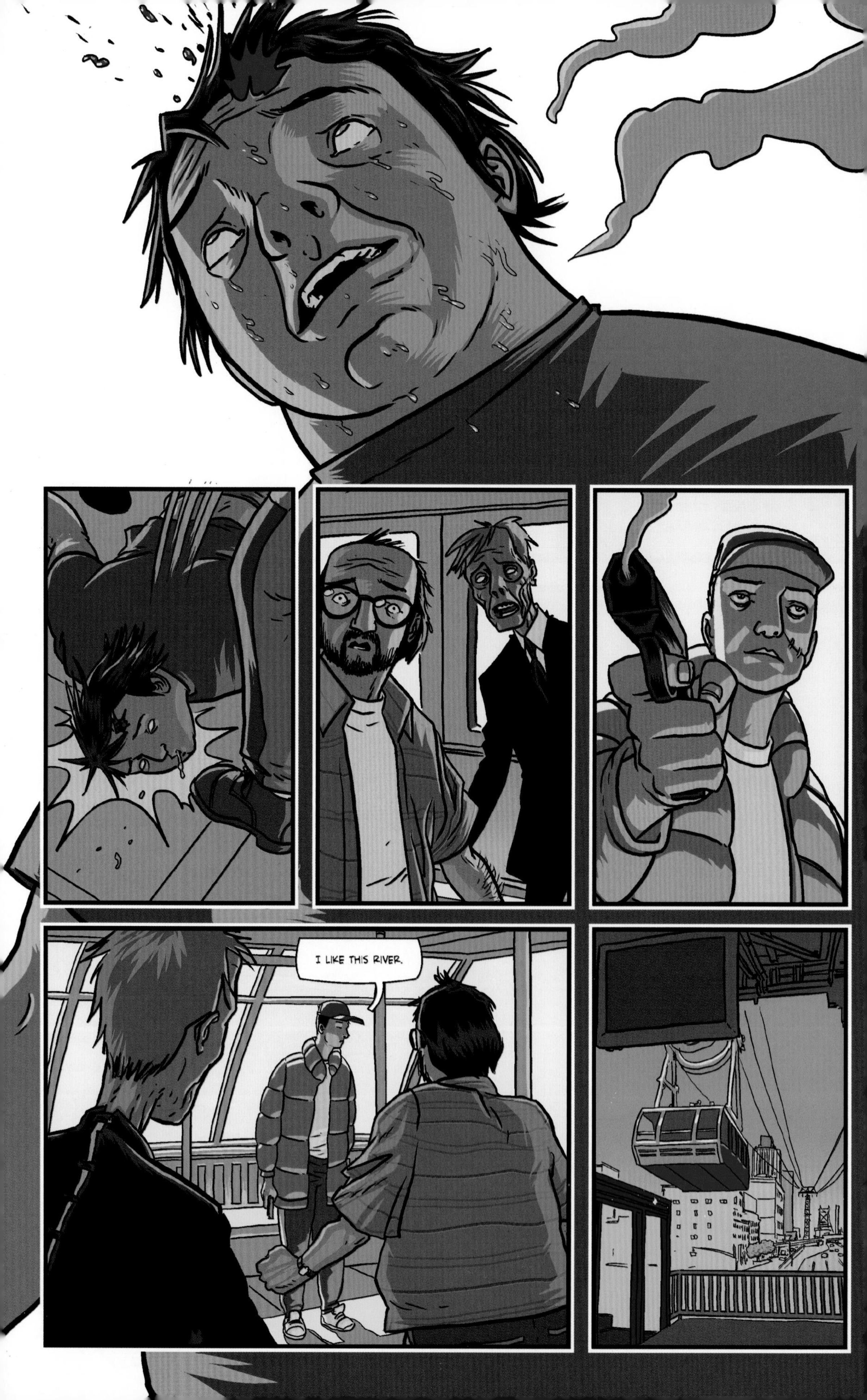
I LIKE THIS RIVER.

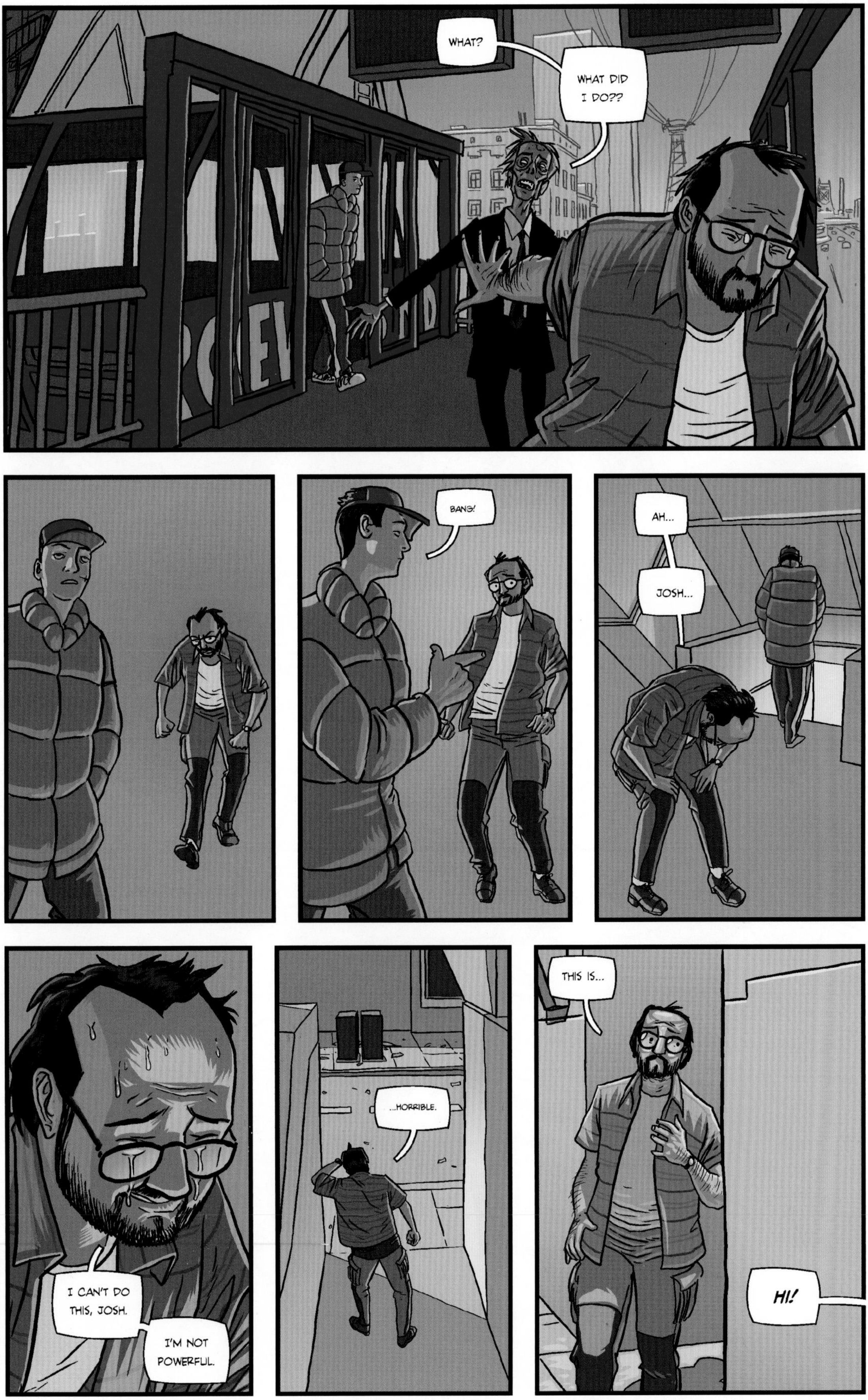
WHAT?
WHAT DID I DO??
BANG!
AH...
JOSH...
I CAN'T DO THIS, JOSH.
I'M NOT POWERFUL.
...HORRIBLE.
THIS IS...
HI!

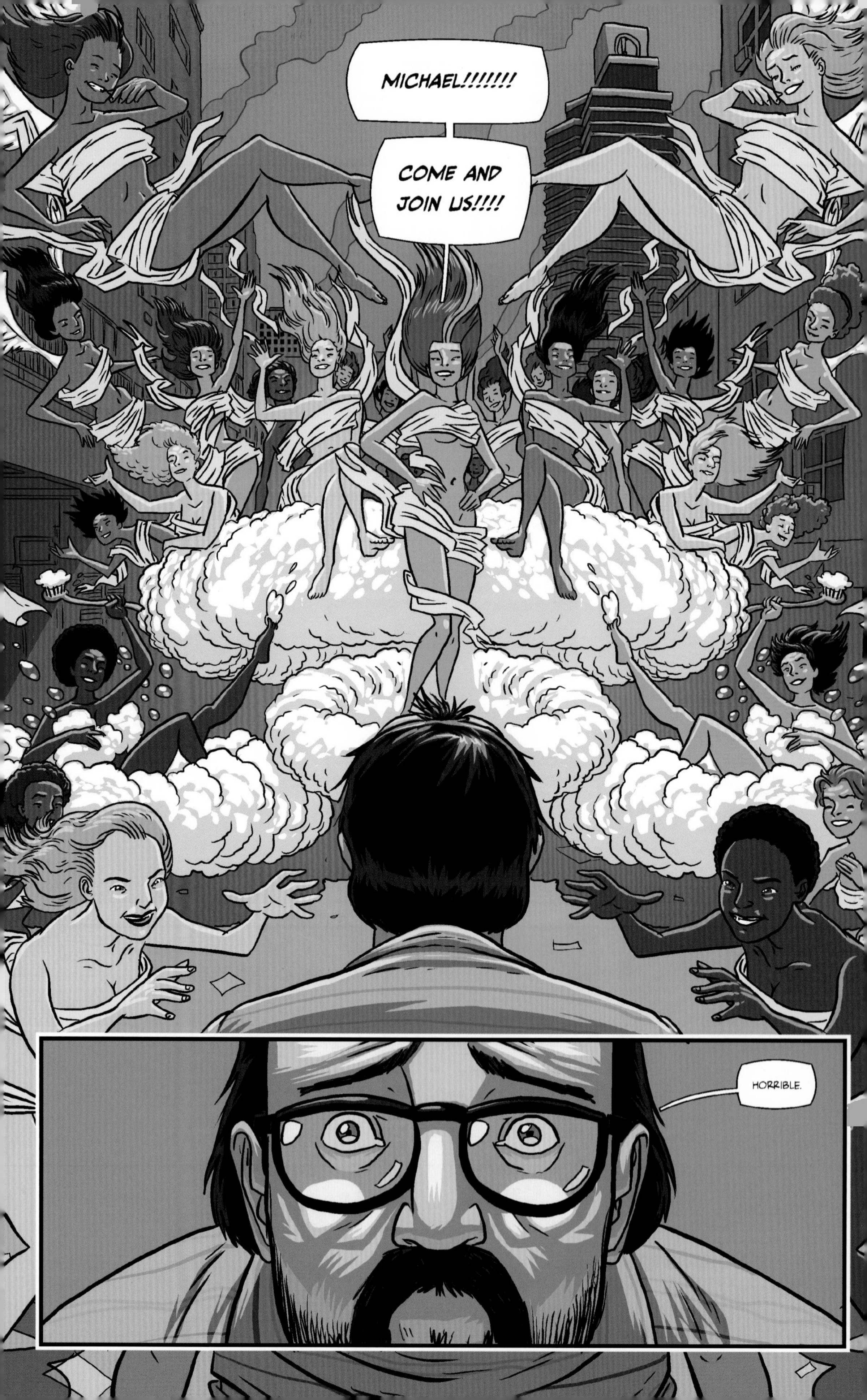
MICHAEL!!!!!!!
COME AND JOIN US!!!!
HORRIBLE.

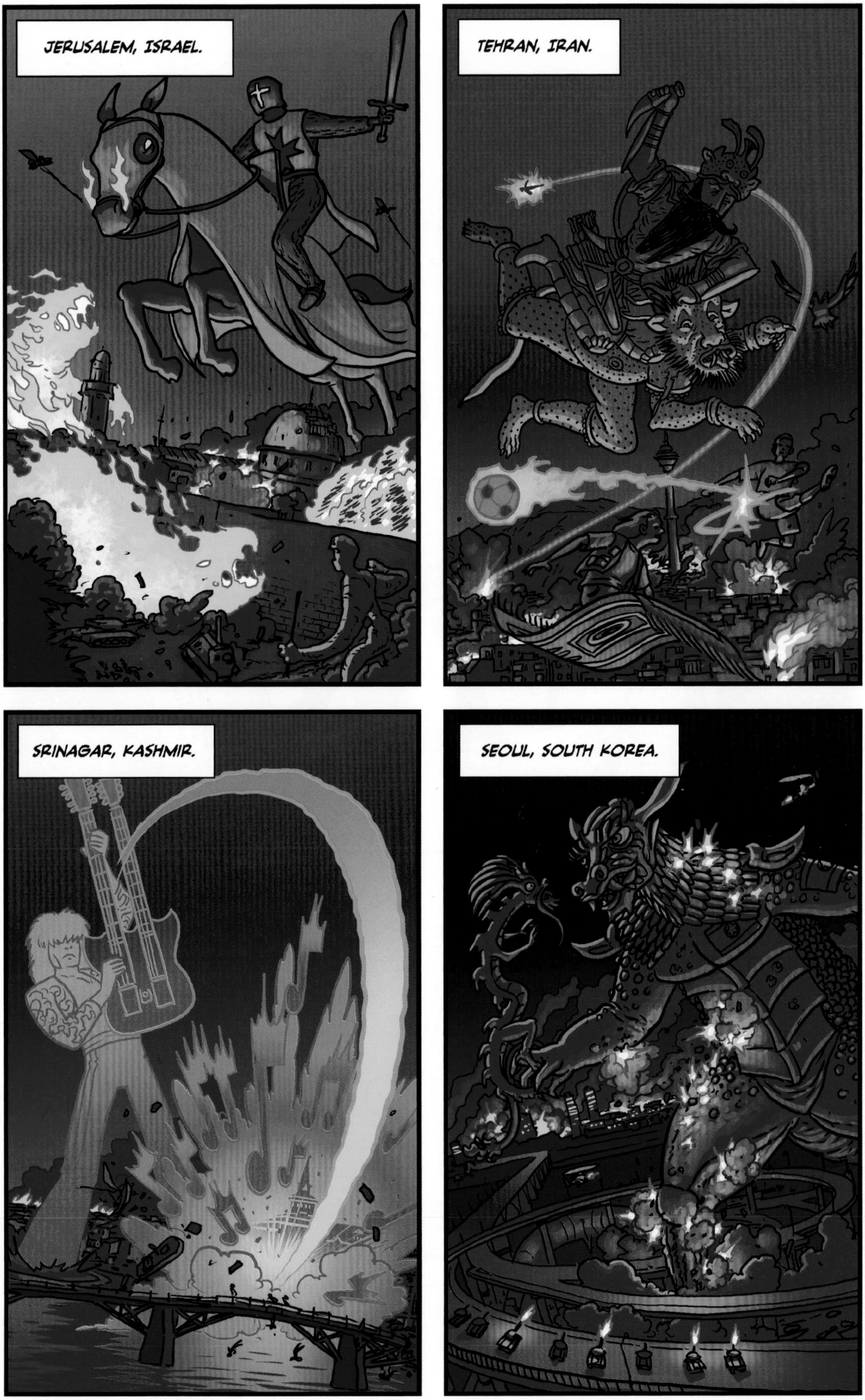
JERUSALEM, ISRAEL.
TEHRAN, IRAN.
SRINAGAR, KASHMIR.
SEOUL, SOUTH KOREA.

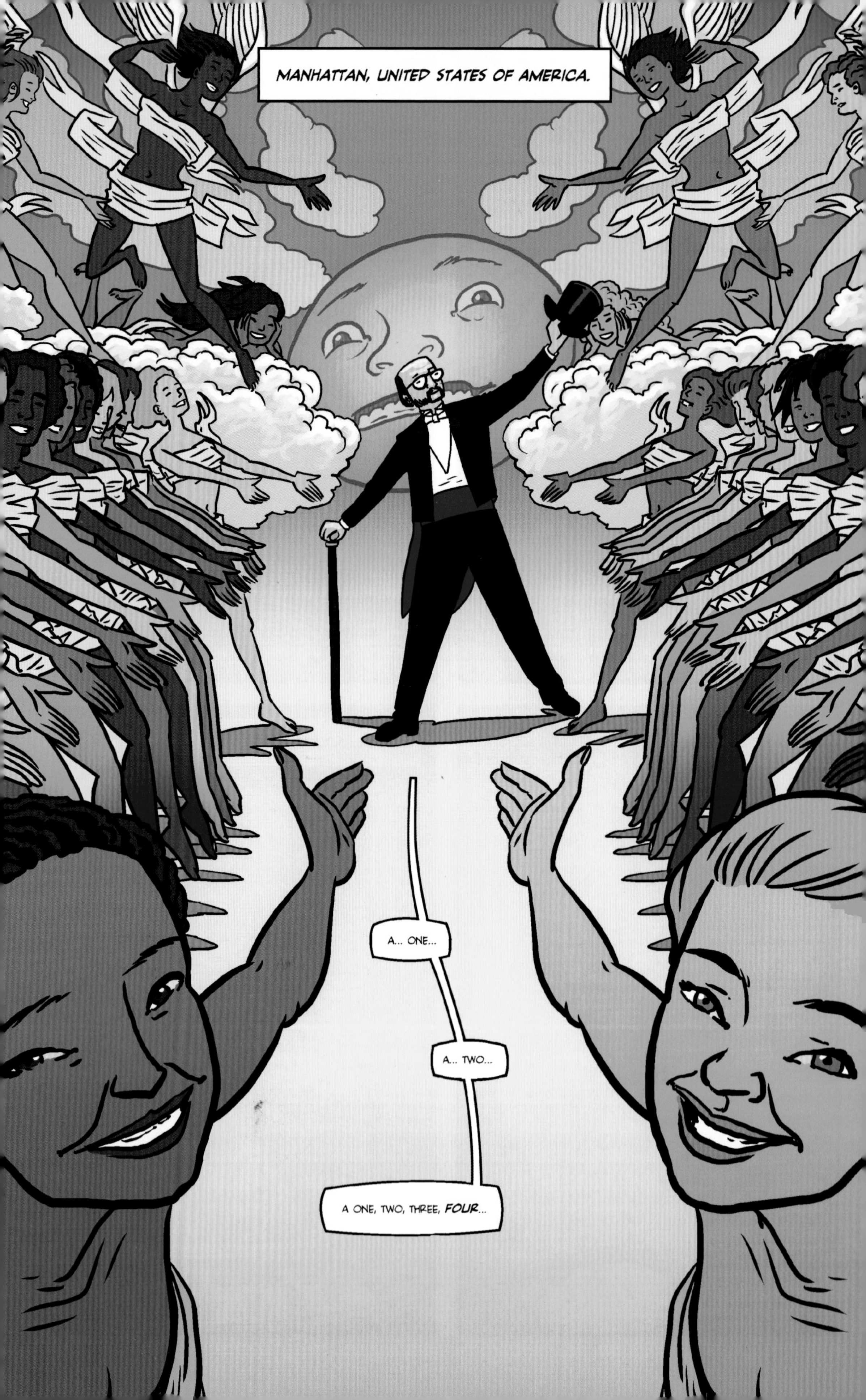
MANHATTAN, UNITED STATES OF AMERICA.
A... ONE...
A... TWO...
A ONE, TWO, THREE, FOUR...

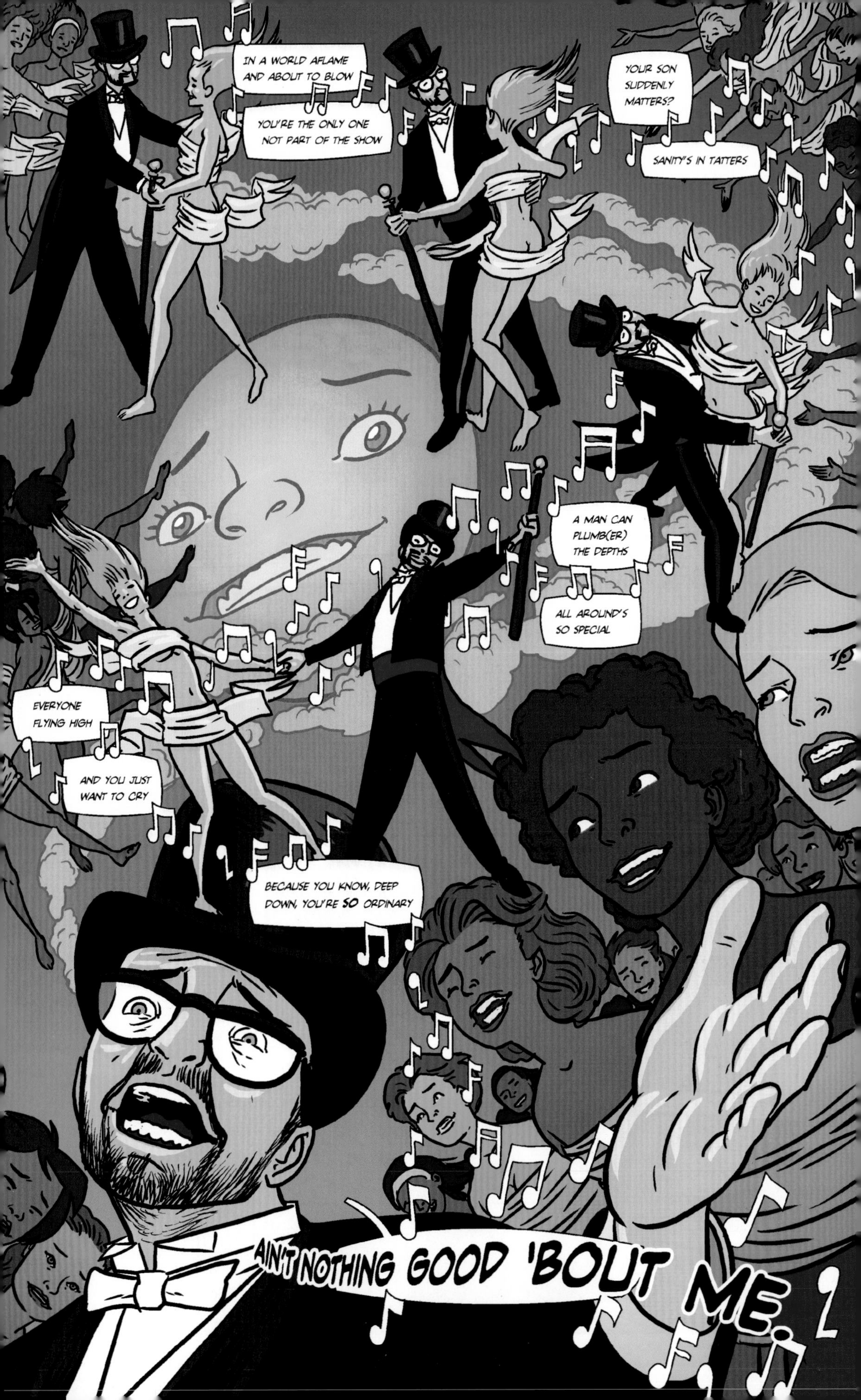
IN A WORLD AFLAME AND ABOUT TO BLOW
YOU'RE THE ONLY ONE NOT PART OF THE SHOW
YOUR SON SUDDENLY MATTERS?
SANITY'S IN TATTERS
A MAN CAN PLUMB(ER) THE DEPTHS
ALL AROUND'S SO SPECIAL
EVERYONE FLYING HIGH
AND YOU JUST WANT TO CRY
BECAUSE YOU KNOW, DEEP DOWN, YOU'RE SO ORDINARY
AIN'T NOTHING GOOD 'BOUT ME.

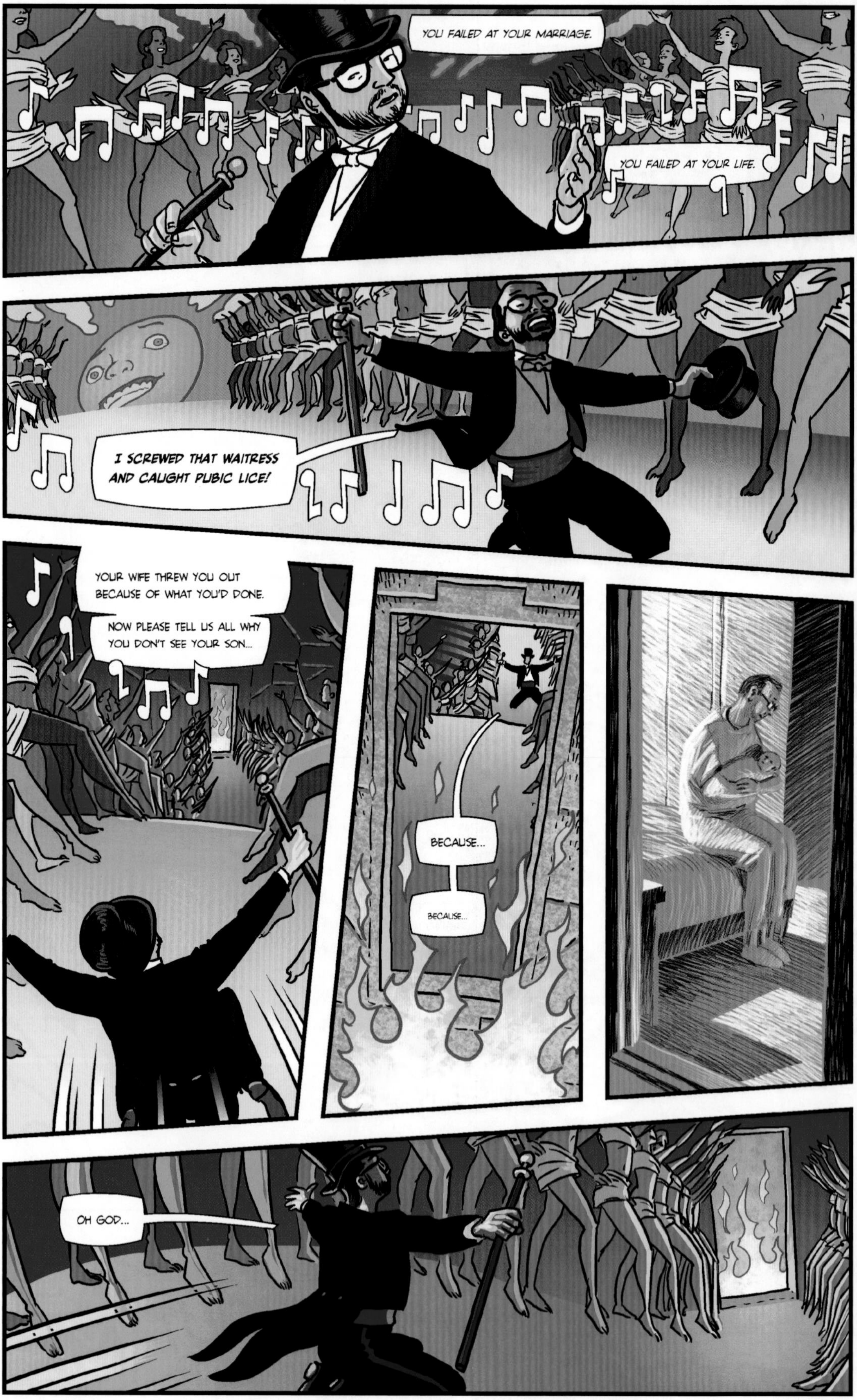
YOU FAILED AT YOUR MARRIAGE.
YOU FAILED AT YOUR LIFE.
I SCREWED THAT WAITRESS AND CAUGHT PUBIC LICE!
YOUR WIFE THREW YOU OUT BECAUSE OF WHAT YOU'D DONE.
NOW PLEASE TELL US ALL WHY YOU DON'T SEE YOUR SON...
BECAUSE...
BECAUSE...
OH GOD...

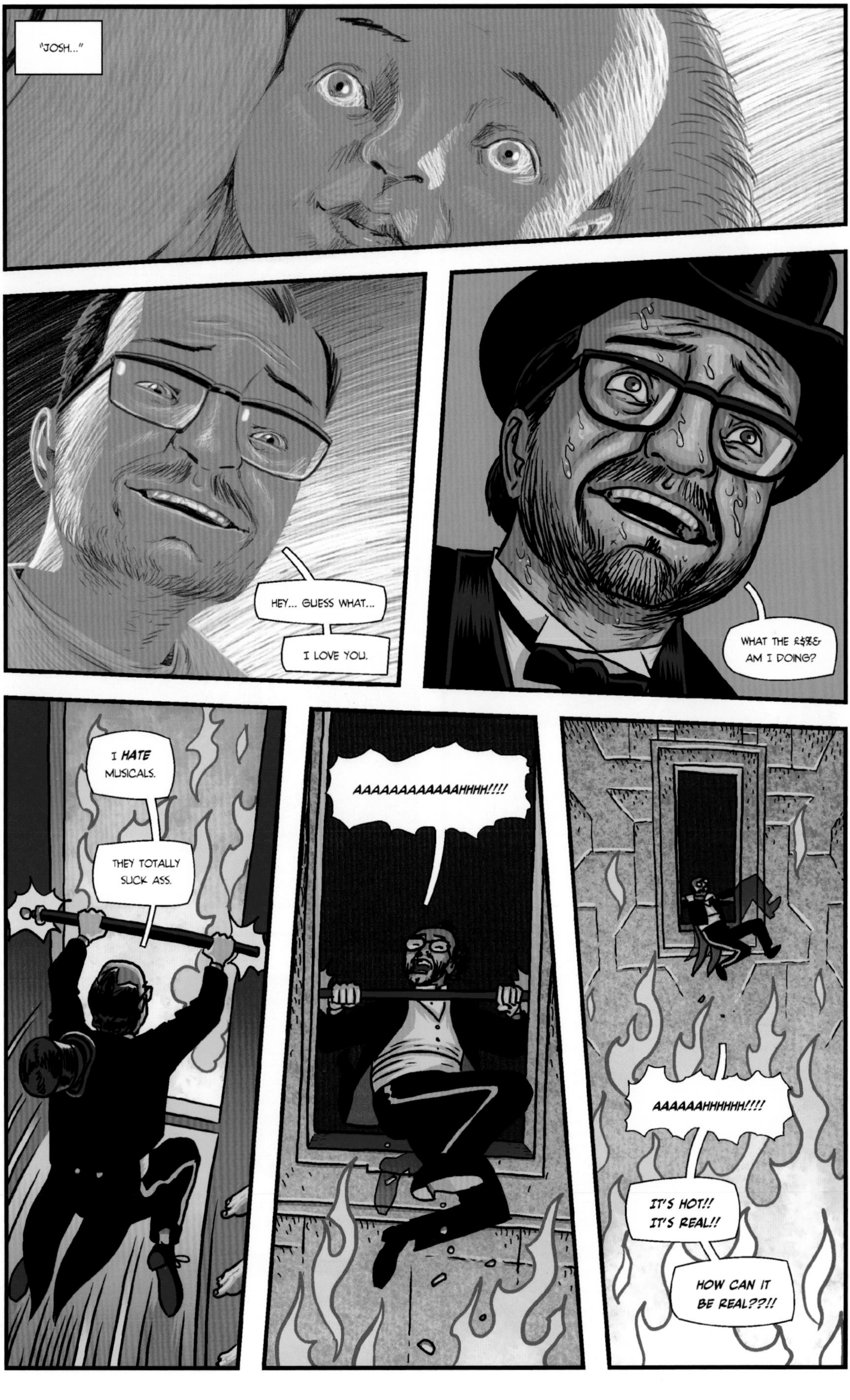
"JOSH..."
HEY... GUESS WHAT...
I LOVE YOU.
WHAT THE £$%& AM I DOING?
I *HATE* MUSICALS.
THEY TOTALLY SUCK ASS.
AAAAAAAAAAAAAHHHH!!!!
AAAAAAHHHHHH!!!!
IT'S HOT!! IT'S REAL!!
HOW CAN IT BE REAL??!!

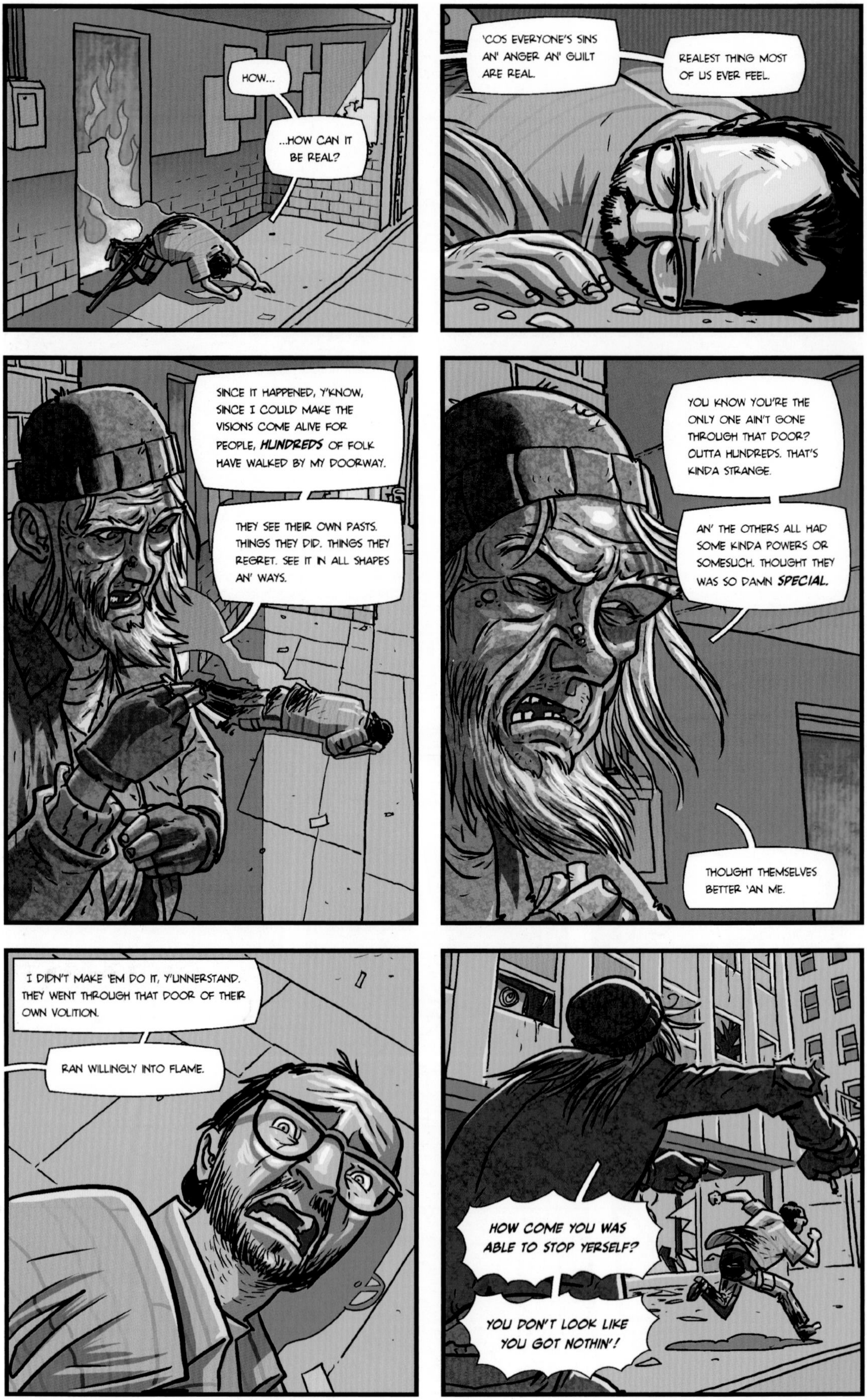
HOW...
...HOW CAN IT BE REAL?
'COS EVERYONE'S SINS AN' ANGER AN' GUILT ARE REAL.
REALEST THING MOST OF US EVER FEEL.
SINCE IT HAPPENED, Y'KNOW, SINCE I COULD MAKE THE VISIONS COME ALIVE FOR PEOPLE, HUNDREDS OF FOLK HAVE WALKED BY MY DOORWAY.
THEY SEE THEIR OWN PASTS. THINGS THEY DID. THINGS THEY REGRET. SEE IT IN ALL SHAPES AN' WAYS.
YOU KNOW YOU'RE THE ONLY ONE AIN'T GONE THROUGH THAT DOOR? OUTTA HUNDREDS. THAT'S KINDA STRANGE.
AN' THE OTHERS ALL HAD SOME KINDA POWERS OR SOMESUCH. THOUGHT THEY WAS SO DAMN SPECIAL.
THOUGHT THEMSELVES BETTER 'AN ME.
I DIDN'T MAKE 'EM DO IT, Y'UNNERSTAND. THEY WENT THROUGH THAT DOOR OF THEIR OWN VOLITION.
RAN WILLINGLY INTO FLAME.
HOW COME YOU WAS ABLE TO STOP YERSELF?
YOU DON'T LOOK LIKE YOU GOT NOTHIN'!

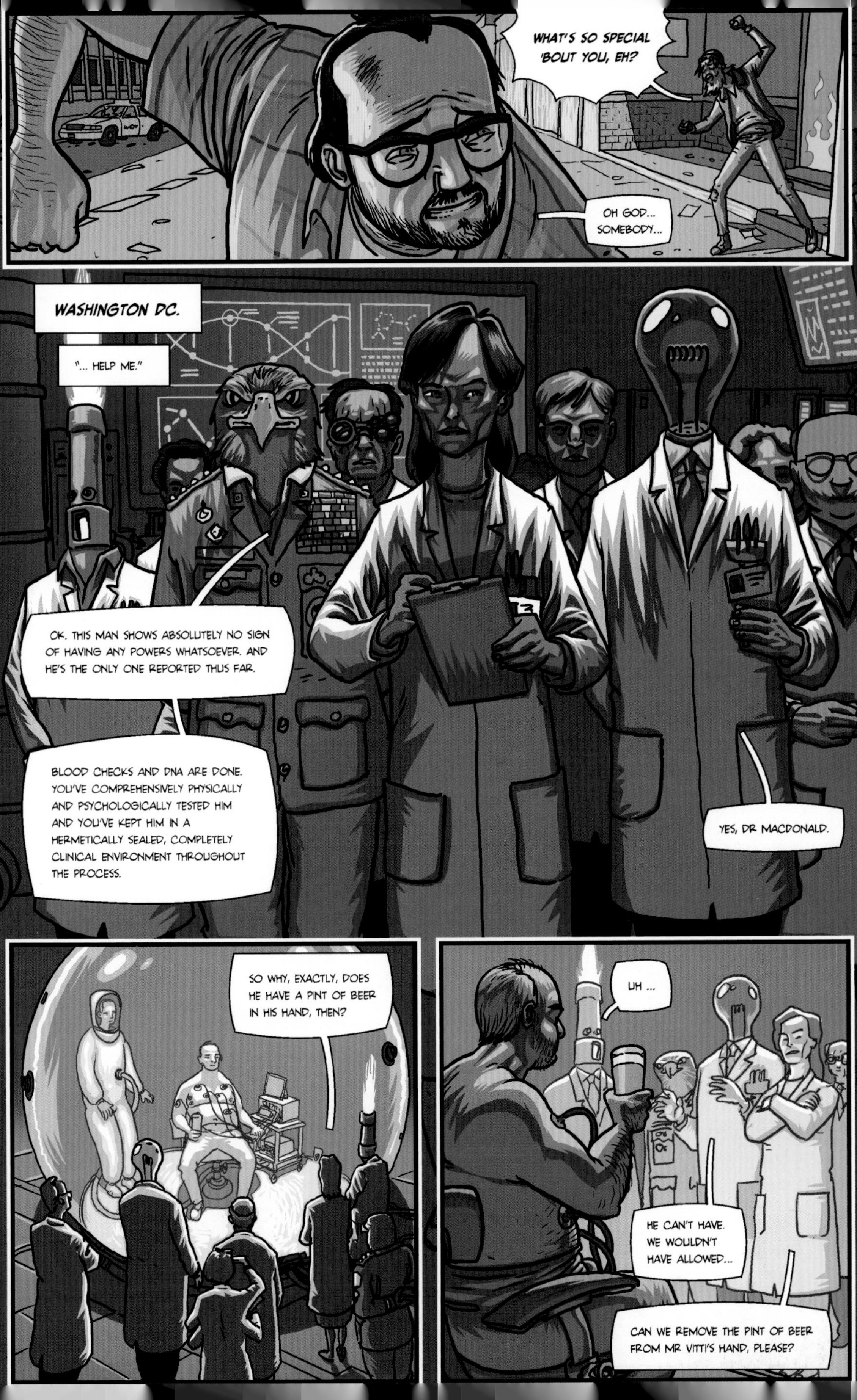
WHAT'S SO SPECIAL 'BOUT YOU, EH?
OH GOD... SOMEBODY...
WASHINGTON DC.
"... HELP ME."
OK. THIS MAN SHOWS ABSOLUTELY NO SIGN OF HAVING ANY POWERS WHATSOEVER. AND HE'S THE ONLY ONE REPORTED THUS FAR.
BLOOD CHECKS AND DNA ARE DONE. YOU'VE COMPREHENSIVELY PHYSICALLY AND PSYCHOLOGICALLY TESTED HIM AND YOU'VE KEPT HIM IN A HERMETICALLY SEALED, COMPLETELY CLINICAL ENVIRONMENT THROUGHOUT THE PROCESS.
YES, DR MACDONALD.
SO WHY, EXACTLY, DOES HE HAVE A PINT OF BEER IN HIS HAND, THEN?
UH ...
HE CAN'T HAVE. WE WOULDN'T HAVE ALLOWED...
CAN WE REMOVE THE PINT OF BEER FROM MR VITTI'S HAND, PLEASE?

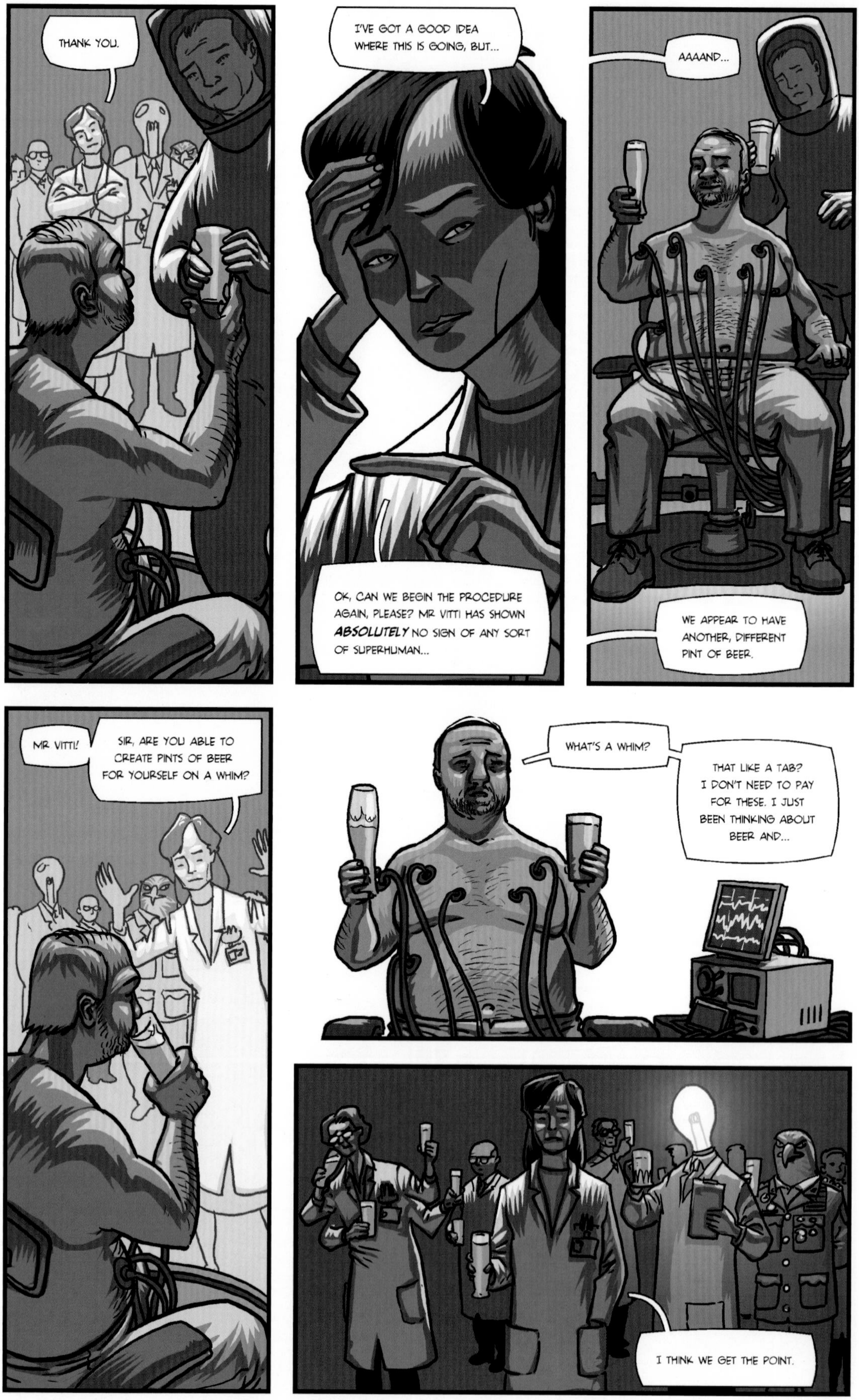
THANK YOU.
I'VE GOT A GOOD IDEA WHERE THIS IS GOING, BUT...
OK, CAN WE BEGIN THE PROCEDURE AGAIN, PLEASE? MR VITTI HAS SHOWN ABSOLUTELY NO SIGN OF ANY SORT OF SUPERHUMAN...
AAAAND...
WE APPEAR TO HAVE ANOTHER, DIFFERENT PINT OF BEER.
MR VITTI!
SIR, ARE YOU ABLE TO CREATE PINTS OF BEER FOR YOURSELF ON A WHIM?
WHAT'S A WHIM?
THAT LIKE A TAB? I DON'T NEED TO PAY FOR THESE. I JUST BEEN THINKING ABOUT BEER AND...
I THINK WE GET THE POINT.

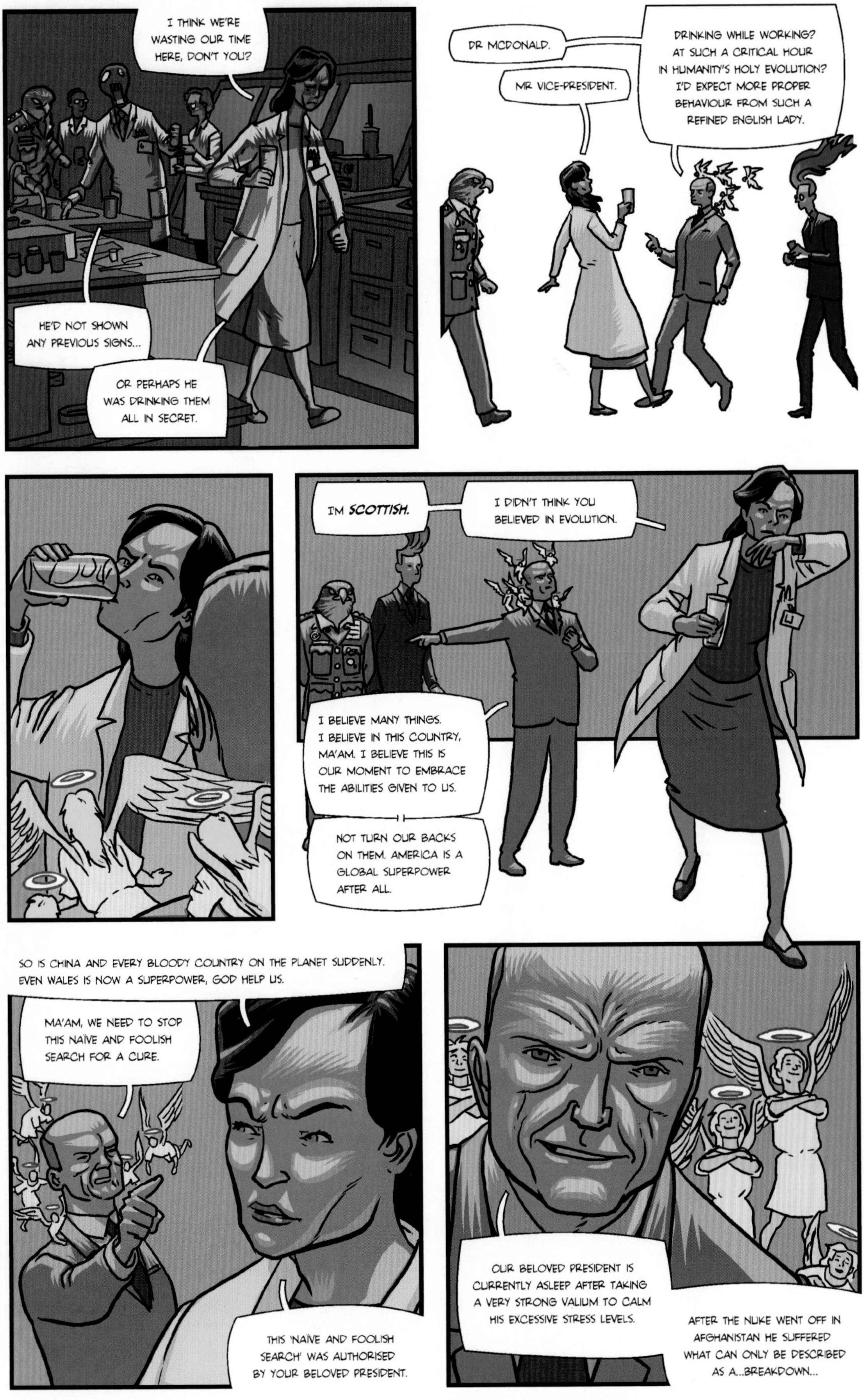
I THINK WE'RE WASTING OUR TIME HERE, DON'T YOU?
HE'D NOT SHOWN ANY PREVIOUS SIGNS...
OR PERHAPS HE WAS DRINKING THEM ALL IN SECRET.
DR MCDONALD.
MR VICE-PRESIDENT.
DRINKING WHILE WORKING? AT SUCH A CRITICAL HOUR IN HUMANITY'S HOLY EVOLUTION? I'D EXPECT MORE PROPER BEHAVIOUR FROM SUCH A REFINED ENGLISH LADY.
I'M *SCOTTISH.*
I DIDN'T THINK YOU BELIEVED IN EVOLUTION.
I BELIEVE MANY THINGS. I BELIEVE IN THIS COUNTRY, MA'AM. I BELIEVE THIS IS OUR MOMENT TO EMBRACE THE ABILITIES GIVEN TO US.
NOT TURN OUR BACKS ON THEM. AMERICA IS A GLOBAL SUPERPOWER AFTER ALL.
SO IS CHINA AND EVERY BLOODY COUNTRY ON THE PLANET SUDDENLY. EVEN WALES IS NOW A SUPERPOWER, GOD HELP US.
MA'AM, WE NEED TO STOP THIS NAÏVE AND FOOLISH SEARCH FOR A CURE.
THIS 'NAÏVE AND FOOLISH SEARCH' WAS AUTHORISED BY YOUR BELOVED PRESIDENT.
OUR BELOVED PRESIDENT IS CURRENTLY ASLEEP AFTER TAKING A VERY STRONG VALIUM TO CALM HIS EXCESSIVE STRESS LEVELS.
AFTER THE NUKE WENT OFF IN AFGHANISTAN HE SUFFERED WHAT CAN ONLY BE DESCRIBED AS A...BREAKDOWN...

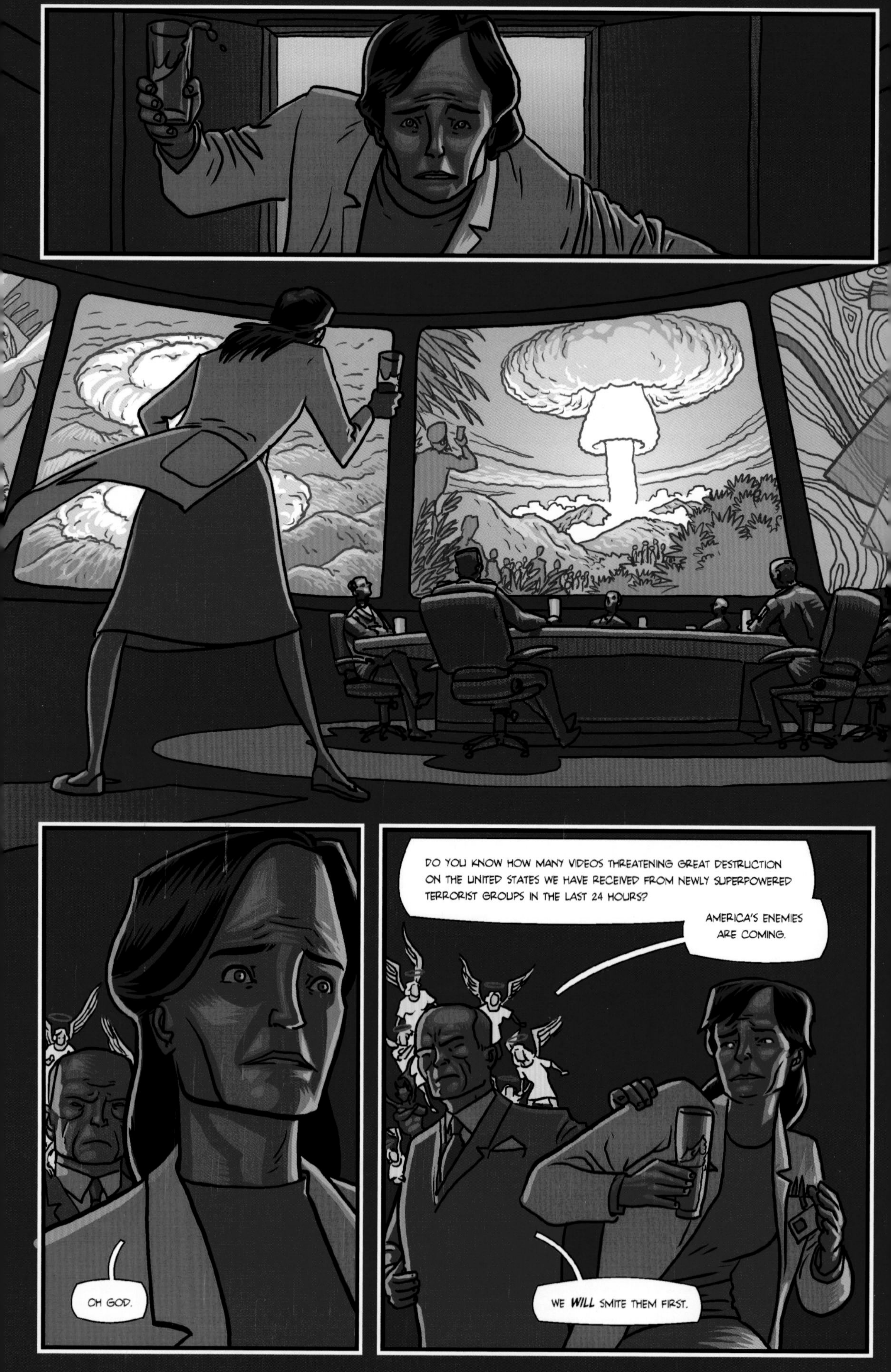
OH GOD.
DO YOU KNOW HOW MANY VIDEOS THREATENING GREAT DESTRUCTION ON THE UNITED STATES WE HAVE RECEIVED FROM NEWLY SUPERPOWERED TERRORIST GROUPS IN THE LAST 24 HOURS?
AMERICA'S ENEMIES ARE COMING.
WE **WILL** SMITE THEM FIRST.

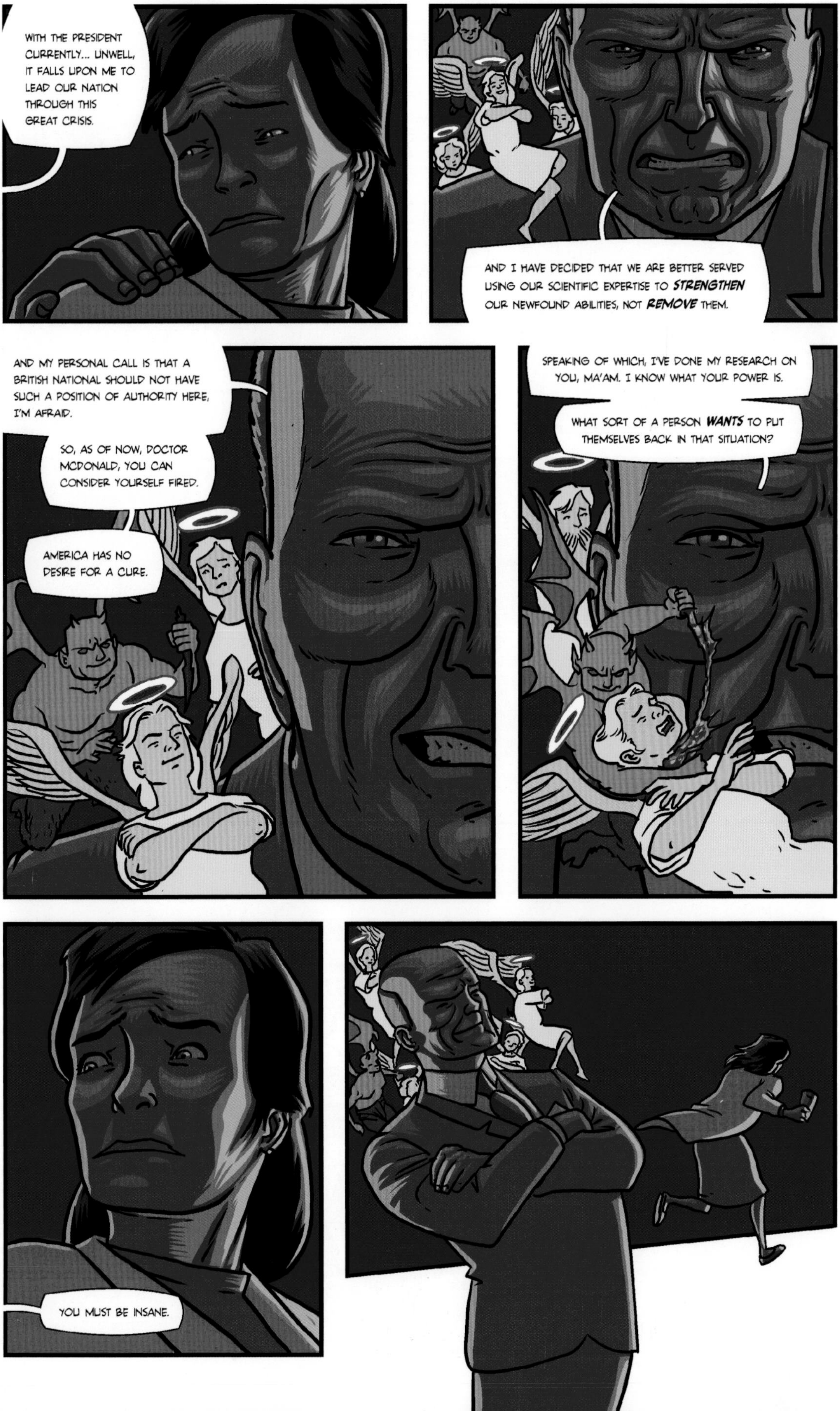
WITH THE PRESIDENT CURRENTLY... UNWELL, IT FALLS UPON ME TO LEAD OUR NATION THROUGH THIS GREAT CRISIS.
AND I HAVE DECIDED THAT WE ARE BETTER SERVED USING OUR SCIENTIFIC EXPERTISE TO STRENGTHEN OUR NEWFOUND ABILITIES, NOT REMOVE THEM.
AND MY PERSONAL CALL IS THAT A BRITISH NATIONAL SHOULD NOT HAVE SUCH A POSITION OF AUTHORITY HERE, I'M AFRAID.
SO, AS OF NOW, DOCTOR MCDONALD, YOU CAN CONSIDER YOURSELF FIRED.
AMERICA HAS NO DESIRE FOR A CURE.
SPEAKING OF WHICH, I'VE DONE MY RESEARCH ON YOU, MA'AM. I KNOW WHAT YOUR POWER IS.
WHAT SORT OF A PERSON WANTS TO PUT THEMSELVES BACK IN THAT SITUATION?
YOU MUST BE INSANE.

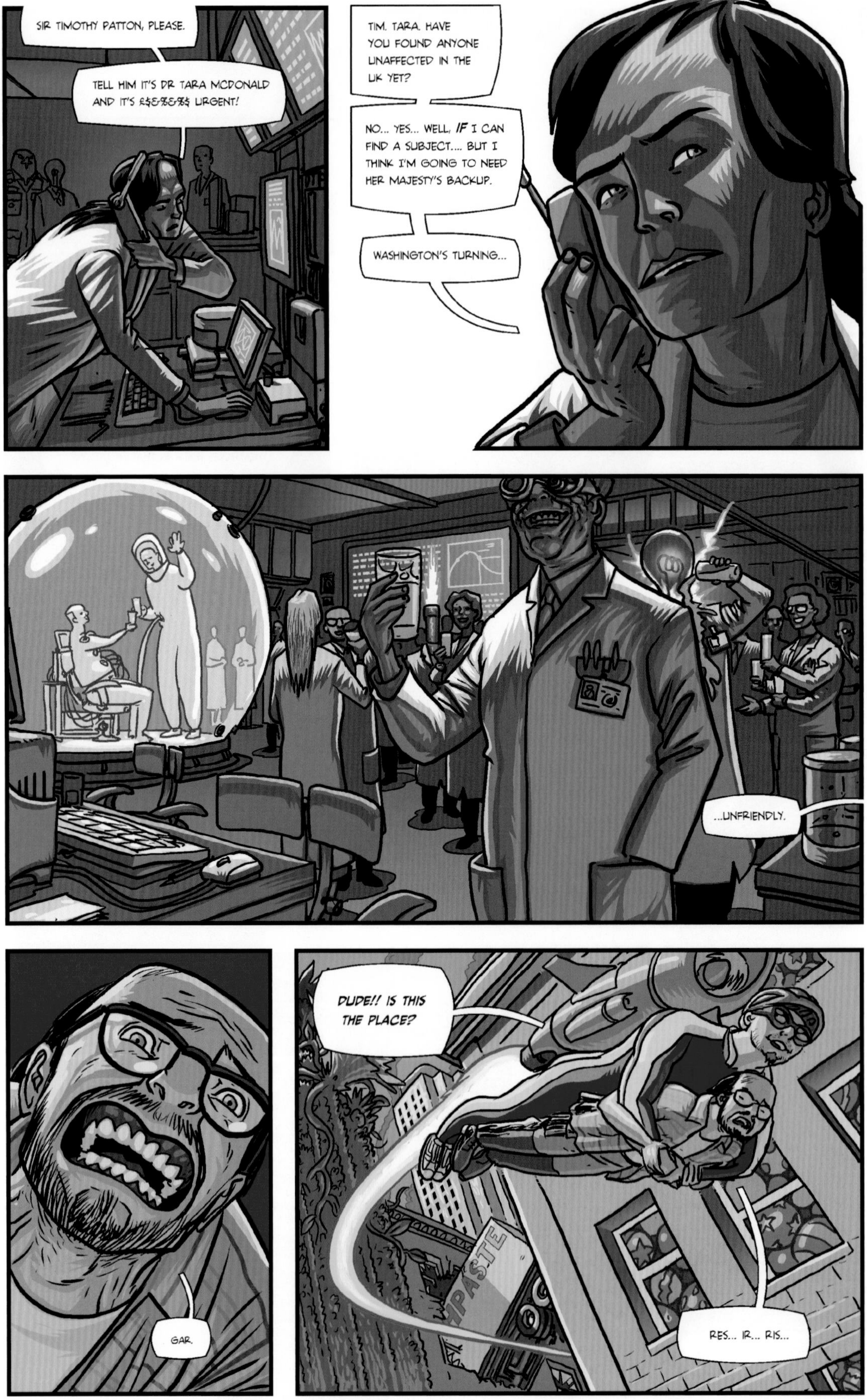
SIR TIMOTHY PATTON, PLEASE.
TELL HIM IT'S DR TARA MCDONALD AND IT'S £$&%&%$ URGENT!
TIM. TARA. HAVE YOU FOUND ANYONE UNAFFECTED IN THE UK YET?
NO... YES... WELL, *IF* I CAN FIND A SUBJECT.... BUT I THINK I'M GOING TO NEED HER MAJESTY'S BACKUP.
WASHINGTON'S TURNING...
...UNFRIENDLY.
GAR.
DUDE!! IS THIS THE PLACE?
RES... IR... RIS...
PASTE

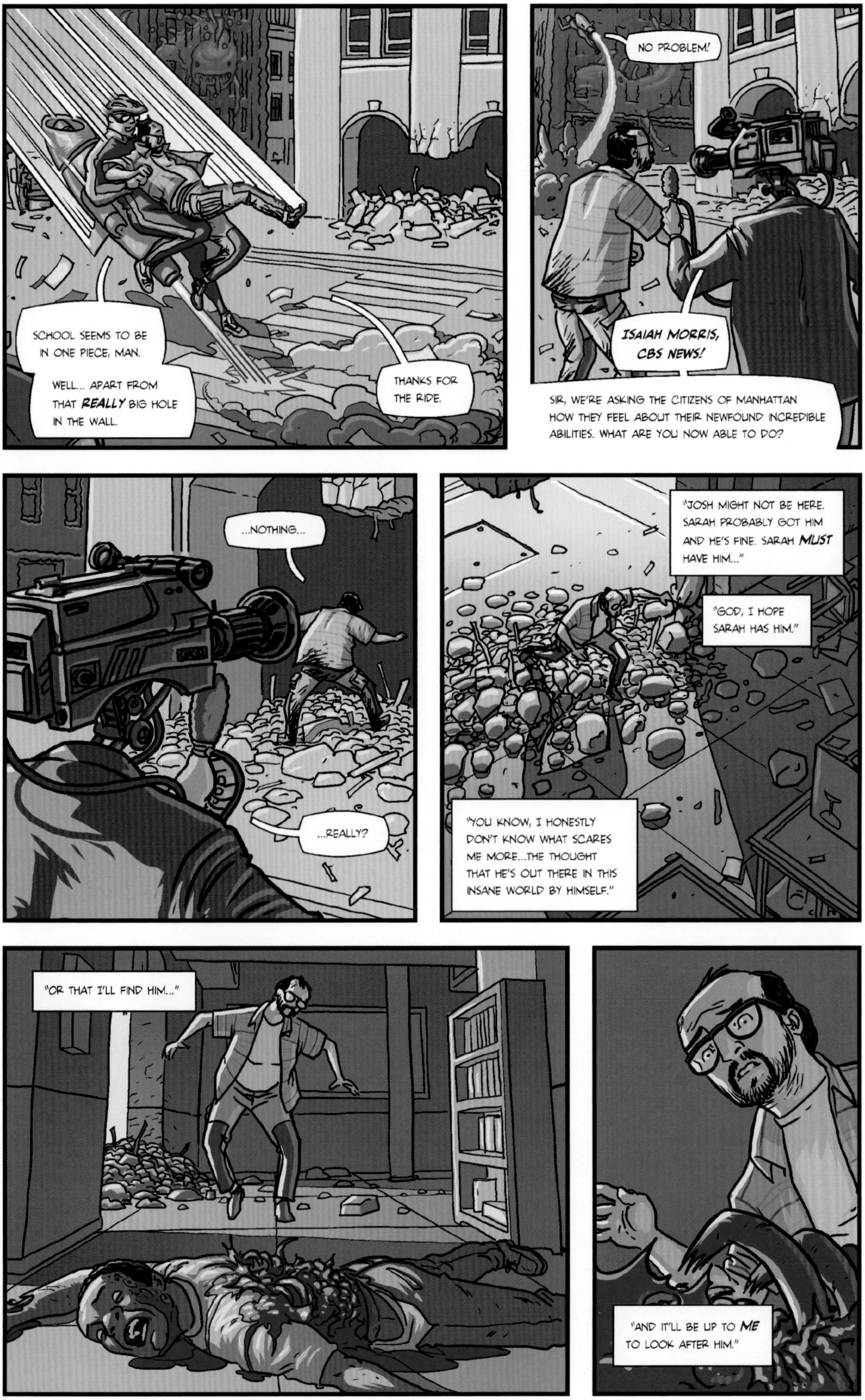

SCHOOL SEEMS TO BE IN ONE PIECE, MAN.
WELL... APART FROM THAT REALLY BIG HOLE IN THE WALL.
THANKS FOR THE RIDE.
NO PROBLEM!
ISAIAH MORRIS, CBS NEWS!
SIR, WE'RE ASKING THE CITIZENS OF MANHATTAN HOW THEY FEEL ABOUT THEIR NEWFOUND INCREDIBLE ABILITIES. WHAT ARE YOU NOW ABLE TO DO?
...NOTHING...
...REALLY?
"JOSH MIGHT NOT BE HERE. SARAH PROBABLY GOT HIM AND HE'S FINE. SARAH MUST HAVE HIM..."
"GOD, I HOPE SARAH HAS HIM."
"YOU KNOW, I HONESTLY DON'T KNOW WHAT SCARES ME MORE...THE THOUGHT THAT HE'S OUT THERE IN THIS INSANE WORLD BY HIMSELF."
"OR THAT I'LL FIND HIM..."
"AND IT'LL BE UP TO ME TO LOOK AFTER HIM."

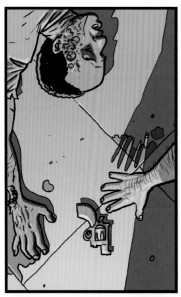

NO...

NO GUN.

AH!!

AHHH!!!

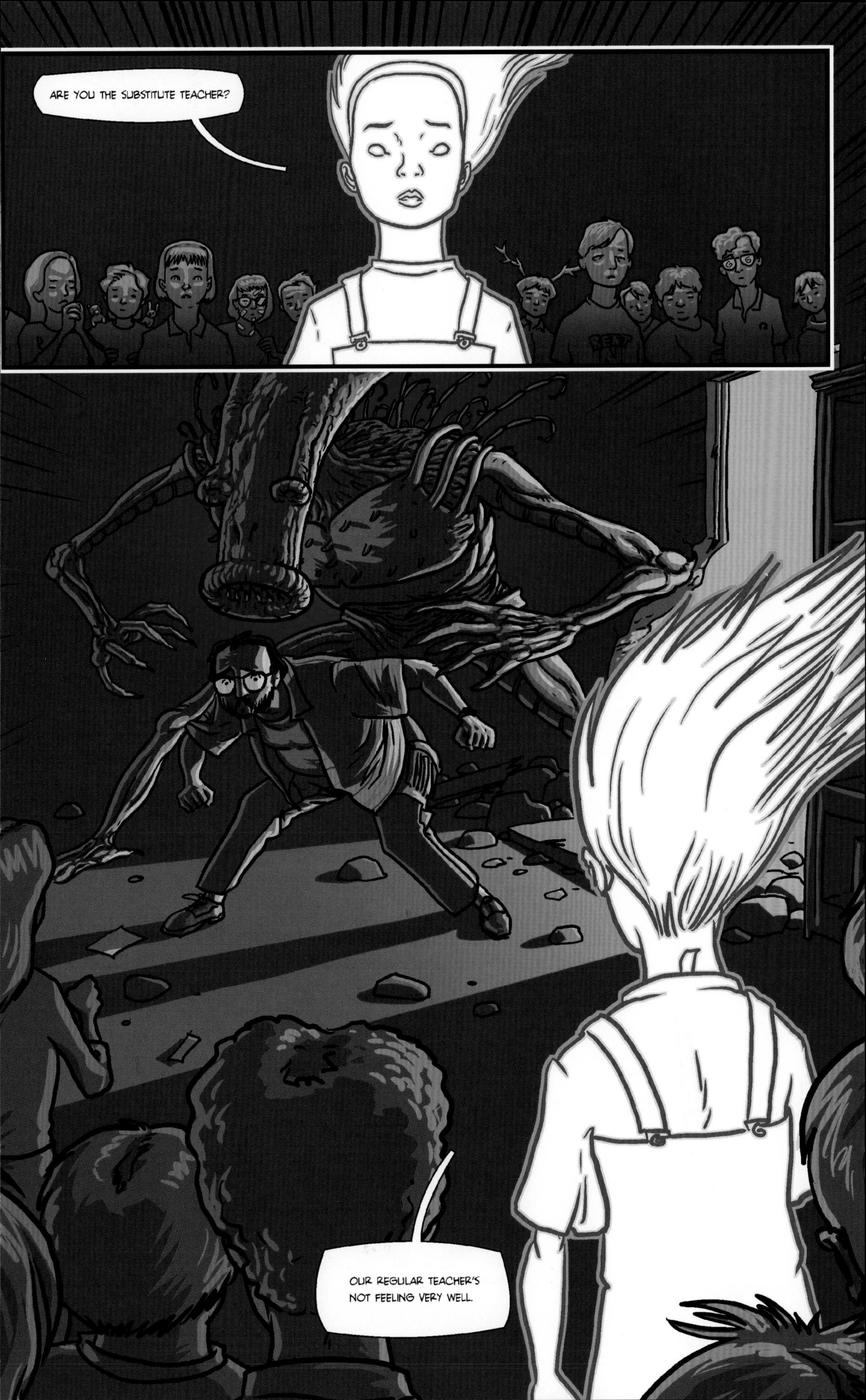
ARE YOU THE SUBSTITUTE TEACHER?
OUR REGULAR TEACHER'S NOT FEELING VERY WELL.

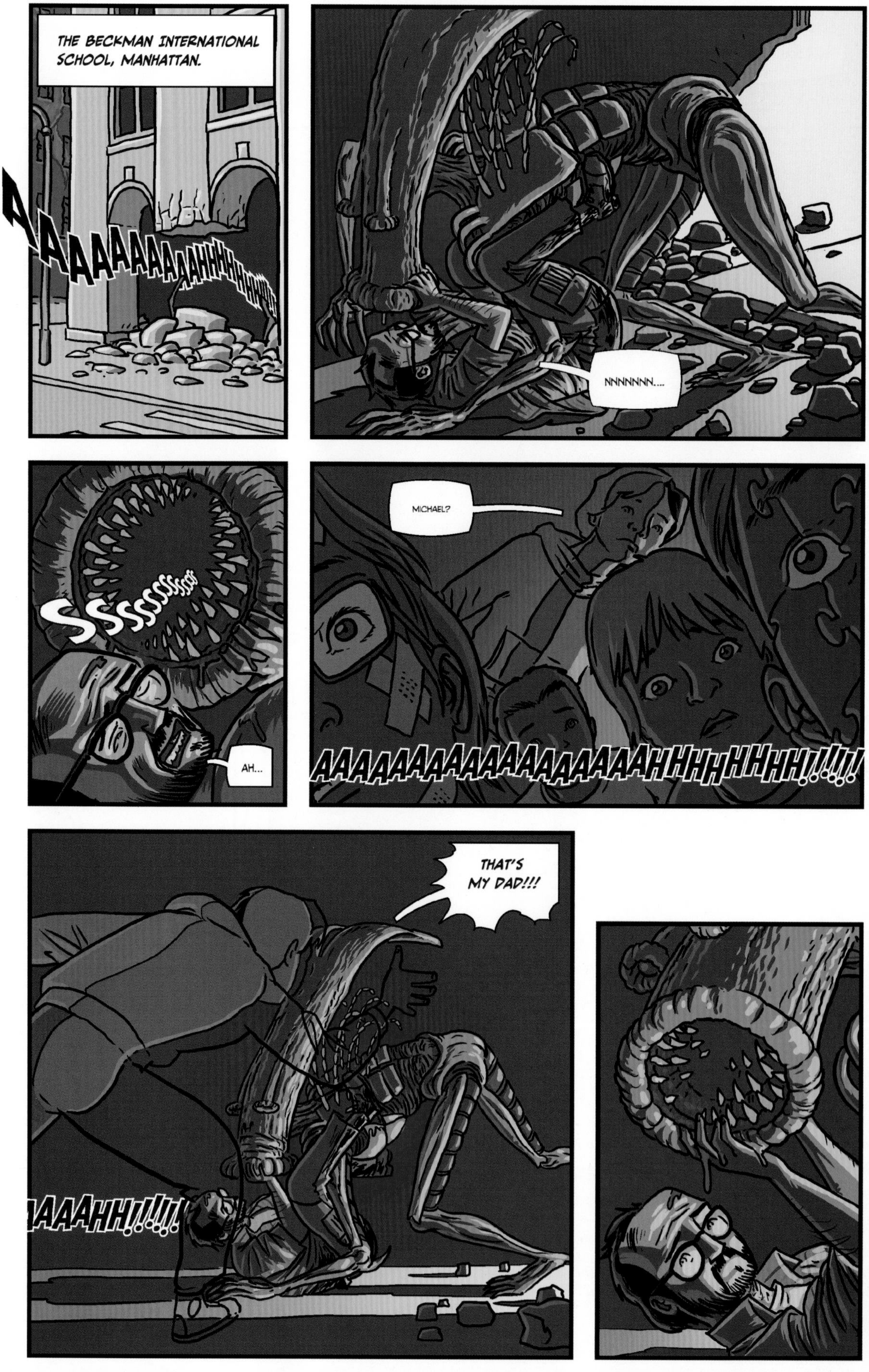

THE BECKMAN INTERNATIONAL SCHOOL, MANHATTAN.
AAAAAAAAAHHHHHHHH!!!
NNNNNNN....
SSSSSSSSSSS
AH...
MICHAEL?
AAAAAAAAAAAAAAAAAAAHHHHHHHH!!!!!
THAT'S MY DAD!!!
AAAAHH!!!!!

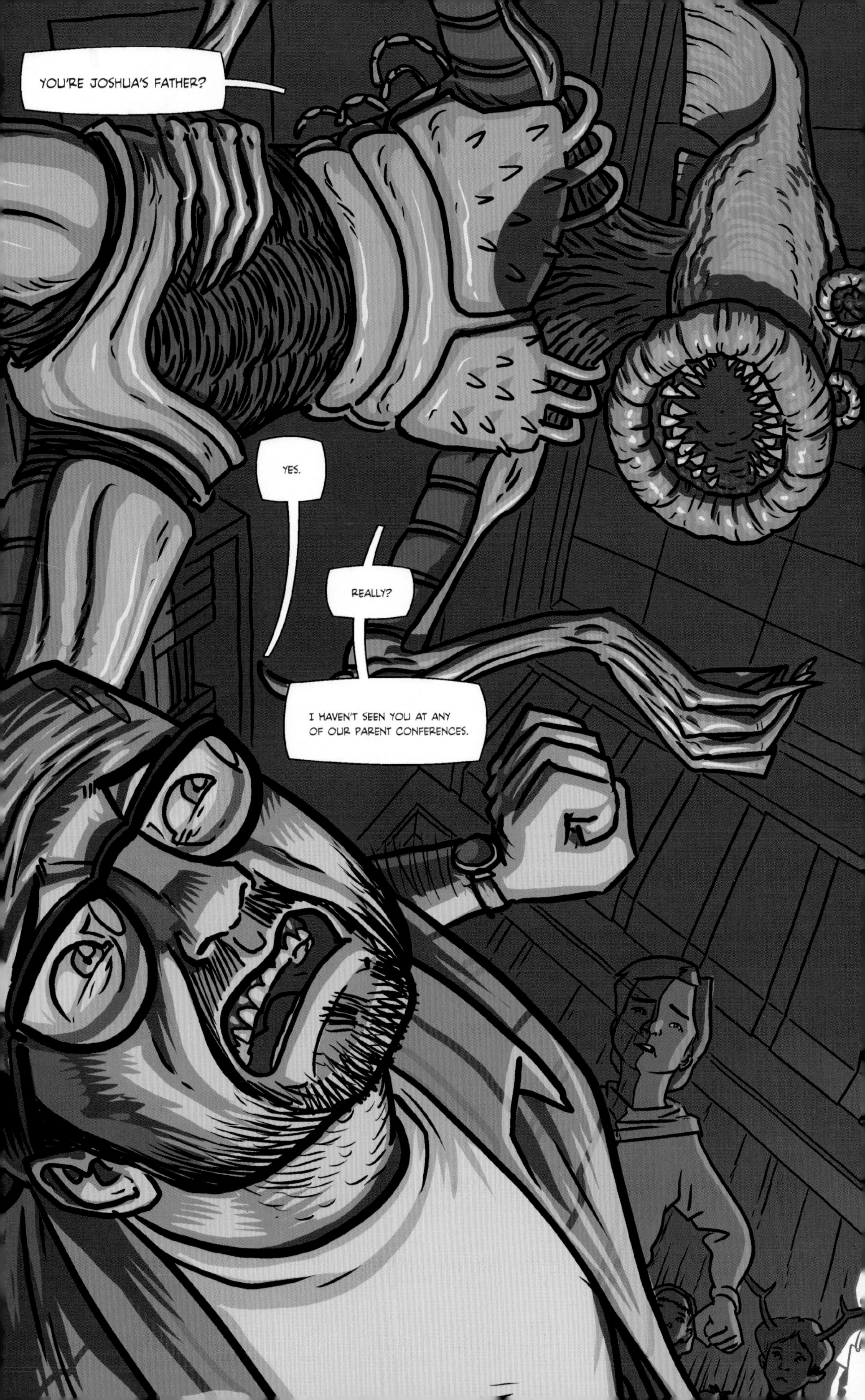
YOU'RE JOSHUA'S FATHER?
YES.
REALLY?
I HAVEN'T SEEN YOU AT ANY OF OUR PARENT CONFERENCES.

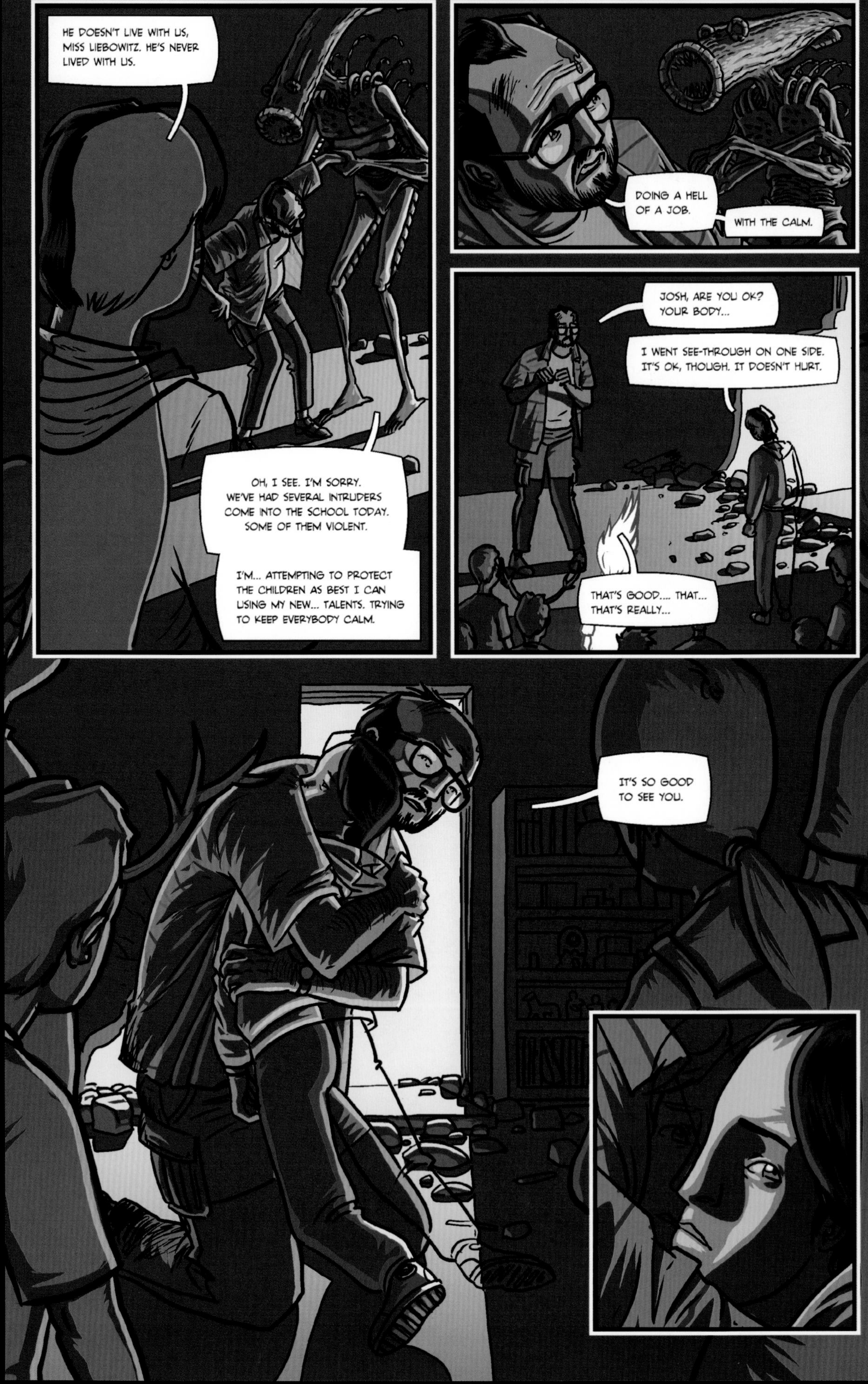
HE DOESN'T LIVE WITH US, MISS LIEBOWITZ. HE'S NEVER LIVED WITH US.
OH, I SEE. I'M SORRY. WE'VE HAD SEVERAL INTRUDERS COME INTO THE SCHOOL TODAY. SOME OF THEM VIOLENT.
I'M... ATTEMPTING TO PROTECT THE CHILDREN AS BEST I CAN USING MY NEW... TALENTS. TRYING TO KEEP EVERYBODY CALM.
DOING A HELL OF A JOB.
WITH THE CALM.
JOSH, ARE YOU OK? YOUR BODY...
I WENT SEE-THROUGH ON ONE SIDE. IT'S OK, THOUGH. IT DOESN'T HURT.
THAT'S GOOD.... THAT... THAT'S REALLY...
IT'S SO GOOD TO SEE YOU.

HAVE YOU HEARD ANYTHING FROM YOUR MOM, JOSH?

NO. SOME PARENTS CAME BUT... NONE OF US HAVE BEEN PICKED UP. THAT'S WHY WE'RE STILL HERE.

HEY...

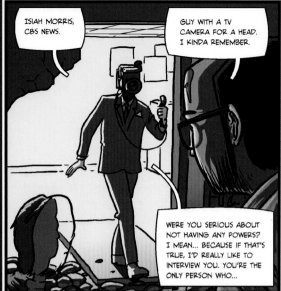

ISIAH MORRIS, CBS NEWS.

GUY WITH A TV CAMERA FOR A HEAD. I KINDA REMEMBER.

WERE YOU SERIOUS ABOUT NOT HAVING ANY POWERS? I MEAN... BECAUSE IF THAT'S TRUE, I'D REALLY LIKE TO INTERVIEW YOU. YOU'RE THE ONLY PERSON WHO...

YOU WANNA SOB STORY? YES!! I GOT NOTHING! HAPPY?!! THE WHOLE WORLD GOT AMAZING SPARKLY £$£#@% POWERS EXCEPT FOR ME!!!

THAT'S HOW FREAKING WORTHLESS I AM!!! YOU GOT THAT ON FILM? YEAH? THEN GET THE &$£ OUT OF HERE!!

OK! OK!

BUT LOOK. HEAR ME OUT?

YOU GIVE ME AND MY NEWS CHANNEL EXCLUSIVE RIGHTS TO INTERVIEW YOU AND WE'LL GIVE YOU WHATEVER YOU WANT.

WE CAN TAKE YOU AND YOUR SON ANYWHERE YOU WANT. WITH A WELL-ARMED ESCORT. FIND ANYONE YOU'RE LOOKING FOR.

IS THERE ANYONE YOU GUYS CURRENTLY HAVE MISSING?

BECAUSE WE CAN HELP YOU FIND THEM.

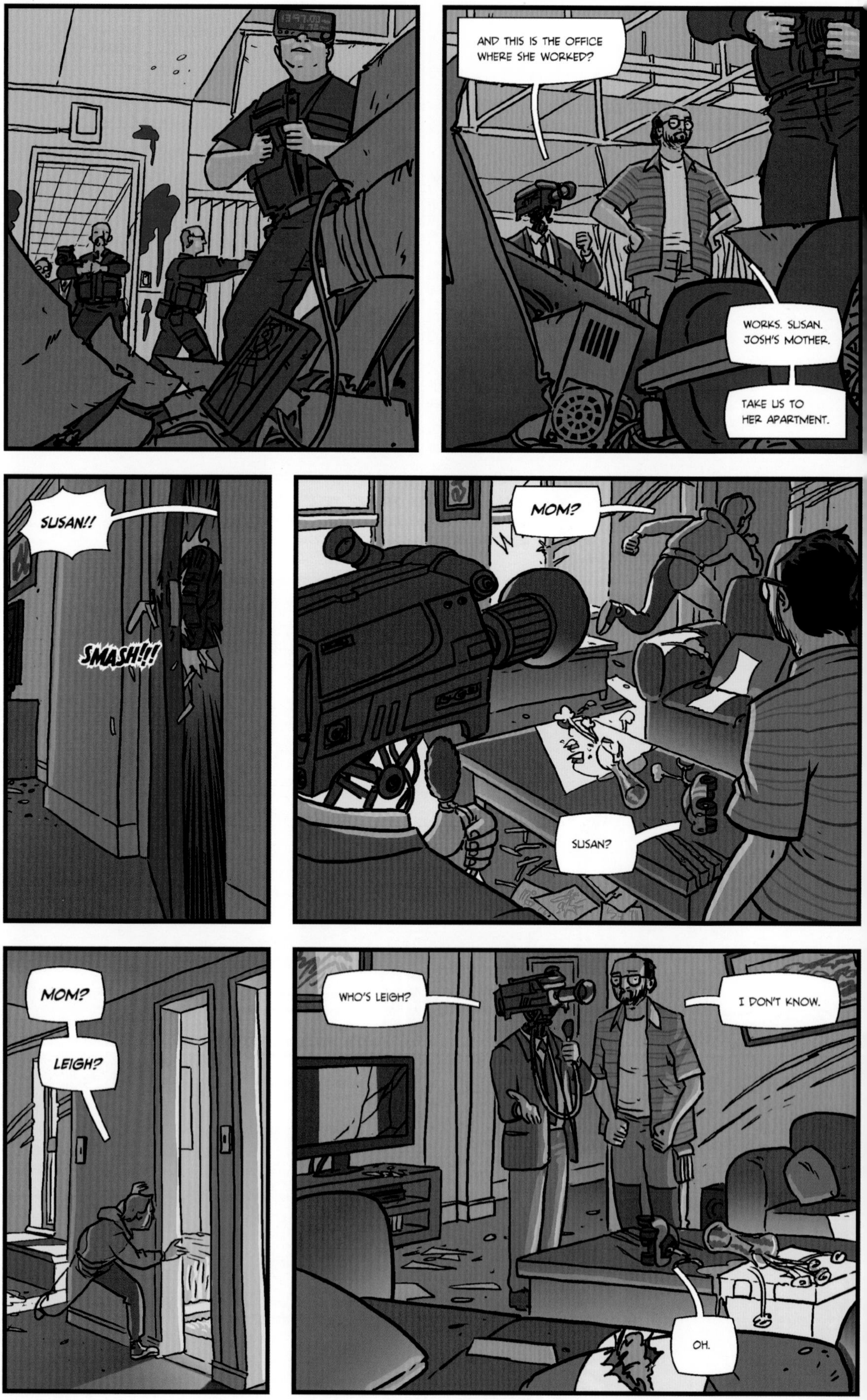

AND THIS IS THE OFFICE WHERE SHE WORKED?
WORKS. SUSAN. JOSH'S MOTHER.
TAKE US TO HER APARTMENT.
SUSAN!!
SMASH!!!
MOM?
SUSAN?
MOM?
LEIGH?
WHO'S LEIGH?
I DON'T KNOW.
OH.

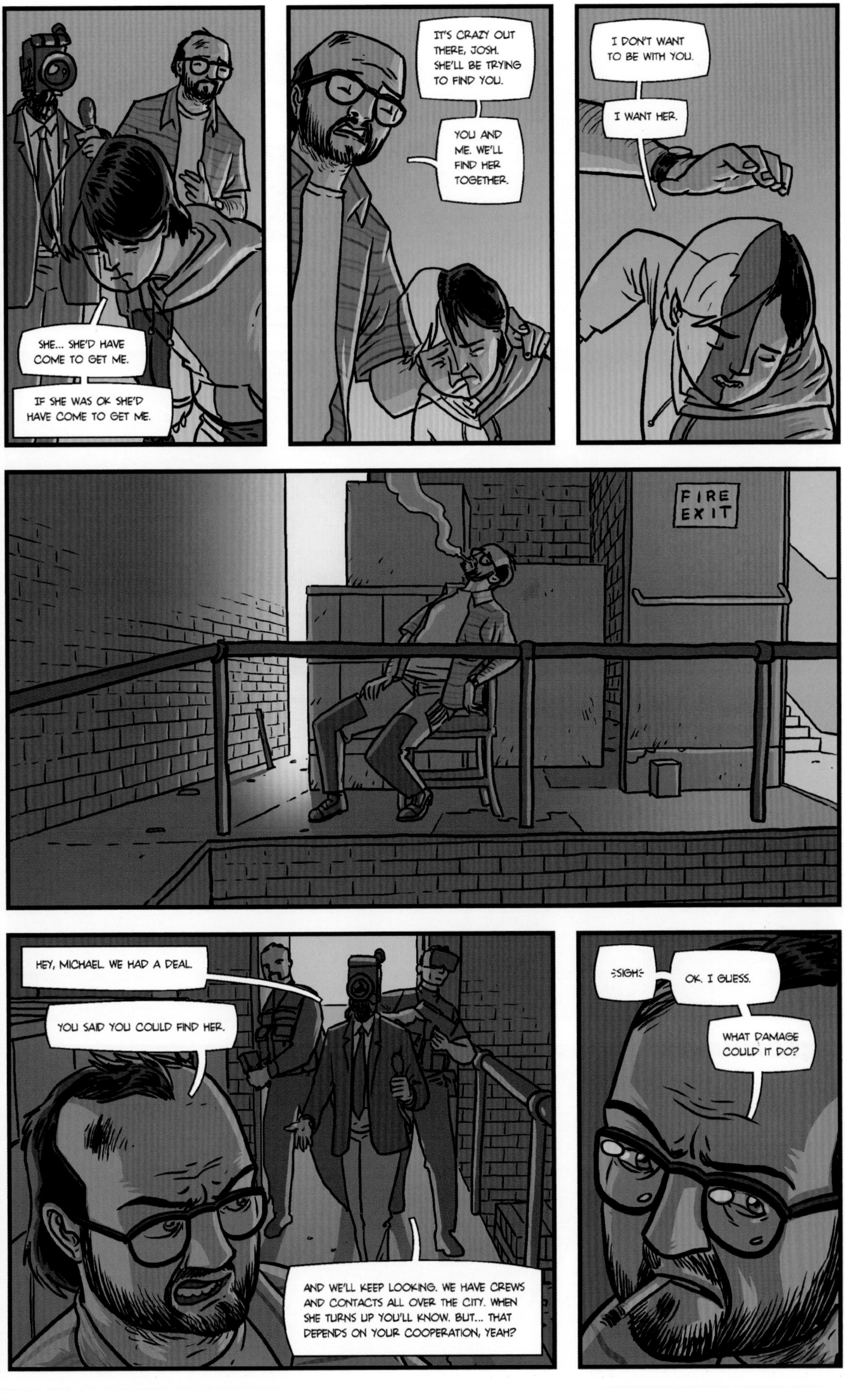
SHE... SHE'D HAVE COME TO GET ME.
IF SHE WAS OK SHE'D HAVE COME TO GET ME.
IT'S CRAZY OUT THERE, JOSH. SHE'LL BE TRYING TO FIND YOU.
YOU AND ME. WE'LL FIND HER TOGETHER.
I DON'T WANT TO BE WITH YOU.
I WANT HER.
FIRE EXIT
HEY, MICHAEL. WE HAD A DEAL.
YOU SAID YOU COULD FIND HER.
AND WE'LL KEEP LOOKING. WE HAVE CREWS AND CONTACTS ALL OVER THE CITY. WHEN SHE TURNS UP YOU'LL KNOW. BUT... THAT DEPENDS ON YOUR COOPERATION, YEAH?
SIGH
OK. I GUESS.
WHAT DAMAGE COULD IT DO?

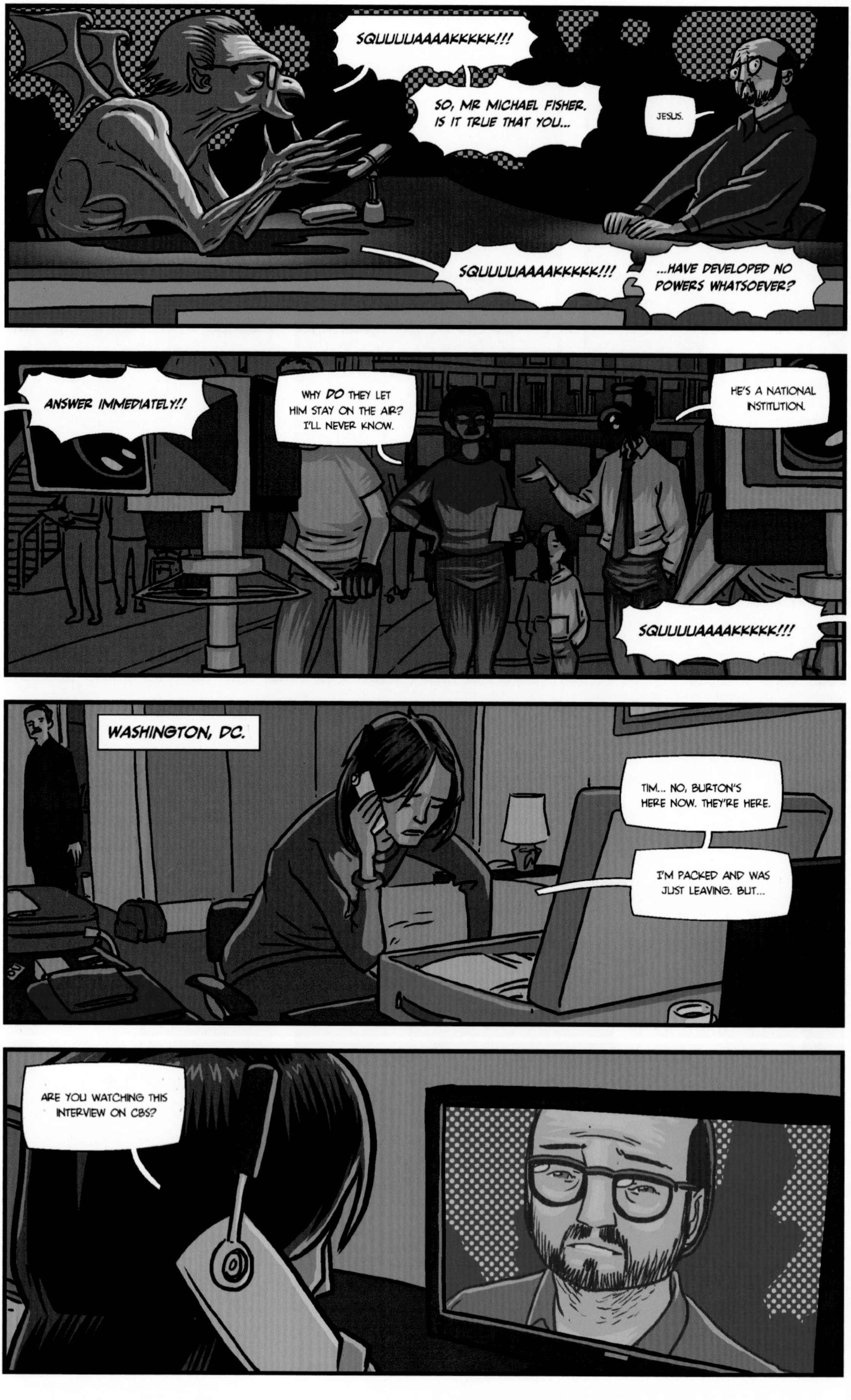
SQUUUUAAAAKKKKK!!!
SO, MR MICHAEL FISHER. IS IT TRUE THAT YOU...
JESUS.
SQUUUUAAAAKKKKK!!!
...HAVE DEVELOPED NO POWERS WHATSOEVER?
ANSWER IMMEDIATELY!!
WHY DO THEY LET HIM STAY ON THE AIR? I'LL NEVER KNOW.
HE'S A NATIONAL INSTITUTION.
SQUUUUAAAAKKKKK!!!
WASHINGTON, DC.
TIM... NO, BURTON'S HERE NOW. THEY'RE HERE.
I'M PACKED AND WAS JUST LEAVING. BUT...
ARE YOU WATCHING THIS INTERVIEW ON CBS?

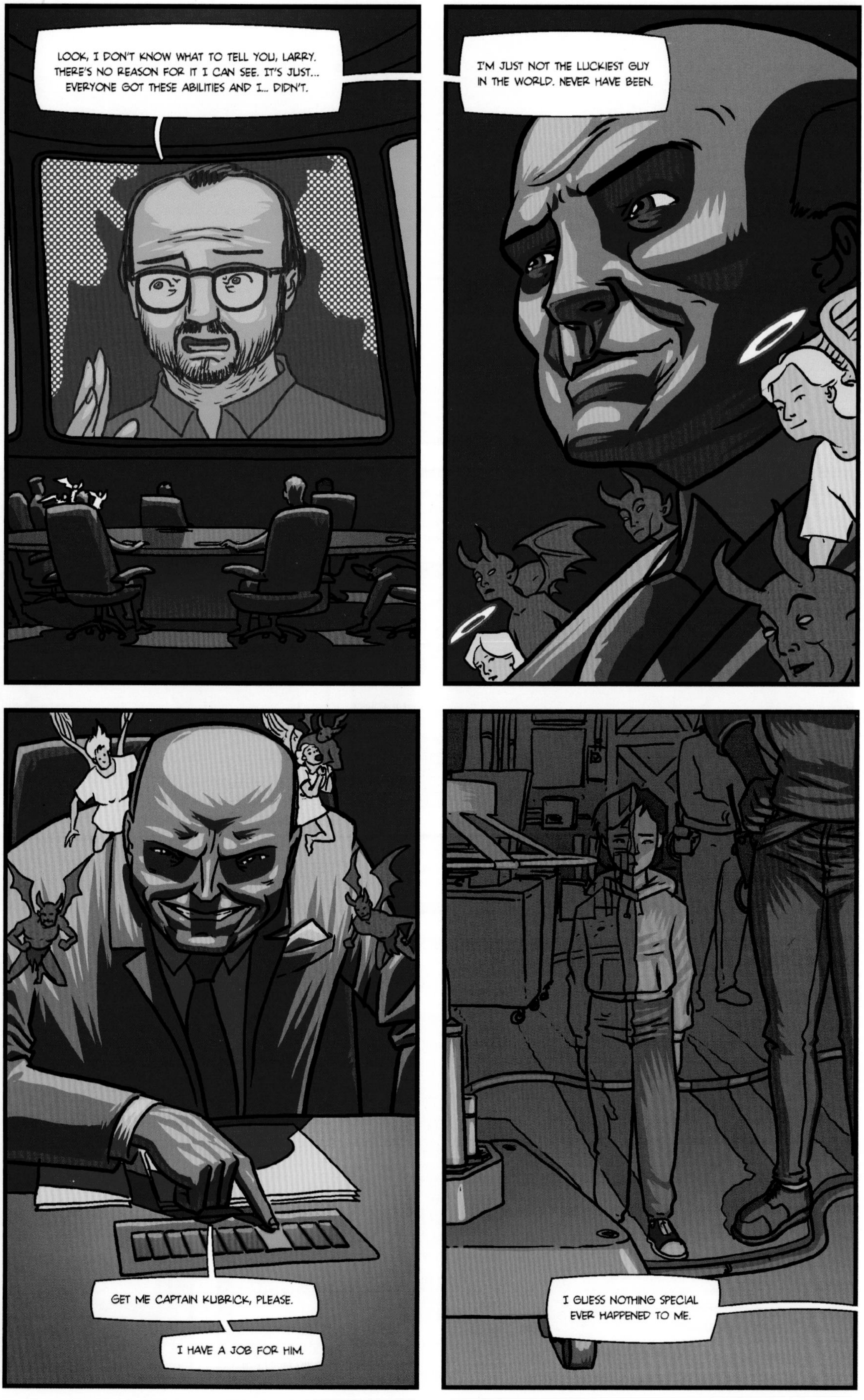
LOOK, I DON'T KNOW WHAT TO TELL YOU, LARRY. THERE'S NO REASON FOR IT I CAN SEE. IT'S JUST... EVERYONE GOT THESE ABILITIES AND I... DIDN'T.
I'M JUST NOT THE LUCKIEST GUY IN THE WORLD. NEVER HAVE BEEN.
GET ME CAPTAIN KUBRICK, PLEASE.
I HAVE A JOB FOR HIM.
I GUESS NOTHING SPECIAL EVER HAPPENED TO ME.

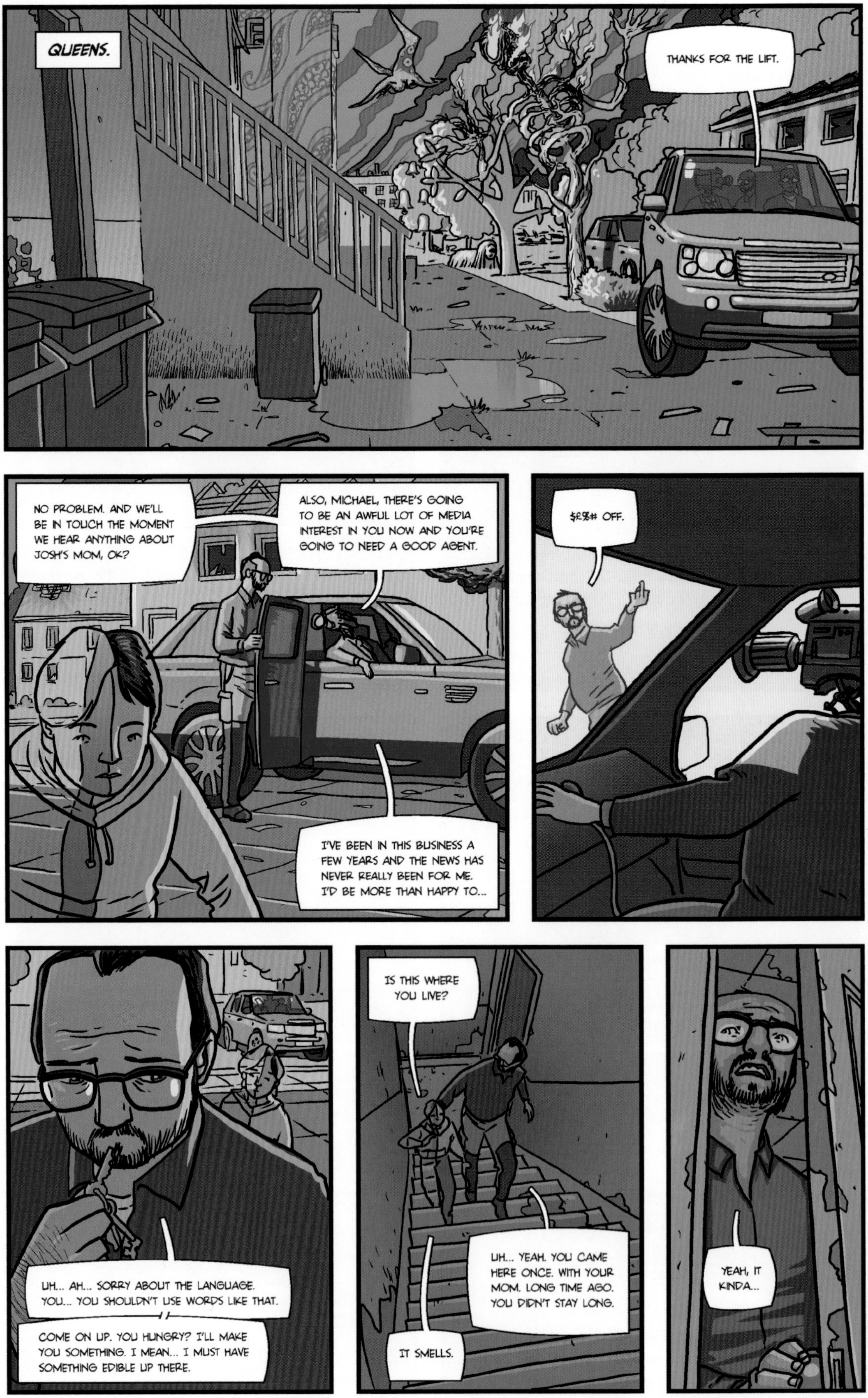
QUEENS.
THANKS FOR THE LIFT.
NO PROBLEM. AND WE'LL BE IN TOUCH THE MOMENT WE HEAR ANYTHING ABOUT JOSH'S MOM, OK?
ALSO, MICHAEL, THERE'S GOING TO BE AN AWFUL LOT OF MEDIA INTEREST IN YOU NOW AND YOU'RE GOING TO NEED A GOOD AGENT.
I'VE BEEN IN THIS BUSINESS A FEW YEARS AND THE NEWS HAS NEVER REALLY BEEN FOR ME. I'D BE MORE THAN HAPPY TO...
$£%# OFF.
UH... AH... SORRY ABOUT THE LANGUAGE. YOU... YOU SHOULDN'T USE WORDS LIKE THAT.
COME ON UP. YOU HUNGRY? I'LL MAKE YOU SOMETHING. I MEAN... I MUST HAVE SOMETHING EDIBLE UP THERE.
IS THIS WHERE YOU LIVE?
IT SMELLS.
UH... YEAH. YOU CAME HERE ONCE. WITH YOUR MOM. LONG TIME AGO. YOU DIDN'T STAY LONG.
YEAH, IT KINDA...

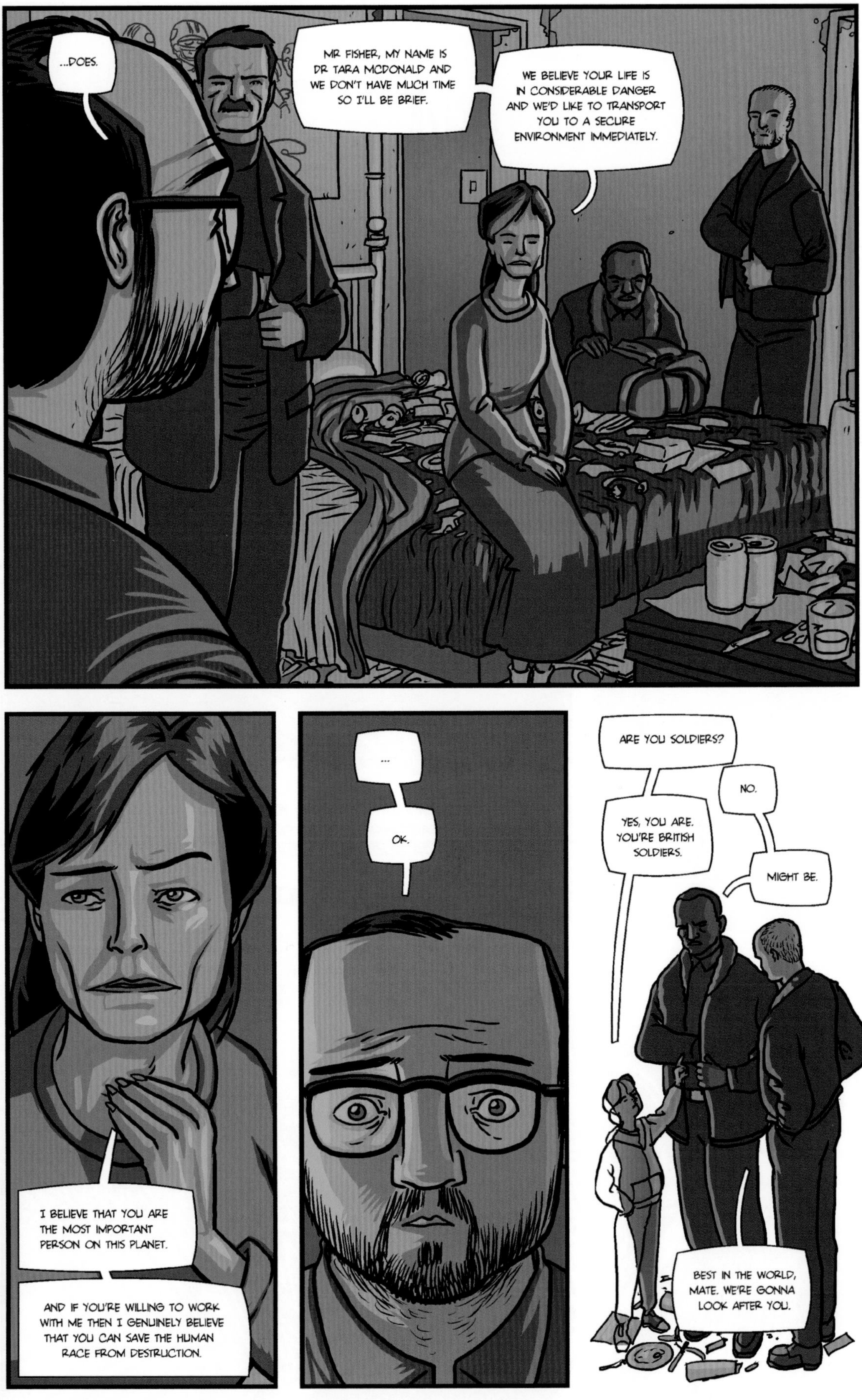
...DOES.
MR FISHER, MY NAME IS DR TARA MCDONALD AND WE DON'T HAVE MUCH TIME SO I'LL BE BRIEF.
WE BELIEVE YOUR LIFE IS IN CONSIDERABLE DANGER AND WE'D LIKE TO TRANSPORT YOU TO A SECURE ENVIRONMENT IMMEDIATELY.
I BELIEVE THAT YOU ARE THE MOST IMPORTANT PERSON ON THIS PLANET.
AND IF YOU'RE WILLING TO WORK WITH ME THEN I GENUINELY BELIEVE THAT YOU CAN SAVE THE HUMAN RACE FROM DESTRUCTION.
...
OK.
ARE YOU SOLDIERS?
YES, YOU ARE. YOU'RE BRITISH SOLDIERS.
NO.
MIGHT BE.
BEST IN THE WORLD, MATE. WE'RE GONNA LOOK AFTER YOU.

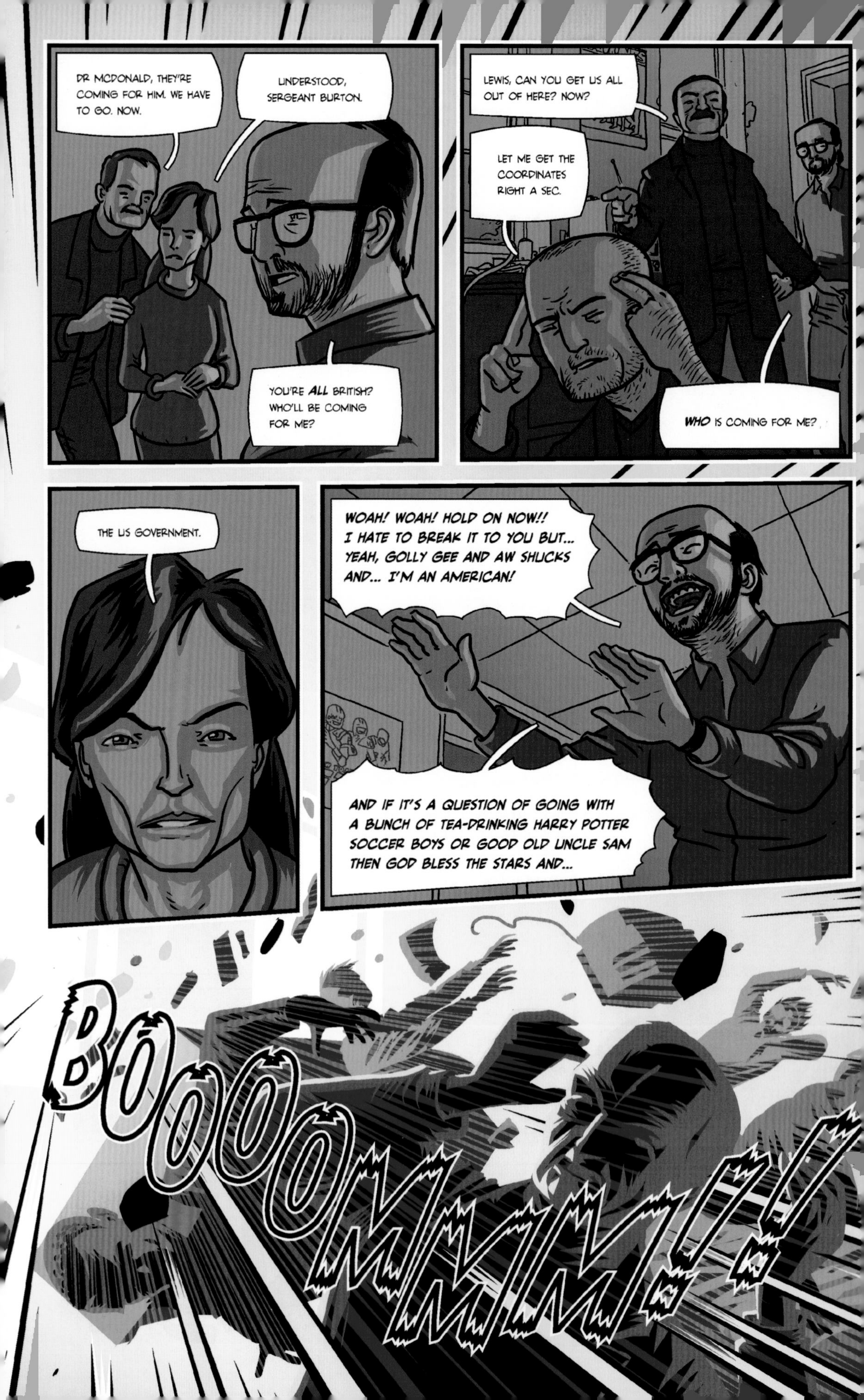
DR MCDONALD, THEY'RE COMING FOR HIM. WE HAVE TO GO. NOW.
UNDERSTOOD, SERGEANT BURTON.
YOU'RE ALL BRITISH? WHO'LL BE COMING FOR ME?
LEWIS, CAN YOU GET US ALL OUT OF HERE? NOW?
LET ME GET THE COORDINATES RIGHT A SEC.
WHO IS COMING FOR ME?
THE US GOVERNMENT.
WOAH! WOAH! HOLD ON NOW!! I HATE TO BREAK IT TO YOU BUT... YEAH, GOLLY GEE AND AW SHUCKS AND... I'M AN AMERICAN!
AND IF IT'S A QUESTION OF GOING WITH A BUNCH OF TEA-DRINKING HARRY POTTER SOCCER BOYS OR GOOD OLD UNCLE SAM THEN GOD BLESS THE STARS AND...
BOOOOOMMMM!!

:COUGH: JOSH?

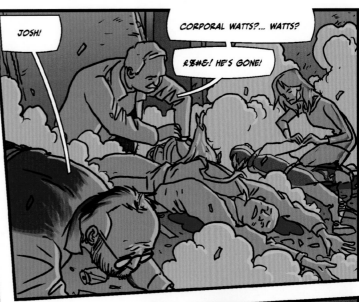

JOSH!

CORPORAL WATTS?... WATTS?

£%#&! HE'S GONE!

EVERYONE! UP!

THEY'LL FOLLOW THAT IN! THEY'RE COMING!!

NOW!!!

JOSH?

HE'S OK. HE'S BREATHING. HE'S UNCONSCIOUS, THANKFULLY.

AW MAN, YOUR LEG. WE NEED.... I CAN MAKE A TORNIQUET.

I CAN'T FEEL IT. IT'S FINE. DON'T WORRY.

NO, THERE'S TOO MUCH BLOOD. WE'VE GOT TO... WE'VE GOT TO...

WE HAVE TO GET YOU AND JOSH OUT OF HERE SAFELY. THANK YOU... BUT I'M NOT BEING BRAVE...

I GENUINELY CAN'T FEEL IT.

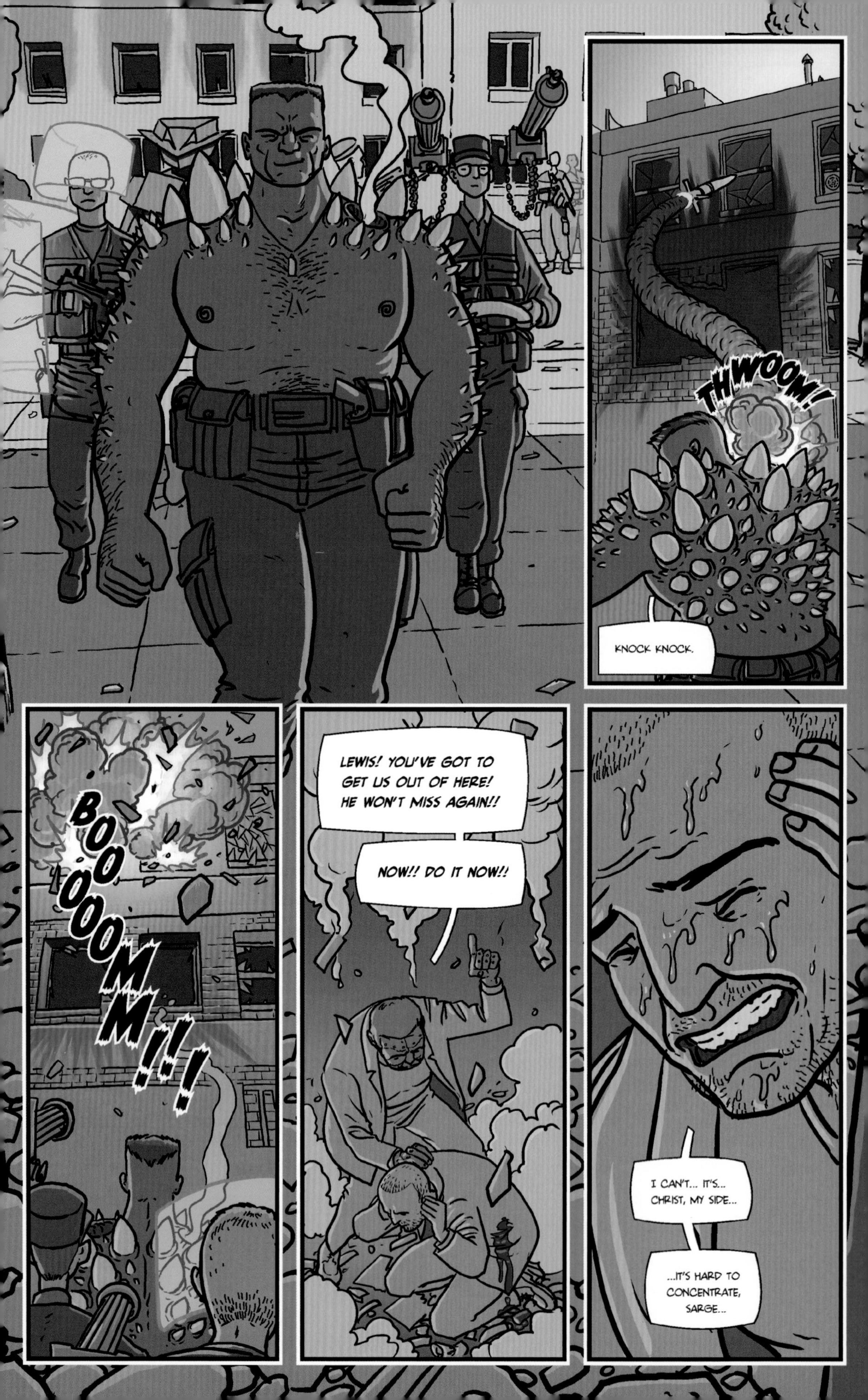
THWOOM!
KNOCK KNOCK.
BOOOOOOMMM!!!
LEWIS! YOU'VE GOT TO GET US OUT OF HERE! HE WON'T MISS AGAIN!!
NOW!! DO IT NOW!!
I CAN'T... IT'S... CHRIST, MY SIDE...
...IT'S HARD TO CONCENTRATE, SARGE...

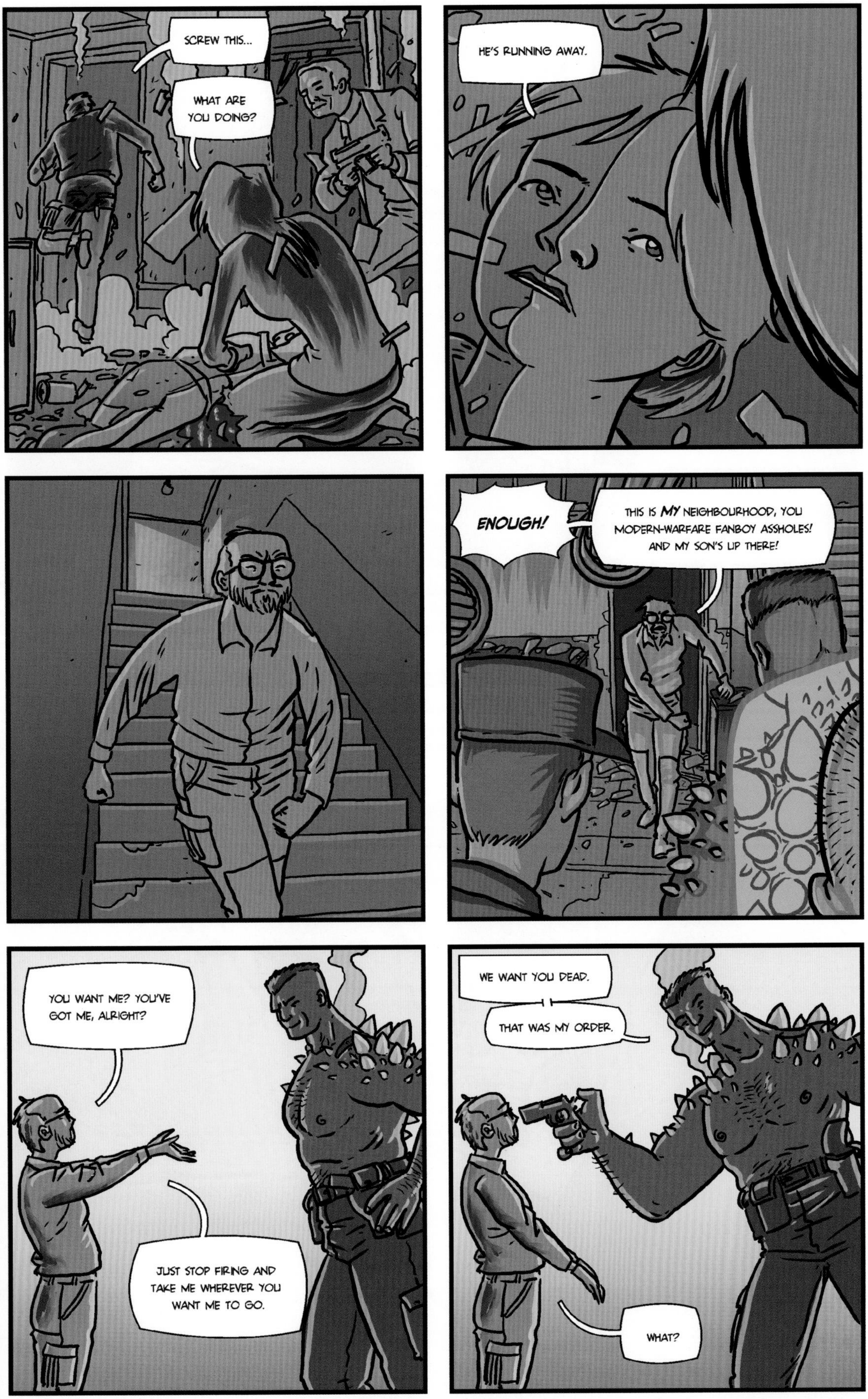
SCREW THIS...
WHAT ARE YOU DOING?
HE'S RUNNING AWAY.
ENOUGH!
THIS IS *MY* NEIGHBOURHOOD, YOU MODERN-WARFARE FANBOY ASSHOLES! AND MY SON'S UP THERE!
YOU WANT ME? YOU'VE GOT ME, ALRIGHT?
JUST STOP FIRING AND TAKE ME WHEREVER YOU WANT ME TO GO.
WE WANT YOU DEAD.
THAT WAS MY ORDER.
WHAT?

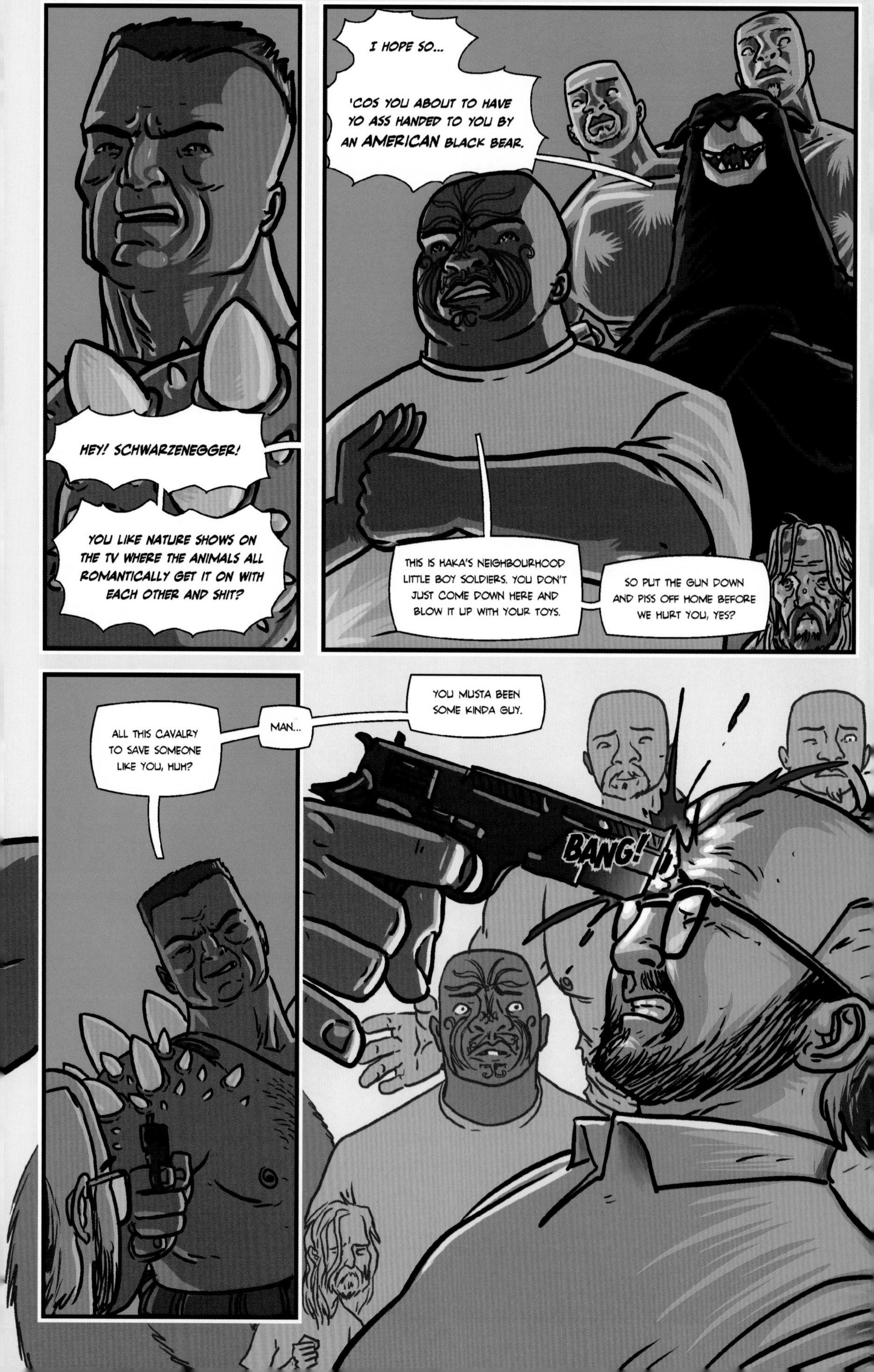
HEY! SCHWARZENEGGER!
YOU LIKE NATURE SHOWS ON THE TV WHERE THE ANIMALS ALL ROMANTICALLY GET IT ON WITH EACH OTHER AND SHIT?
I HOPE SO...
'COS YOU ABOUT TO HAVE YO ASS HANDED TO YOU BY AN AMERICAN BLACK BEAR.
THIS IS HAKA'S NEIGHBOURHOOD LITTLE BOY SOLDIERS. YOU DON'T JUST COME DOWN HERE AND BLOW IT UP WITH YOUR TOYS.
SO PUT THE GUN DOWN AND PISS OFF HOME BEFORE WE HURT YOU, YES?
ALL THIS CAVALRY TO SAVE SOMEONE LIKE YOU, HUH?
MAN...
YOU MUSTA BEEN SOME KINDA GUY.
BANG!

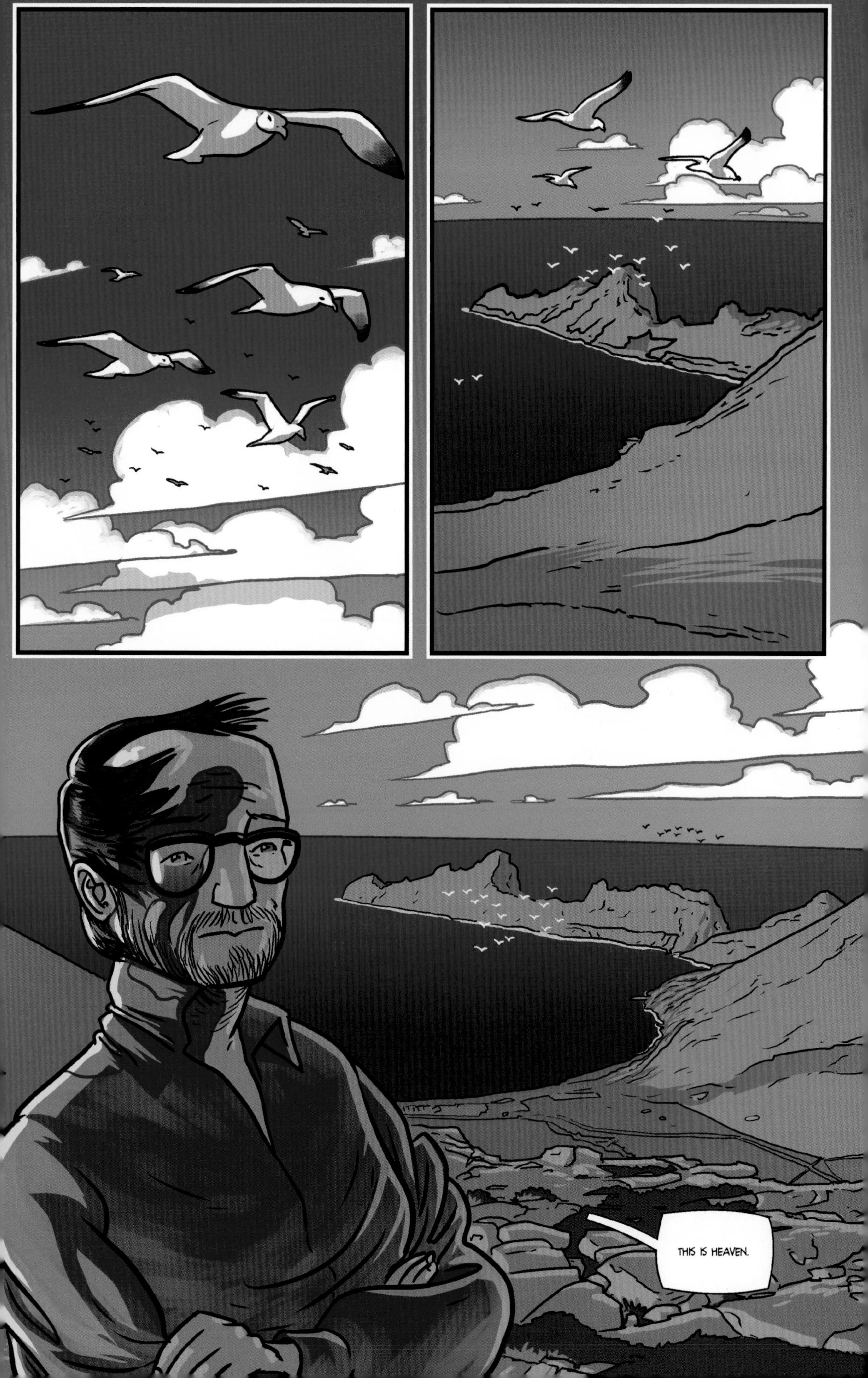
THIS IS HEAVEN.

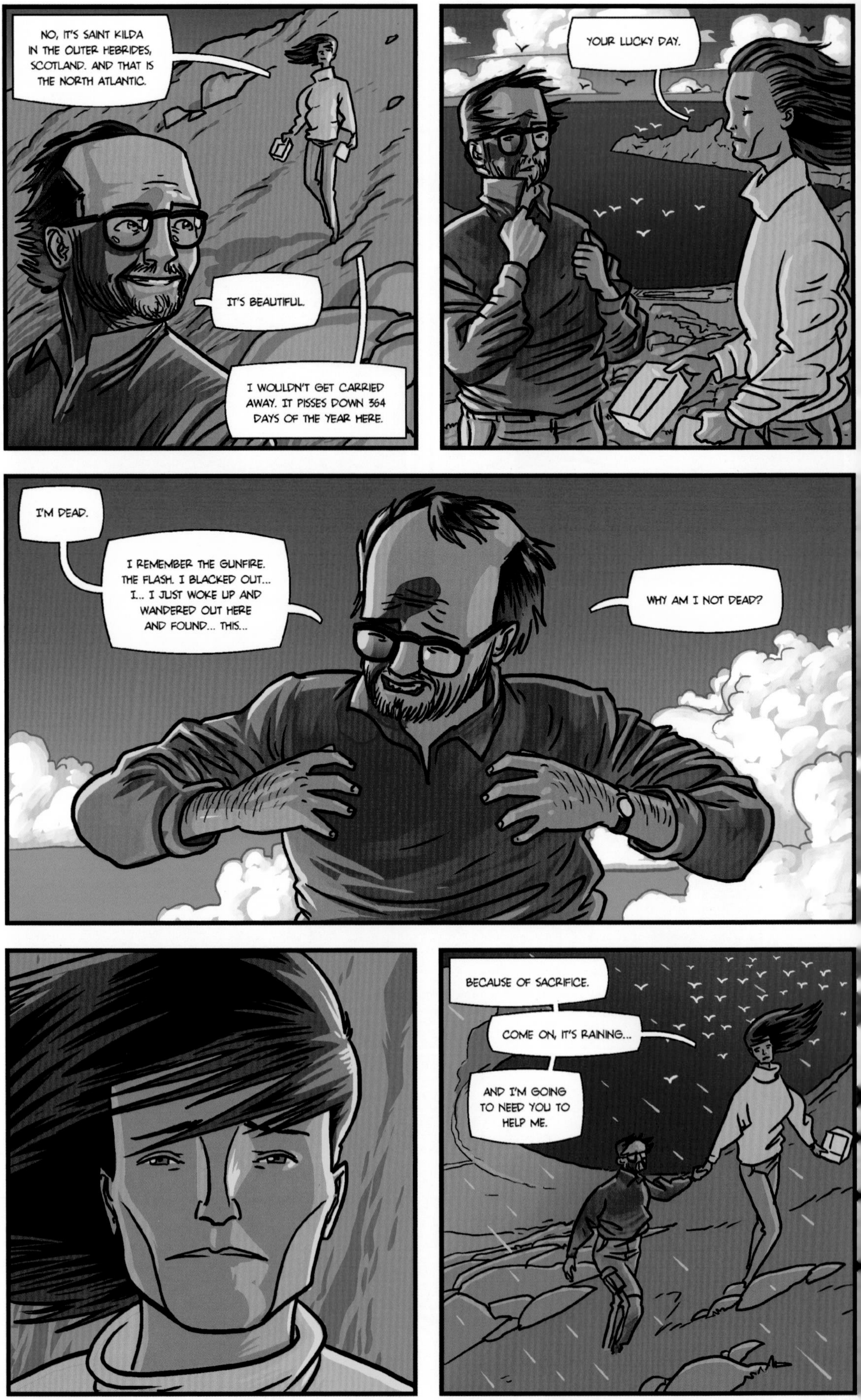
NO, IT'S SAINT KILDA IN THE OUTER HEBRIDES, SCOTLAND. AND THAT IS THE NORTH ATLANTIC.
IT'S BEAUTIFUL.
I WOULDN'T GET CARRIED AWAY. IT PISSES DOWN 364 DAYS OF THE YEAR HERE.
YOUR LUCKY DAY.
I'M DEAD.
I REMEMBER THE GUNFIRE. THE FLASH. I BLACKED OUT... I... I JUST WOKE UP AND WANDERED OUT HERE AND FOUND... THIS...
WHY AM I NOT DEAD?
BECAUSE OF SACRIFICE.
COME ON, IT'S RAINING...
AND I'M GOING TO NEED YOU TO HELP ME.

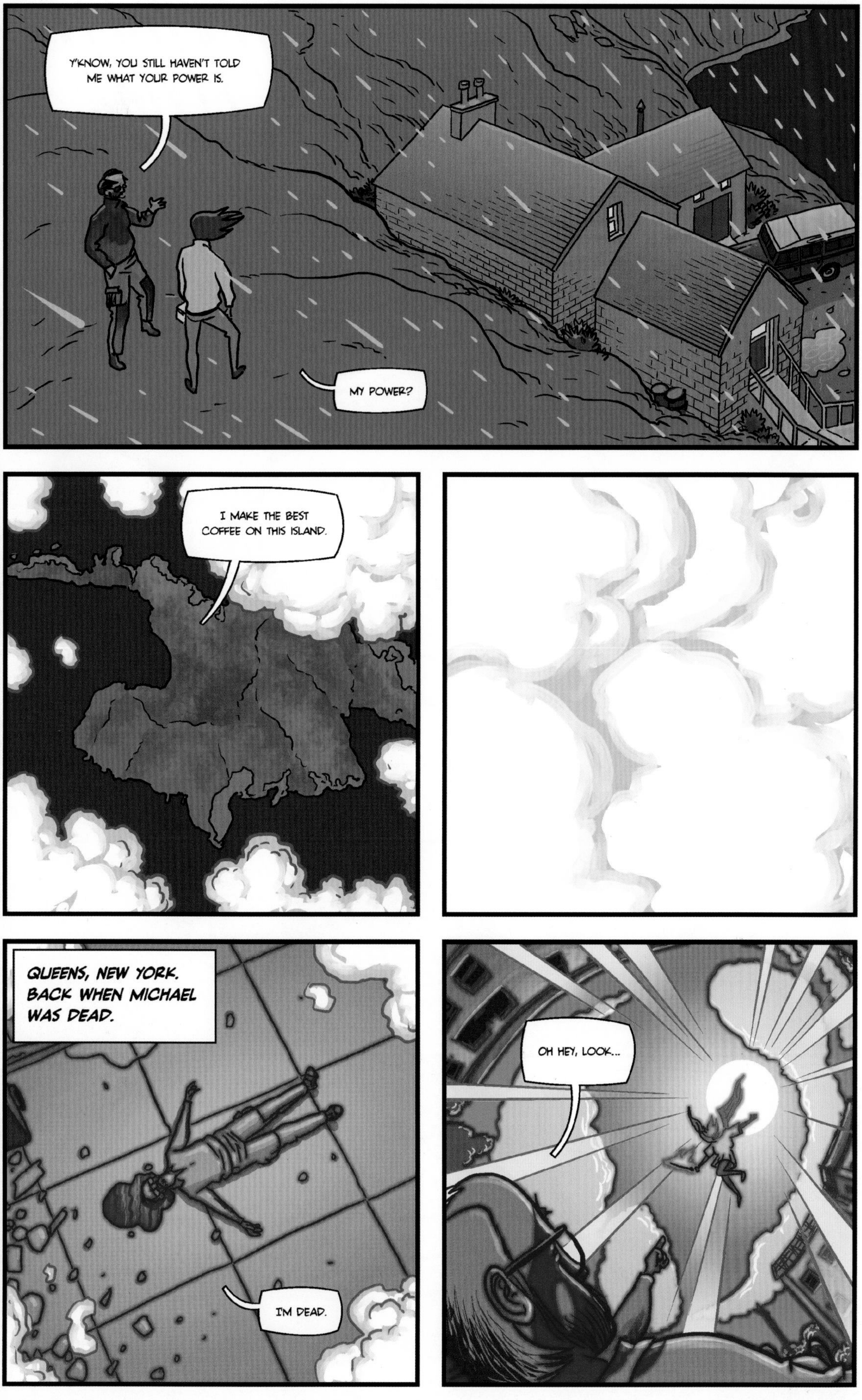

Y'KNOW, YOU STILL HAVEN'T TOLD ME WHAT YOUR POWER IS.
MY POWER?
I MAKE THE BEST COFFEE ON THIS ISLAND.
QUEENS, NEW YORK. BACK WHEN MICHAEL WAS DEAD.
I'M DEAD.
OH HEY, LOOK...

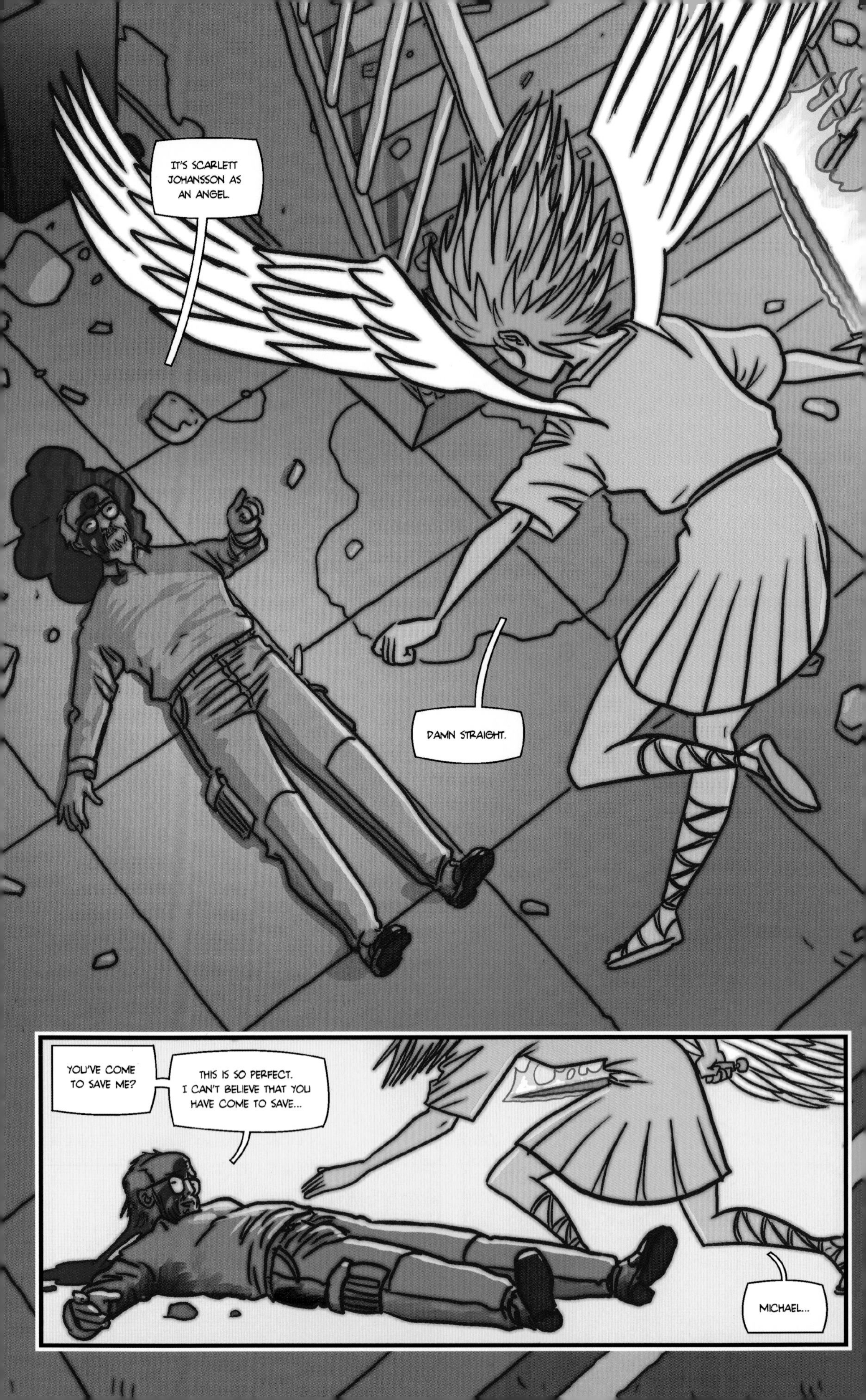
IT'S SCARLETT JOHANSSON AS AN ANGEL.
DAMN STRAIGHT.
YOU'VE COME TO SAVE ME?
THIS IS SO PERFECT. I CAN'T BELIEVE THAT YOU HAVE COME TO SAVE...
MICHAEL...

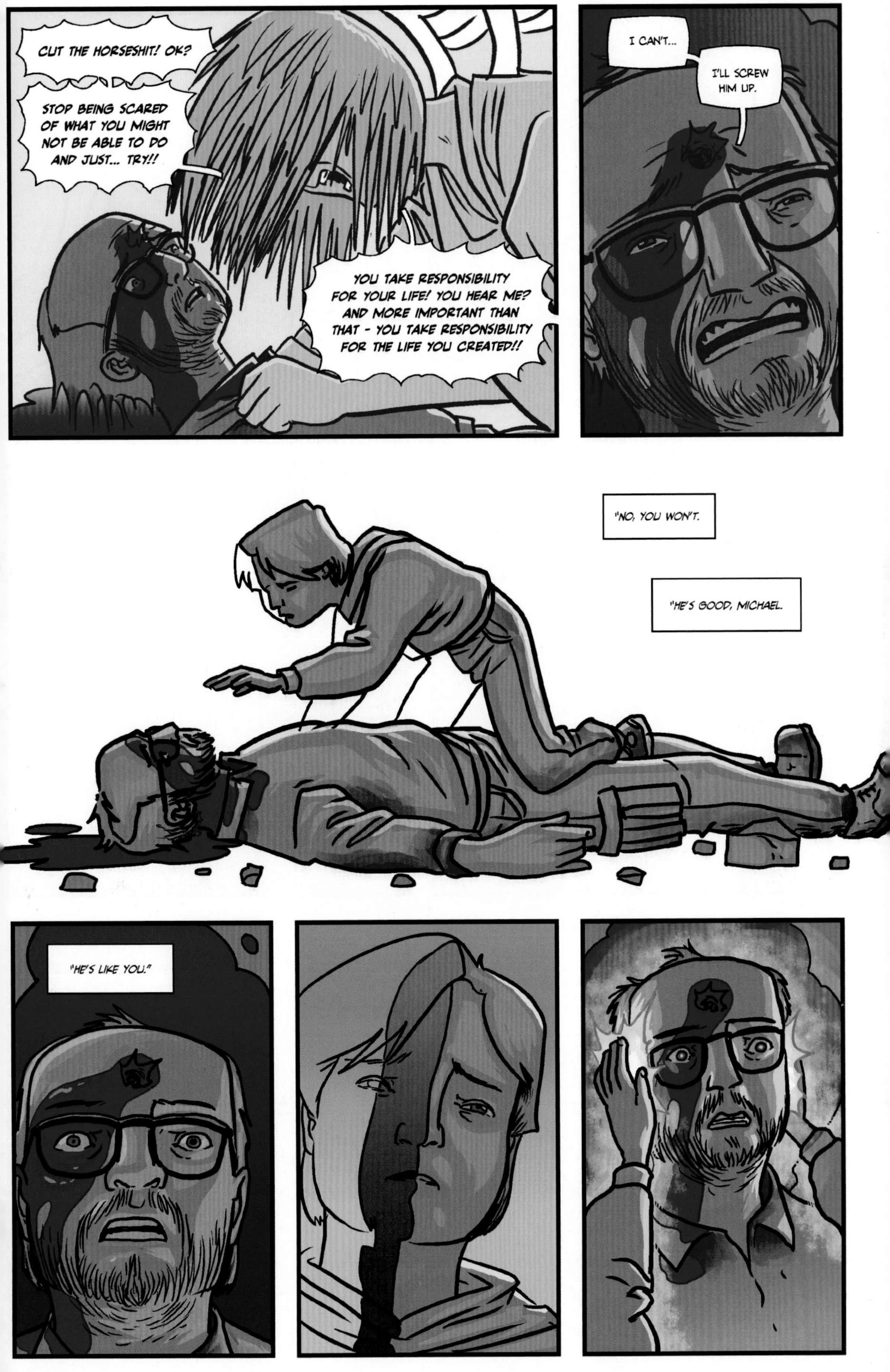
CUT THE HORSESHIT! OK?
STOP BEING SCARED OF WHAT YOU MIGHT NOT BE ABLE TO DO AND JUST... TRY!!
YOU TAKE RESPONSIBILITY FOR YOUR LIFE! YOU HEAR ME? AND MORE IMPORTANT THAN THAT - YOU TAKE RESPONSIBILITY FOR THE LIFE YOU CREATED!!
I CAN'T...
I'LL SCREW HIM UP.
"NO, YOU WON'T.
"HE'S GOOD, MICHAEL.
"HE'S LIKE YOU."

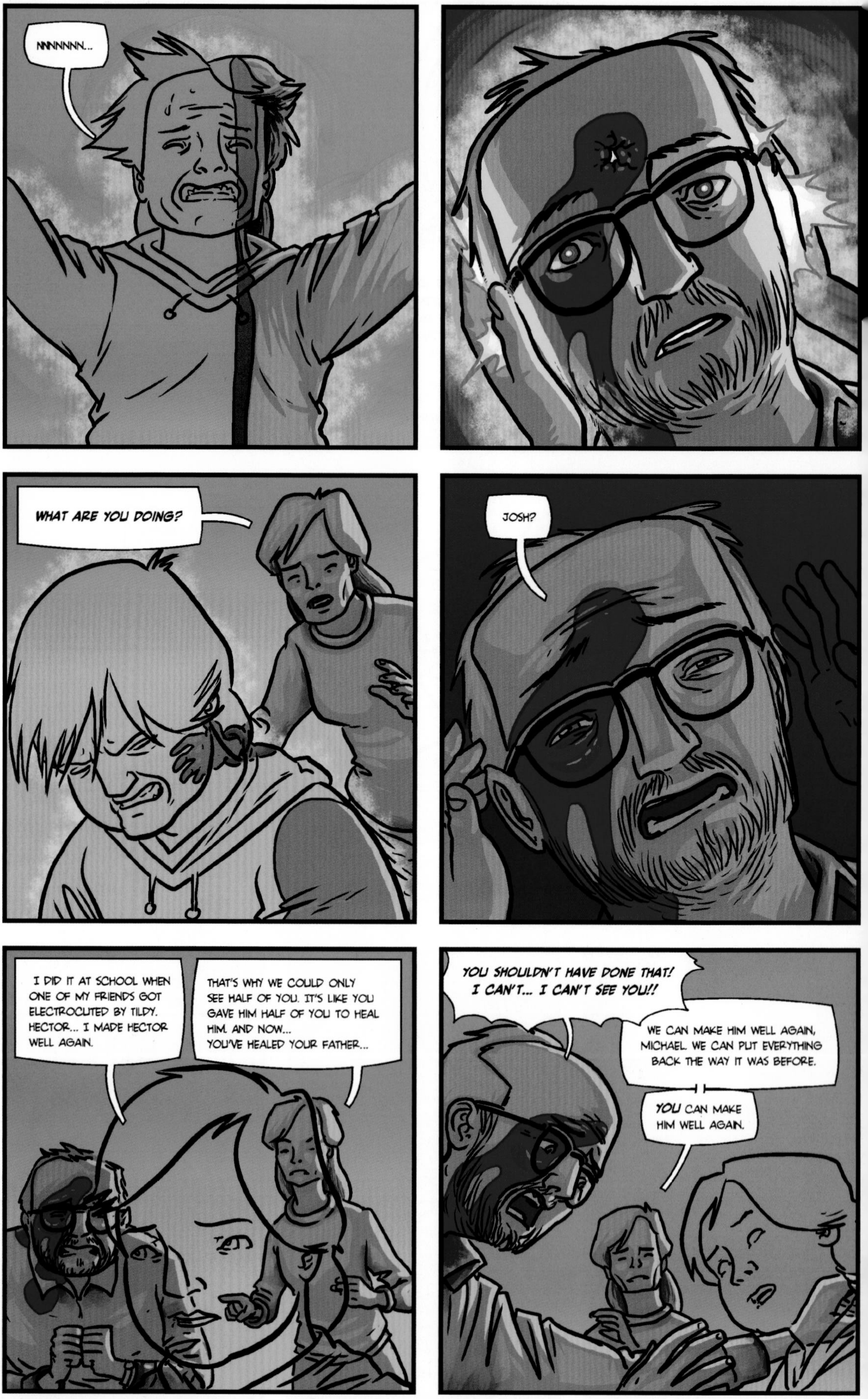

NNNNNNN...
WHAT ARE YOU DOING?
JOSH?
I DID IT AT SCHOOL WHEN ONE OF MY FRIENDS GOT ELECTROCUTED BY TILDY. HECTOR... I MADE HECTOR WELL AGAIN.
THAT'S WHY WE COULD ONLY SEE HALF OF YOU. IT'S LIKE YOU GAVE HIM HALF OF YOU TO HEAL HIM. AND NOW... YOU'VE HEALED YOUR FATHER...
YOU SHOULDN'T HAVE DONE THAT! I CAN'T... I CAN'T SEE YOU!!
WE CAN MAKE HIM WELL AGAIN, MICHAEL. WE CAN PUT EVERYTHING BACK THE WAY IT WAS BEFORE.
YOU CAN MAKE HIM WELL AGAIN.

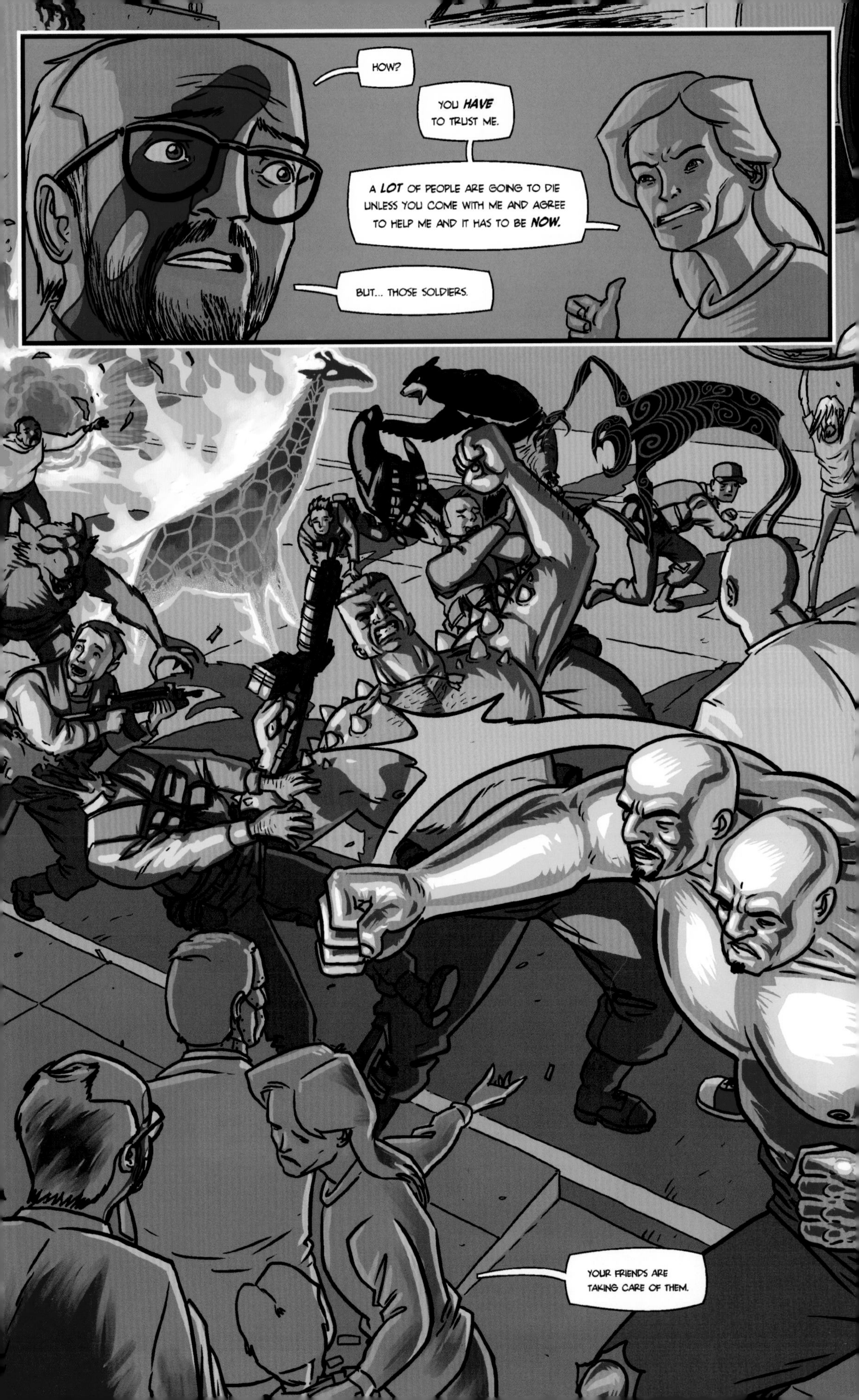
HOW?
YOU **HAVE** TO TRUST ME.
A **LOT** OF PEOPLE ARE GOING TO DIE UNLESS YOU COME WITH ME AND AGREE TO HELP ME AND IT HAS TO BE **NOW.**
BUT... THOSE SOLDIERS.
YOUR FRIENDS ARE TAKING CARE OF THEM.

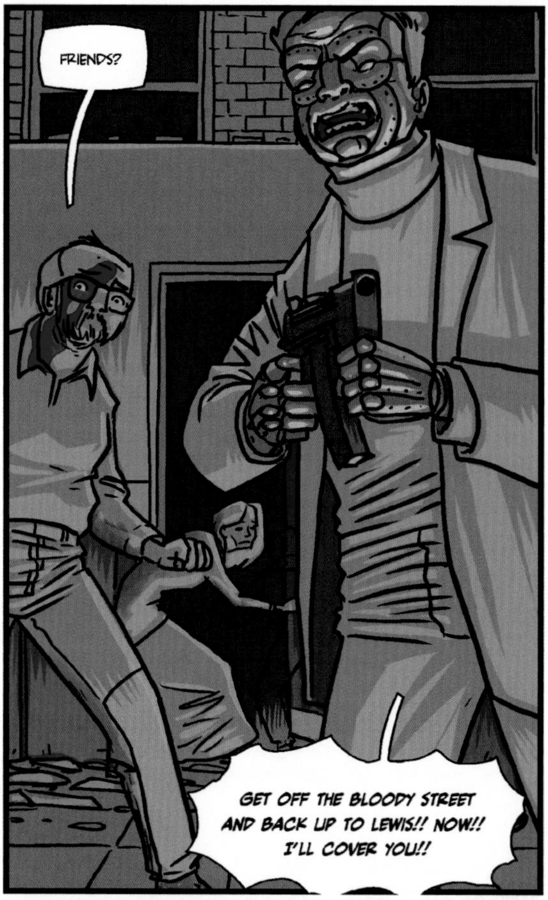
FRIENDS?
GET OFF THE BLOODY STREET AND BACK UP TO LEWIS!! NOW!! I'LL COVER YOU!!

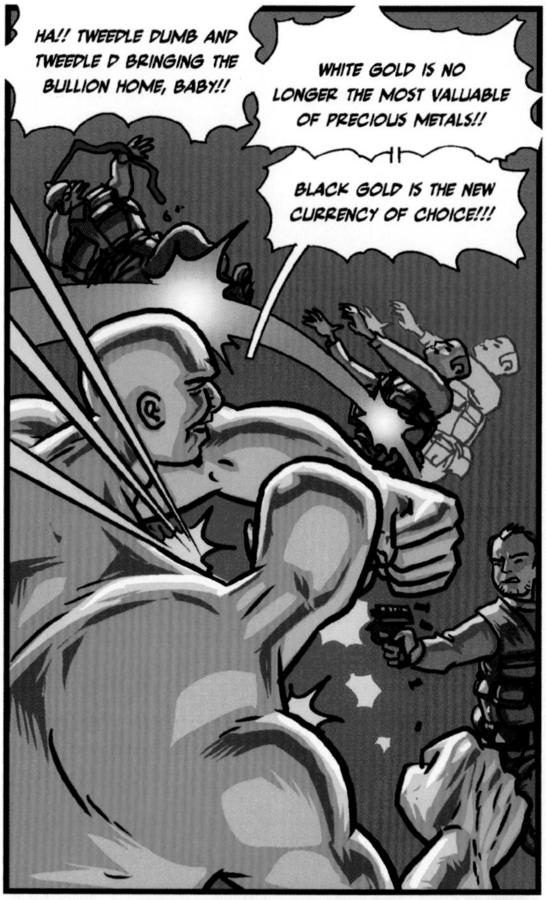
HA!! TWEEDLE DUMB AND TWEEDLE D BRINGING THE BULLION HOME, BABY!!
WHITE GOLD IS NO LONGER THE MOST VALUABLE OF PRECIOUS METALS!!
BLACK GOLD IS THE NEW CURRENCY OF CHOICE!!!

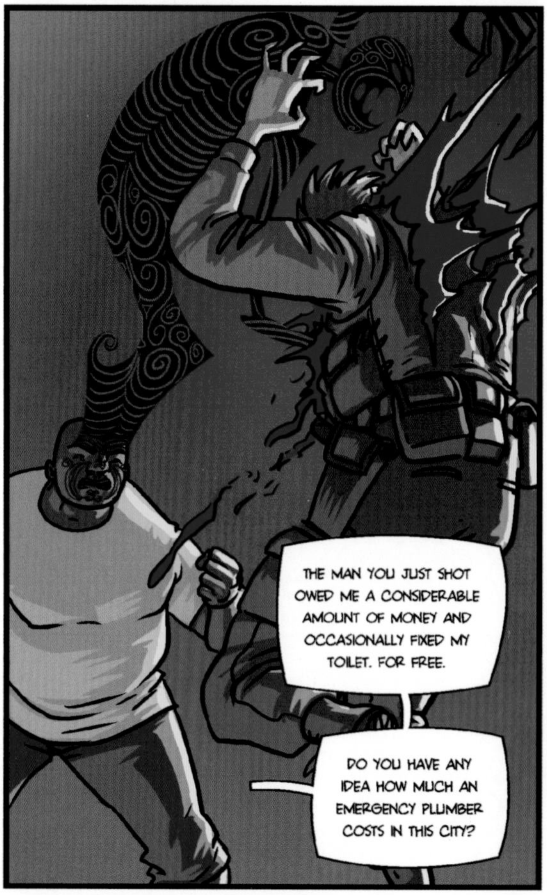
THE MAN YOU JUST SHOT OWED ME A CONSIDERABLE AMOUNT OF MONEY AND OCCASIONALLY FIXED MY TOILET. FOR FREE.
DO YOU HAVE ANY IDEA HOW MUCH AN EMERGENCY PLUMBER COSTS IN THIS CITY?

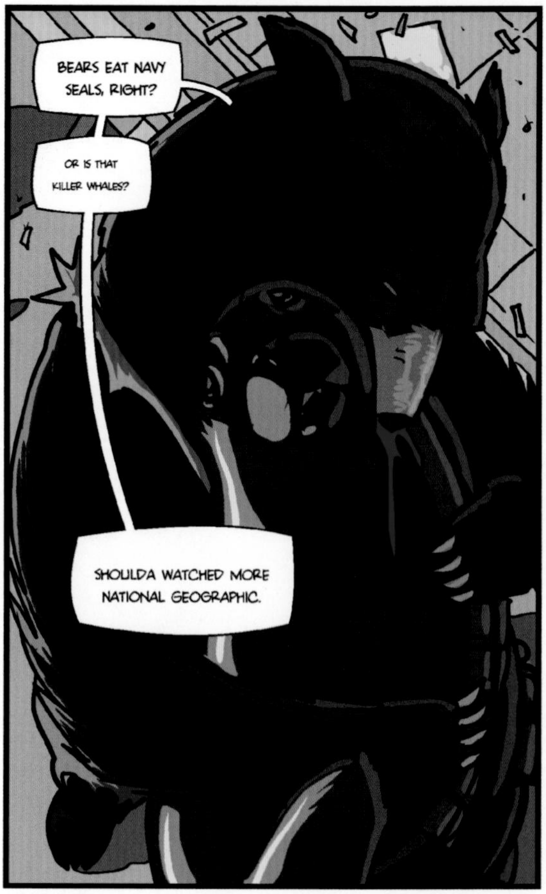
BEARS EAT NAVY SEALS, RIGHT?
OR IS THAT KILLER WHALES?
SHOULDA WATCHED MORE NATIONAL GEOGRAPHIC.

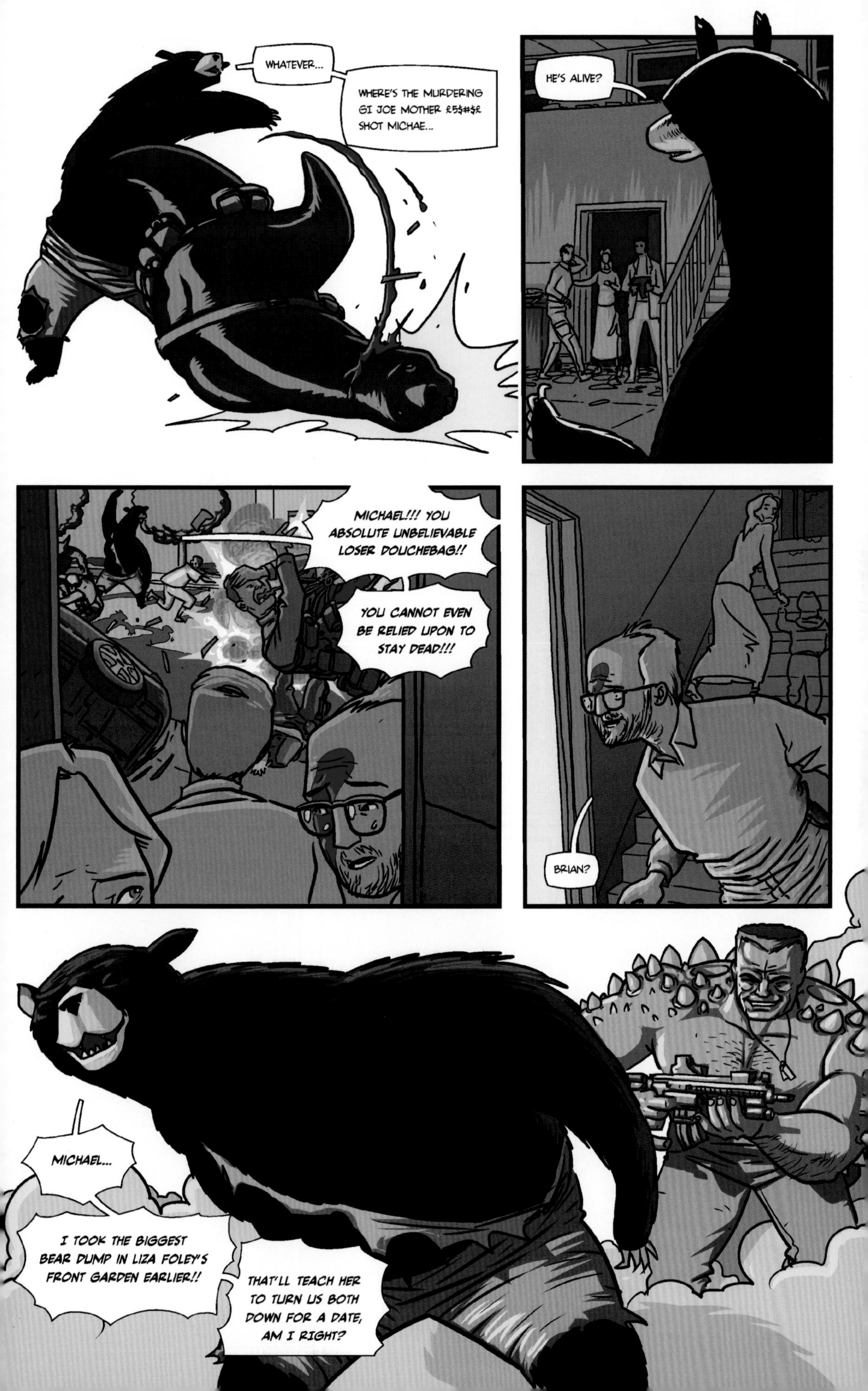
WHATEVER...
WHERE'S THE MURDERING GI JOE MOTHER £5$#$£ SHOT MICHAE...
HE'S ALIVE?
MICHAEL!!! YOU ABSOLUTE UNBELIEVABLE LOSER DOUCHEBAG!!
YOU CANNOT EVEN BE RELIED UPON TO STAY DEAD!!!
BRIAN?
MICHAEL...
I TOOK THE BIGGEST BEAR DUMP IN LIZA FOLEY'S FRONT GARDEN EARLIER!!
THAT'LL TEACH HER TO TURN US BOTH DOWN FOR A DATE, AM I RIGHT?

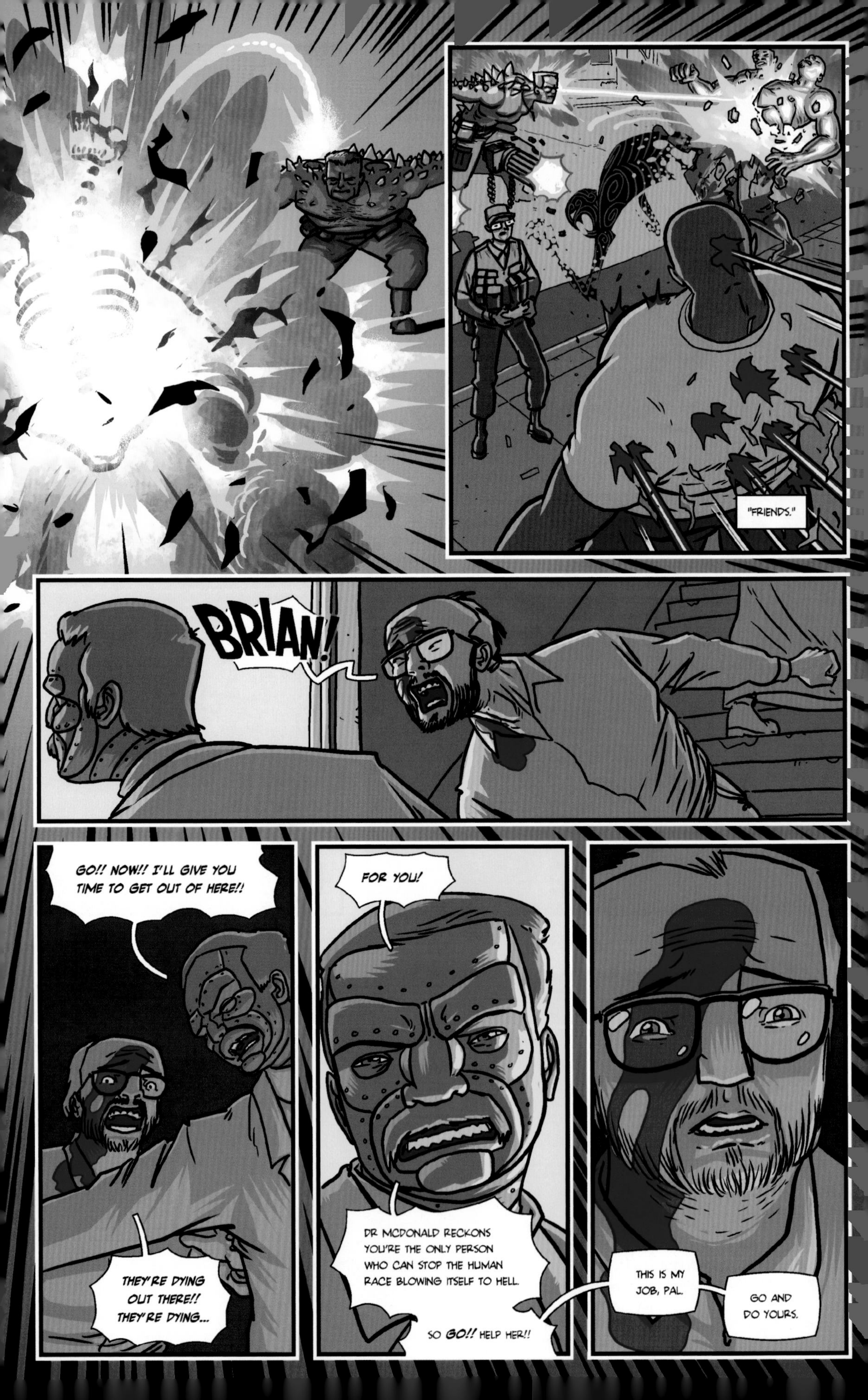
"FRIENDS."
BRIAN!
GO!! NOW!! I'LL GIVE YOU TIME TO GET OUT OF HERE!!
THEY'RE DYING OUT THERE!! THEY'RE DYING...
FOR YOU!
DR MCDONALD RECKONS YOU'RE THE ONLY PERSON WHO CAN STOP THE HUMAN RACE BLOWING ITSELF TO HELL.
SO GO!! HELP HER!!
THIS IS MY JOB, PAL.
GO AND DO YOURS.

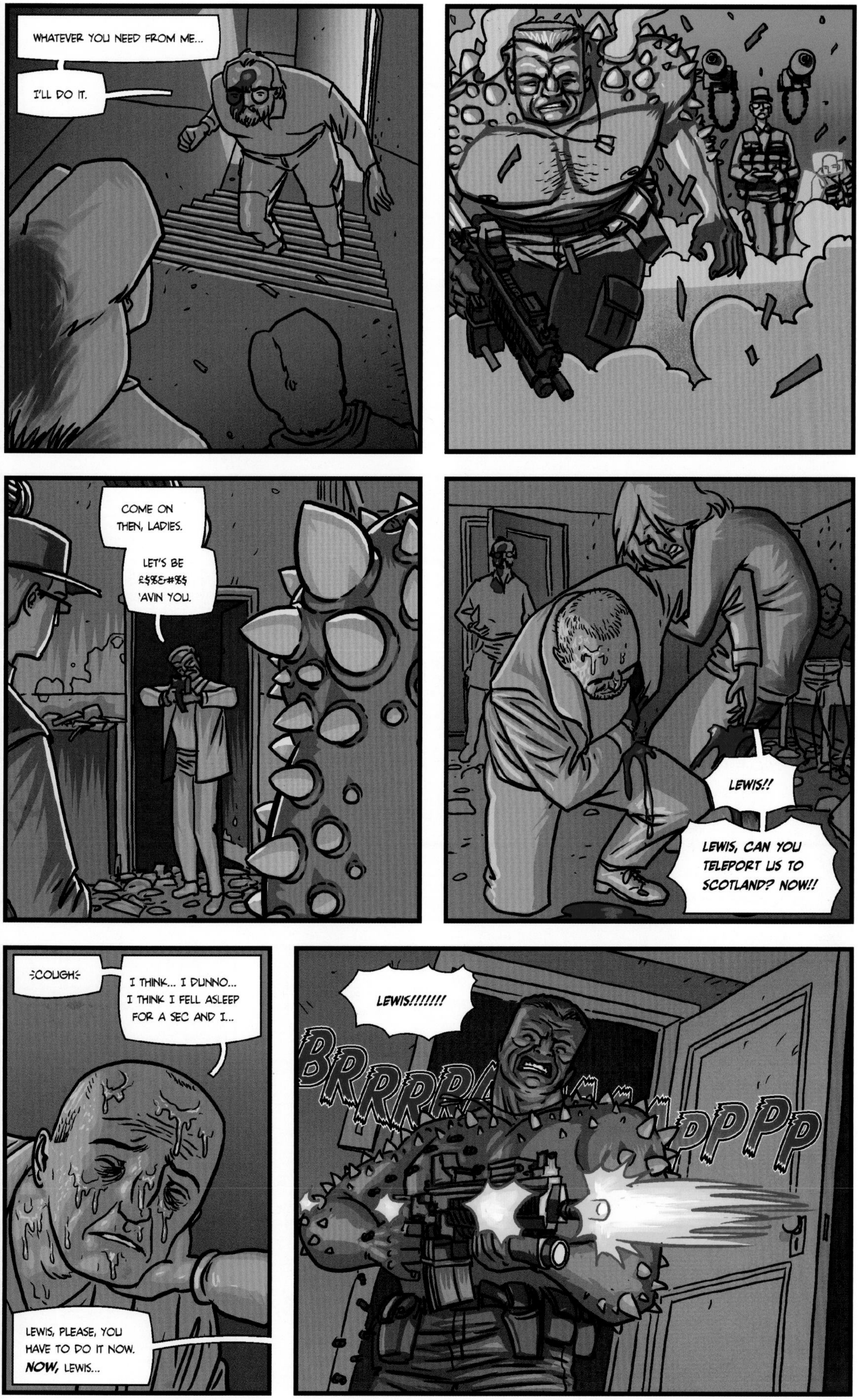
WHATEVER YOU NEED FROM ME...
I'LL DO IT.
COME ON THEN, LADIES.
LET'S BE £$%&#%$ 'AVIN YOU.
LEWIS!!
LEWIS, CAN YOU TELEPORT US TO SCOTLAND? NOW!!
COUGH
I THINK... I DUNNO... I THINK I FELL ASLEEP FOR A SEC AND I...
LEWIS, PLEASE, YOU HAVE TO DO IT NOW. NOW, LEWIS...
LEWIS!!!!!!!
BRRRRRAAAAAPPPPP

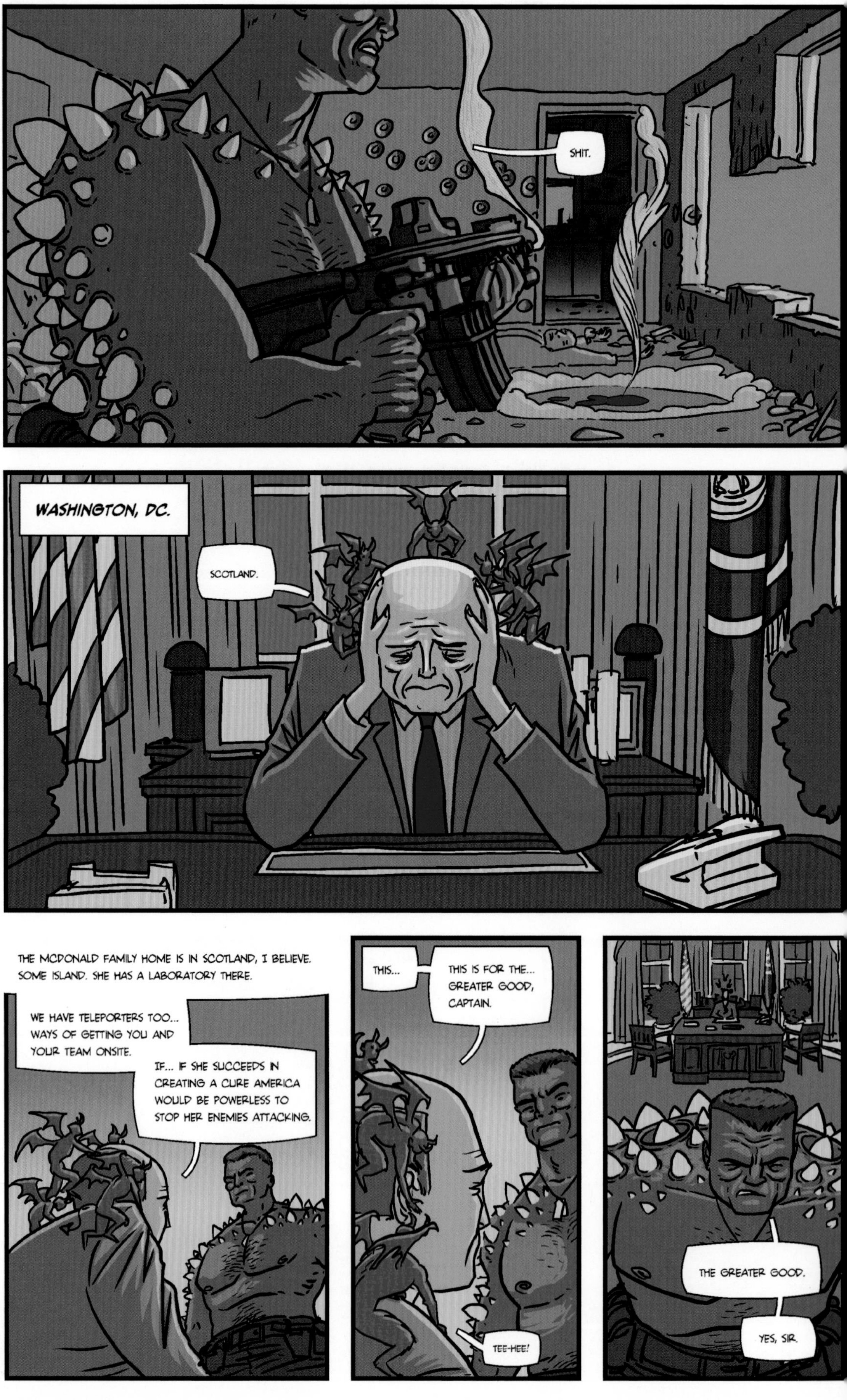
SHIT.
WASHINGTON, DC.
SCOTLAND.
THE MCDONALD FAMILY HOME IS IN SCOTLAND, I BELIEVE. SOME ISLAND. SHE HAS A LABORATORY THERE.
WE HAVE TELEPORTERS TOO... WAYS OF GETTING YOU AND YOUR TEAM ONSITE.
IF... IF SHE SUCCEEDS IN CREATING A CURE AMERICA WOULD BE POWERLESS TO STOP HER ENEMIES ATTACKING.
THIS...
THIS IS FOR THE... GREATER GOOD, CAPTAIN.
TEE-HEE!
THE GREATER GOOD.
YES, SIR.

WHATEVER HAPPENS...

YOU BELONG TO US NOW.

I TRIED TO STOP THE BLEEDING...

HE WAS TOO WEAK. HE DIED JUST AFTER WE ARRIVED.

I'M SORRY.

IT MUST HAVE TAKEN ALL HIS REMAINING STRENGTH TO TELEPORT US HERE. YOU'D PASSED OUT WHEN WE APPEARED.

I DID WHEN LEWIS TELEPORTED ME TO QUEENS FROM WASHINGTON. IT'S JARRING. AND WHO KNOWS HOW THE BULLET TRAUMA AFFECTED YOU. YOU'VE BEEN OUT FOR HOURS.

JESUS.

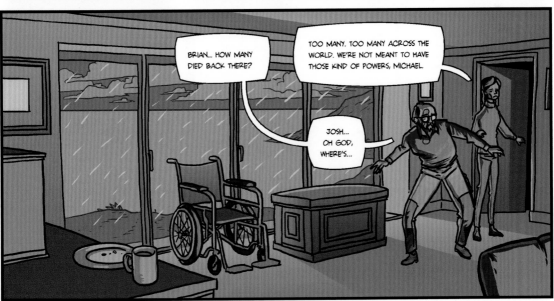

BRIAN... HOW MANY DIED BACK THERE?

TOO MANY. TOO MANY ACROSS THE WORLD. WE'RE NOT MEANT TO HAVE THOSE KIND OF POWERS, MICHAEL.

JOSH... OH GOD, WHERE'S...

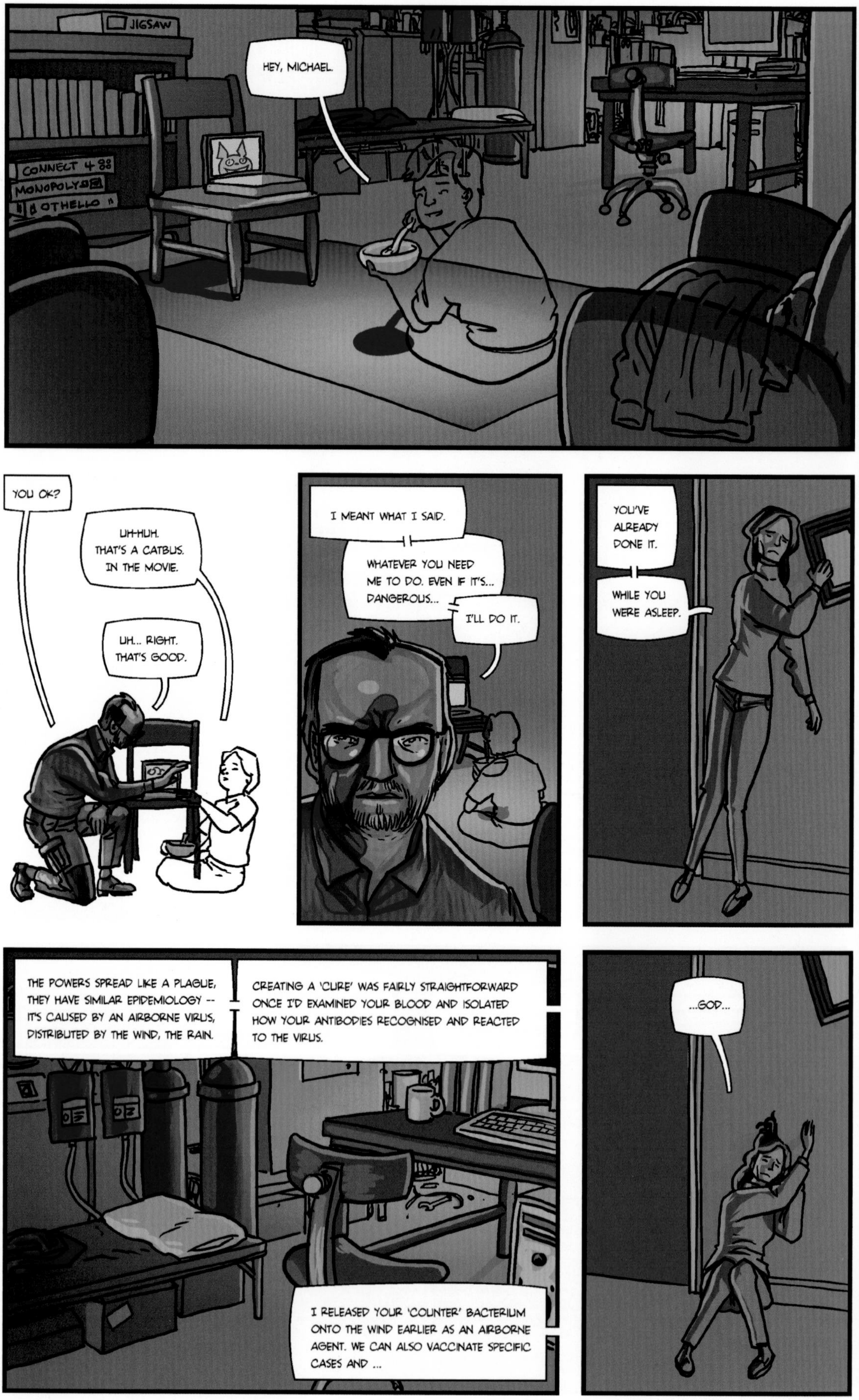
JIGSAW
CONNECT 4
MONOPOLY
OTHELLO
HEY, MICHAEL.
YOU OK?
UH-HUH. THAT'S A CATBUS. IN THE MOVIE.
UH... RIGHT. THAT'S GOOD.
I MEANT WHAT I SAID.
WHATEVER YOU NEED ME TO DO. EVEN IF IT'S... DANGEROUS...
I'LL DO IT.
YOU'VE ALREADY DONE IT.
WHILE YOU WERE ASLEEP.
THE POWERS SPREAD LIKE A PLAGUE, THEY HAVE SIMILAR EPIDEMIOLOGY -- IT'S CAUSED BY AN AIRBORNE VIRUS, DISTRIBUTED BY THE WIND, THE RAIN.
CREATING A 'CURE' WAS FAIRLY STRAIGHTFORWARD ONCE I'D EXAMINED YOUR BLOOD AND ISOLATED HOW YOUR ANTIBODIES RECOGNISED AND REACTED TO THE VIRUS.
I RELEASED YOUR 'COUNTER' BACTERIUM ONTO THE WIND EARLIER AS AN AIRBORNE AGENT. WE CAN ALSO VACCINATE SPECIFIC CASES AND ...
...GOD...

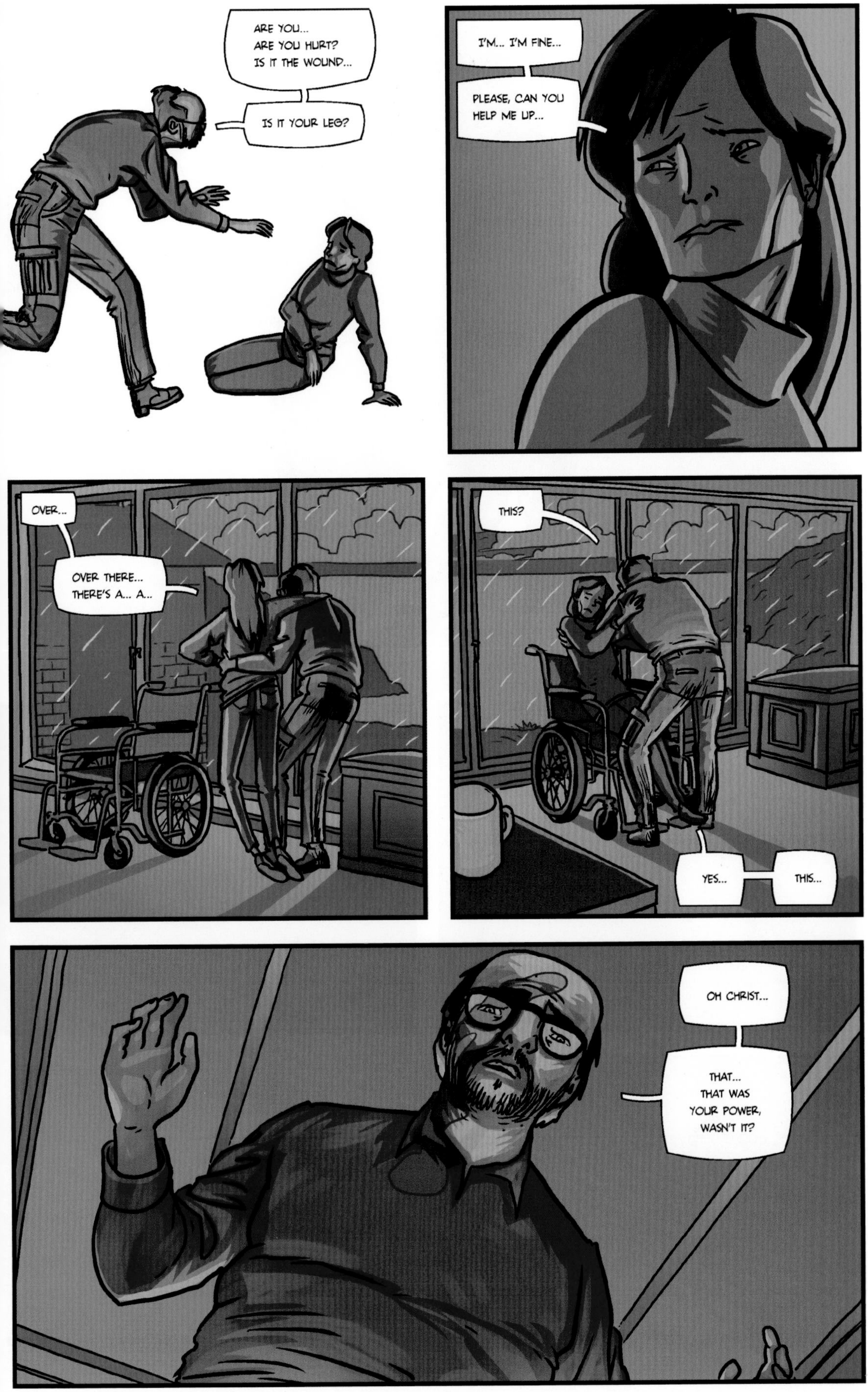
ARE YOU...
ARE YOU HURT?
IS IT THE WOUND...
IS IT YOUR LEG?
I'M... I'M FINE...
PLEASE, CAN YOU HELP ME UP...
OVER...
OVER THERE... THERE'S A... A...
THIS?
YES...
THIS...
OH CHRIST...
THAT... THAT WAS YOUR POWER, WASN'T IT?

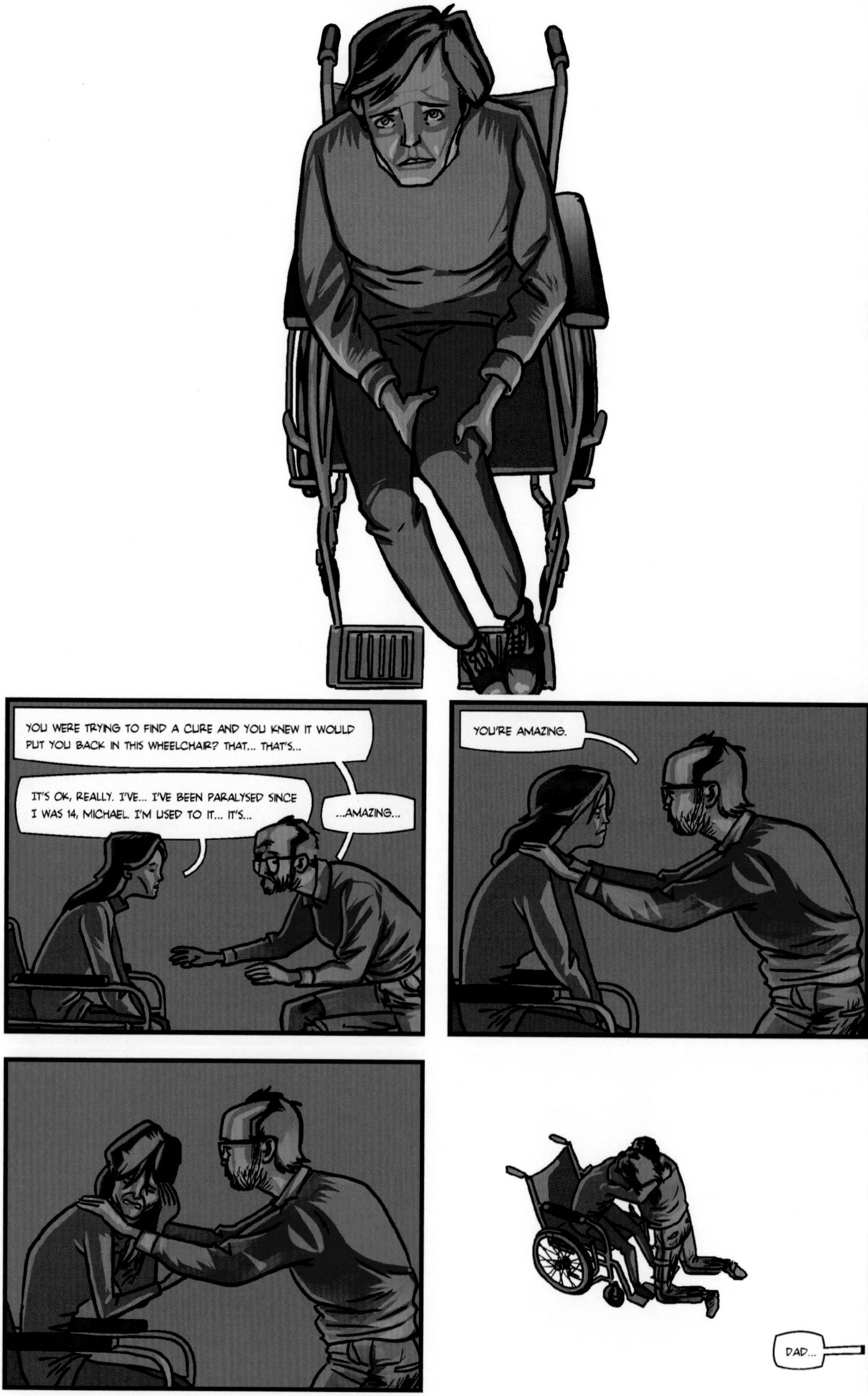
YOU WERE TRYING TO FIND A CURE AND YOU KNEW IT WOULD PUT YOU BACK IN THIS WHEELCHAIR? THAT... THAT'S...
IT'S OK, REALLY. I'VE... I'VE BEEN PARALYSED SINCE I WAS 14, MICHAEL. I'M USED TO IT... IT'S...
...AMAZING...
YOU'RE AMAZING.
DAD...

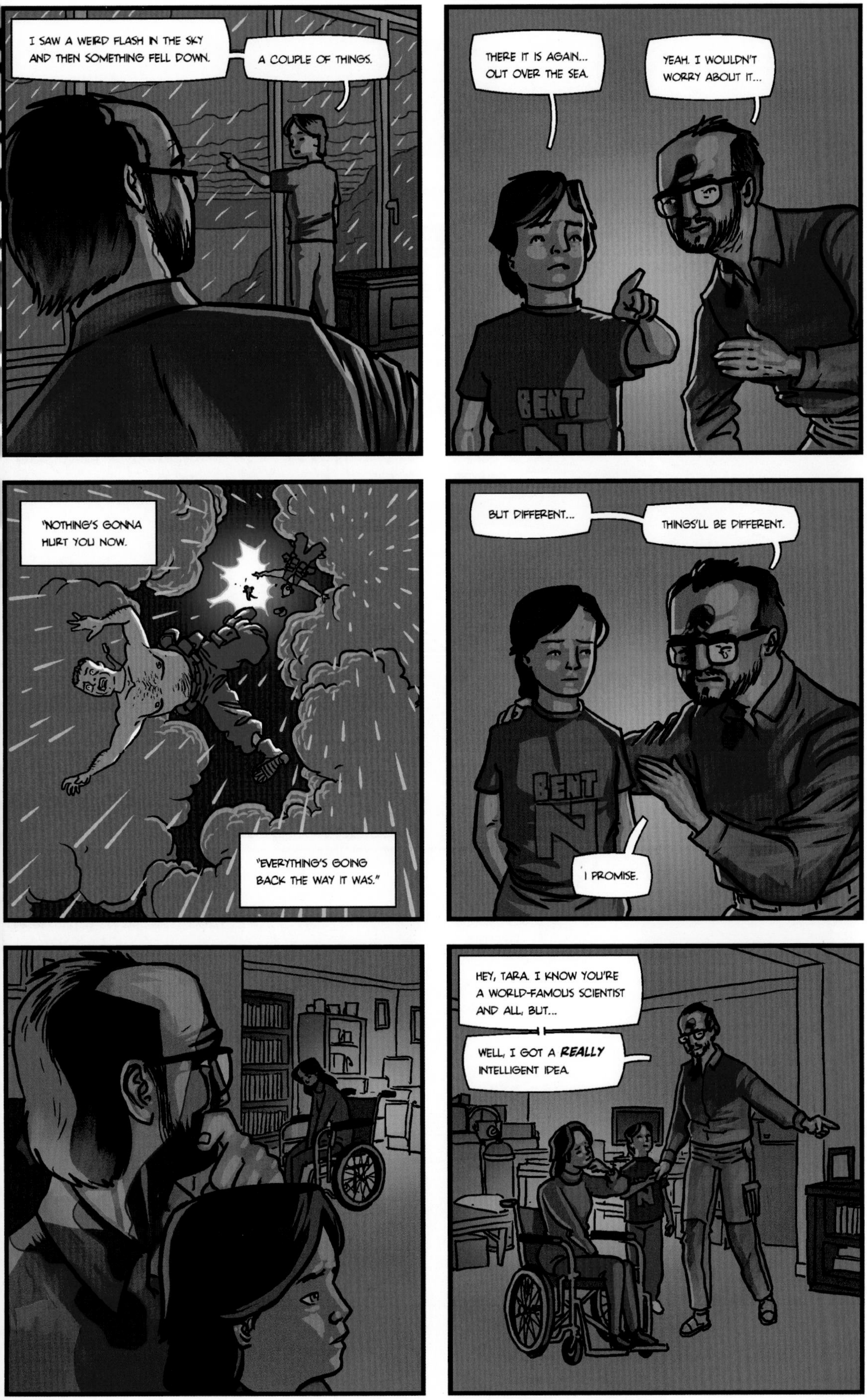
I SAW A WEIRD FLASH IN THE SKY AND THEN SOMETHING FELL DOWN.
A COUPLE OF THINGS.
THERE IT IS AGAIN... OUT OVER THE SEA.
YEAH. I WOULDN'T WORRY ABOUT IT...
BENT
"NOTHING'S GONNA HURT YOU NOW.
"EVERYTHING'S GOING BACK THE WAY IT WAS."
BUT DIFFERENT...
THINGS'LL BE DIFFERENT.
BENT
I PROMISE.
HEY, TARA. I KNOW YOU'RE A WORLD-FAMOUS SCIENTIST AND ALL, BUT...
WELL, I GOT A ***REALLY*** INTELLIGENT IDEA.

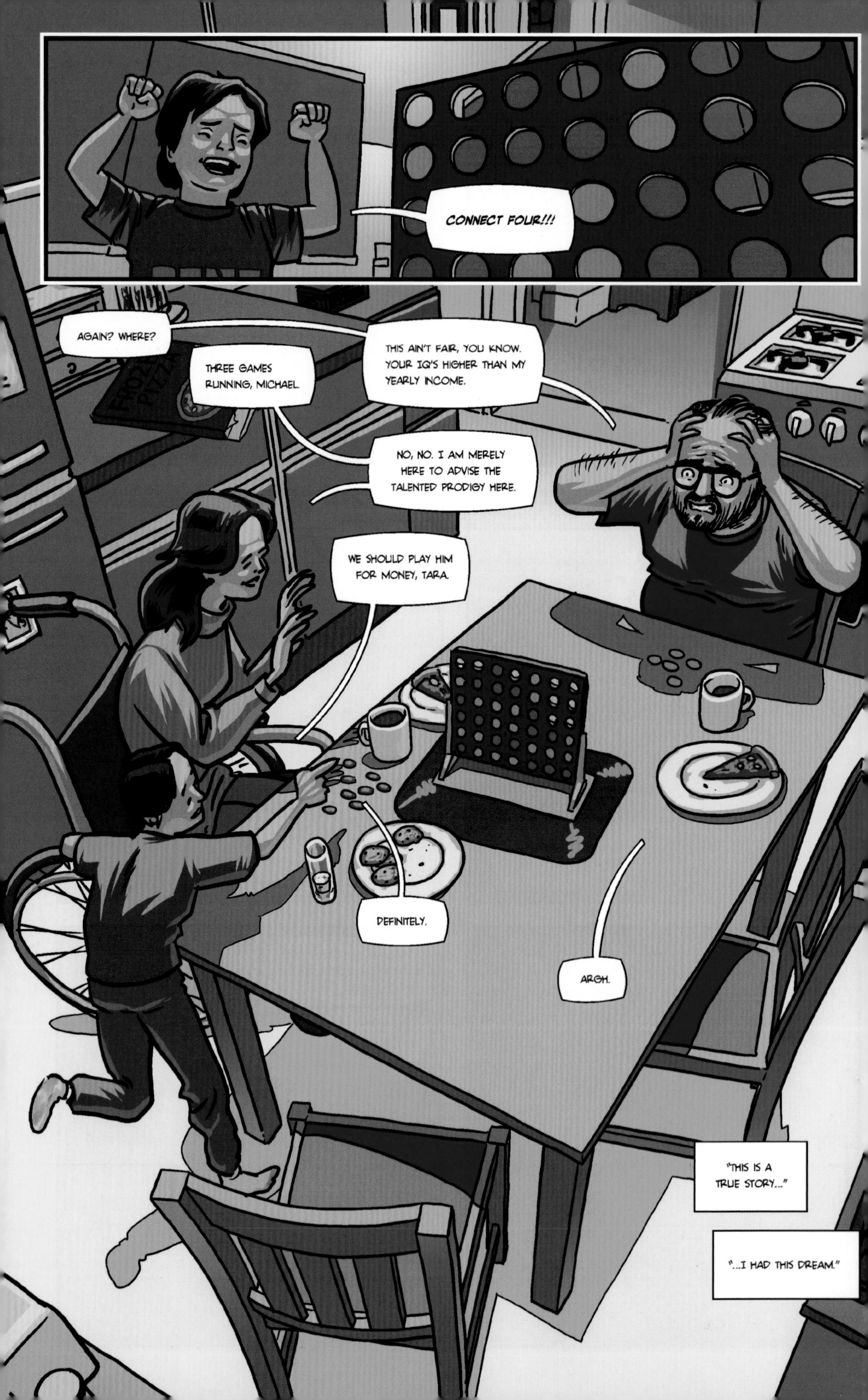
CONNECT FOUR!!!
AGAIN? WHERE?
THREE GAMES RUNNING, MICHAEL.
THIS AIN'T FAIR, YOU KNOW. YOUR IQ'S HIGHER THAN MY YEARLY INCOME.
NO, NO. I AM MERELY HERE TO ADVISE THE TALENTED PRODIGY HERE.
WE SHOULD PLAY HIM FOR MONEY, TARA.
DEFINITELY.
ARGH.
"THIS IS A TRUE STORY..."
"...I HAD THIS DREAM."

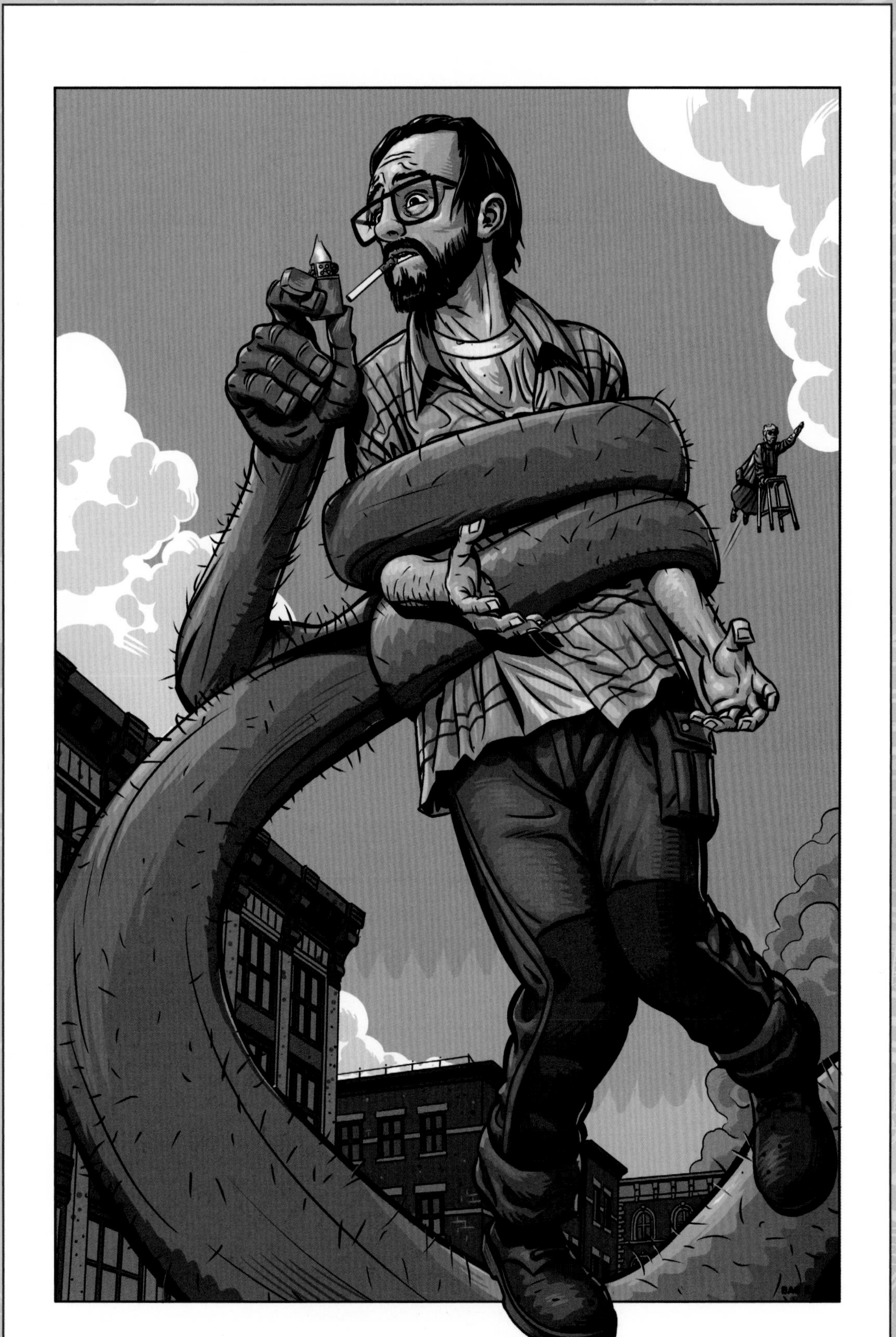

Edmund Bagwell

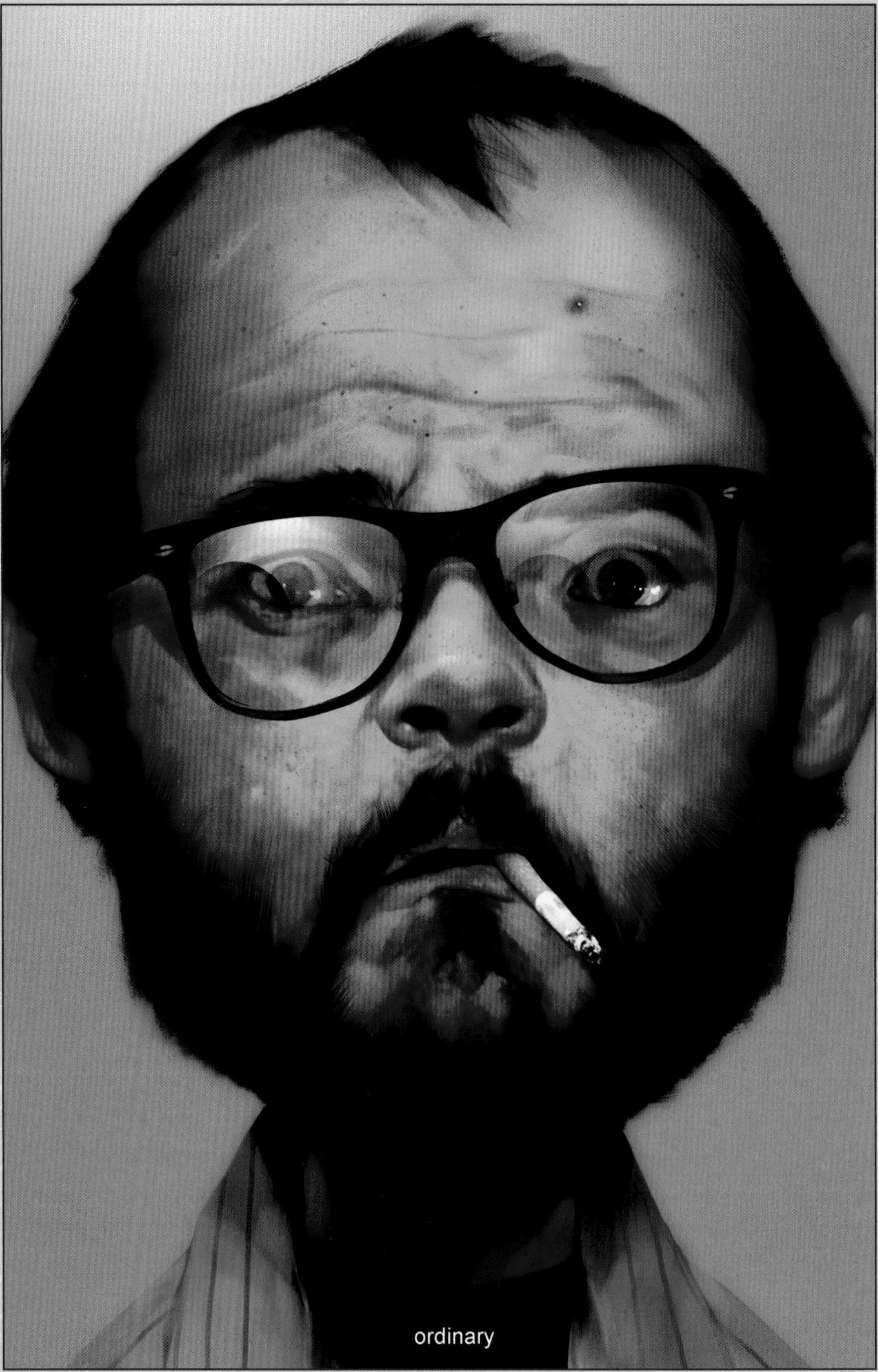
ordinary

Ben Oliver

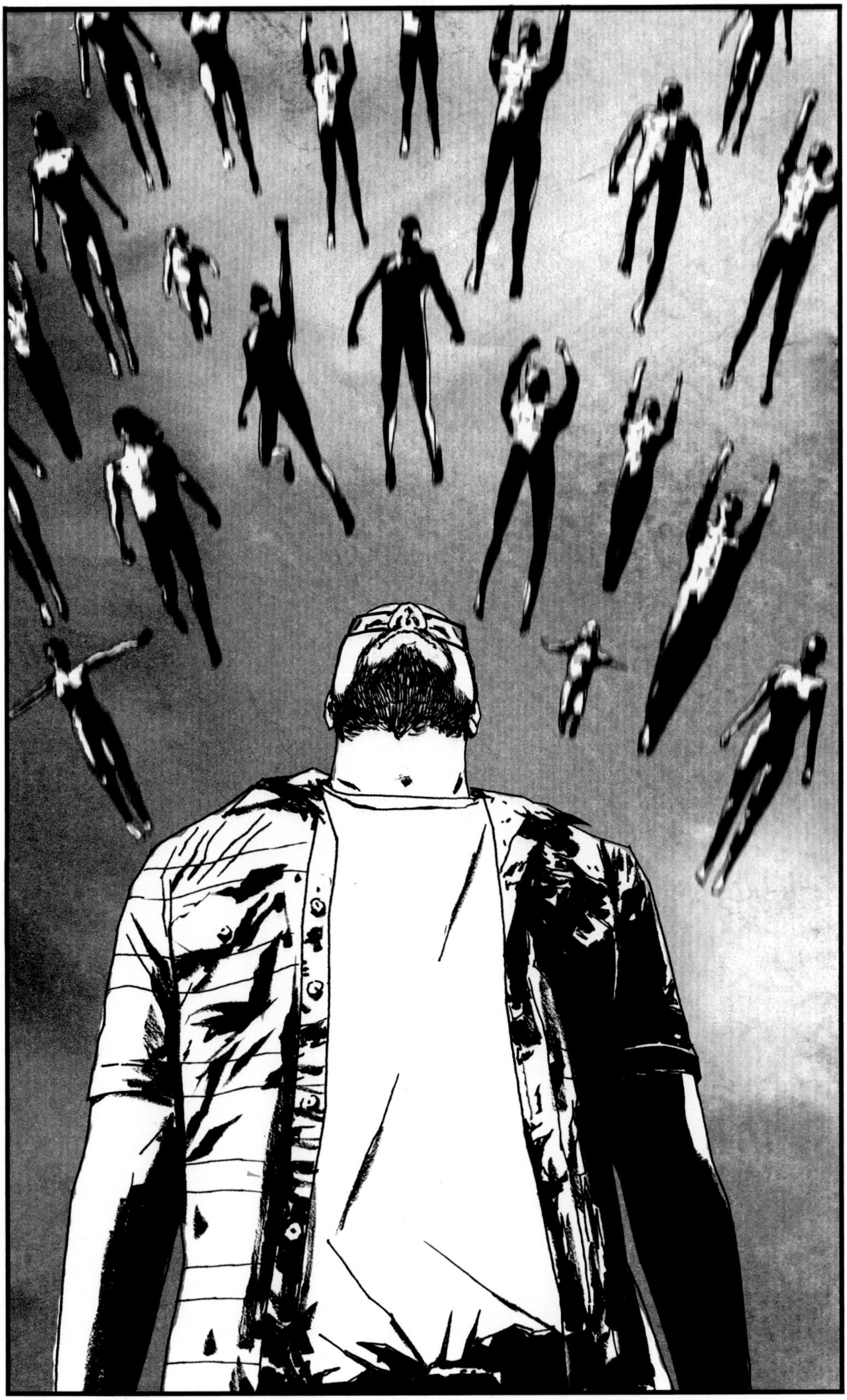

Laurence Campbell

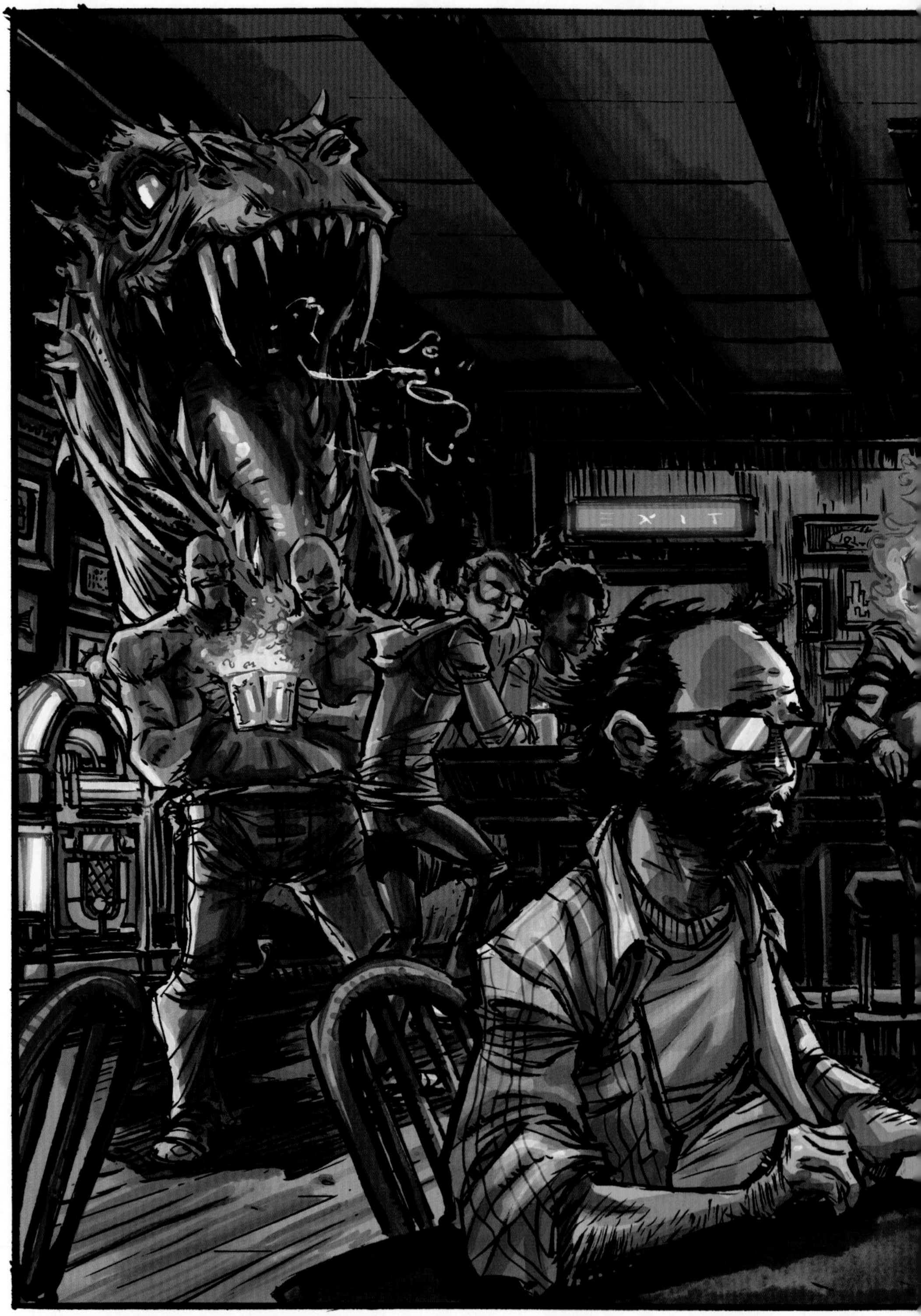

Brian Ching & Michael Atiyeh

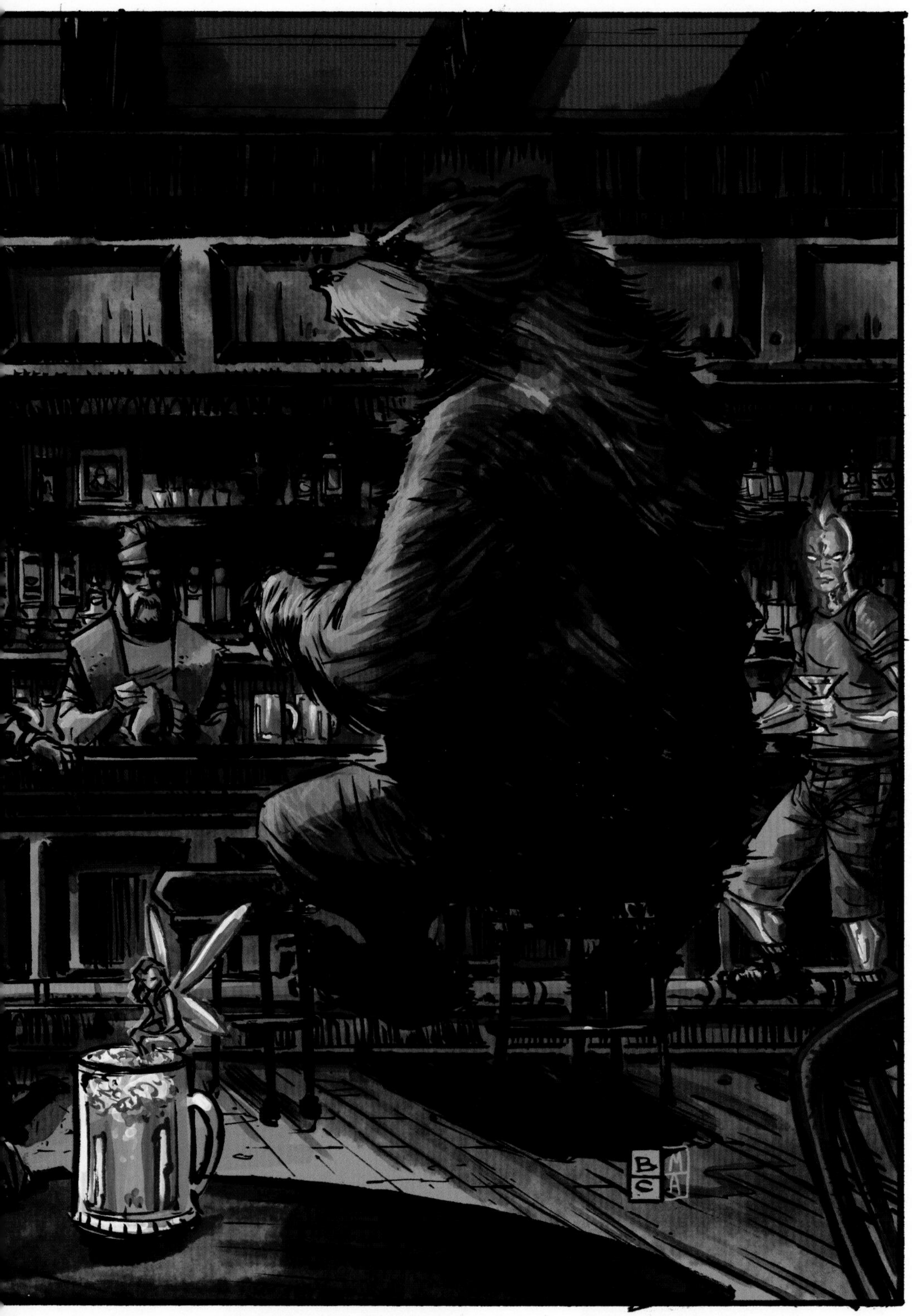

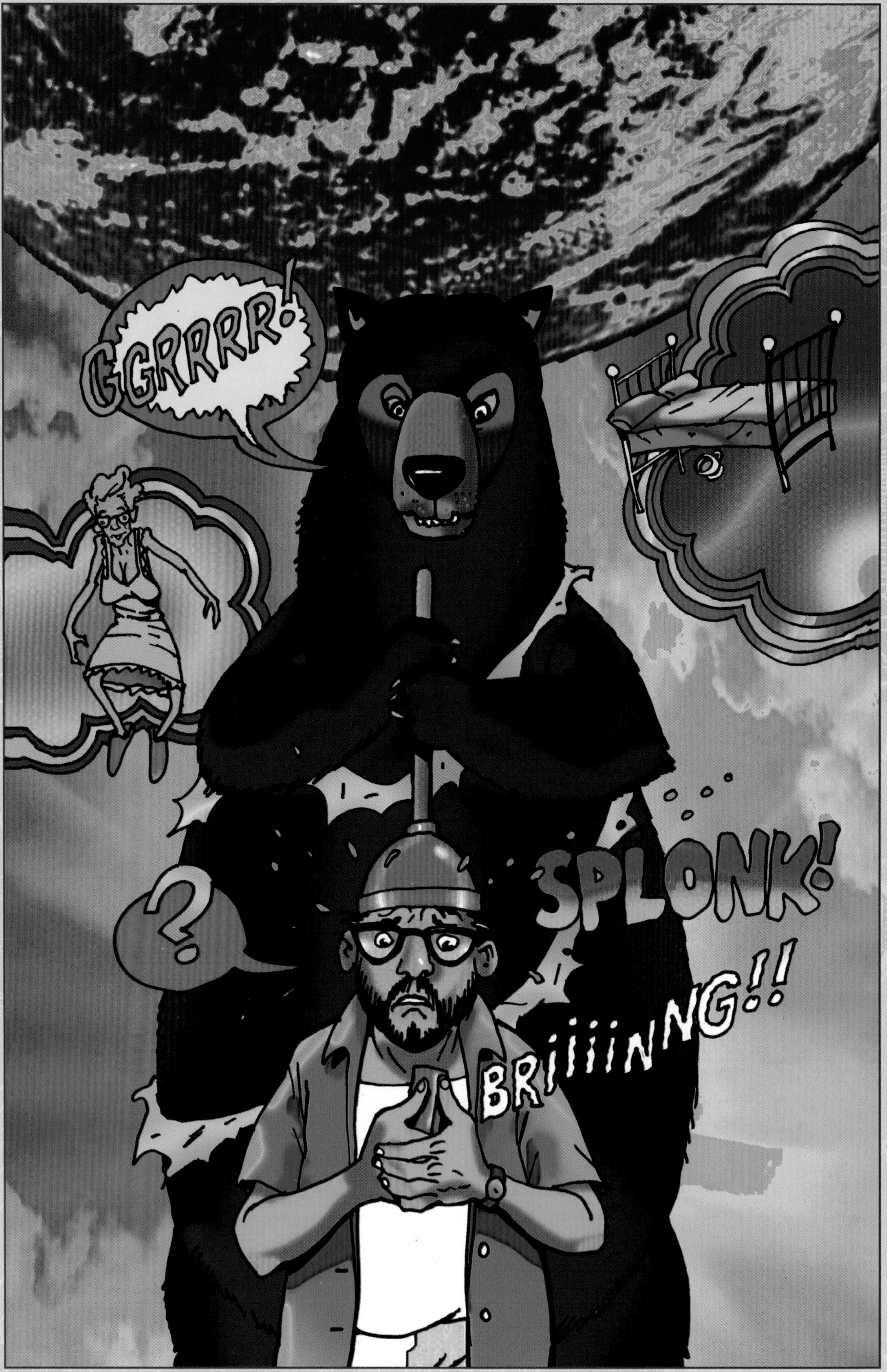
GGRRRR!
?
SPLONK!
BRiiiiNNG!!

Brendan McCarthy

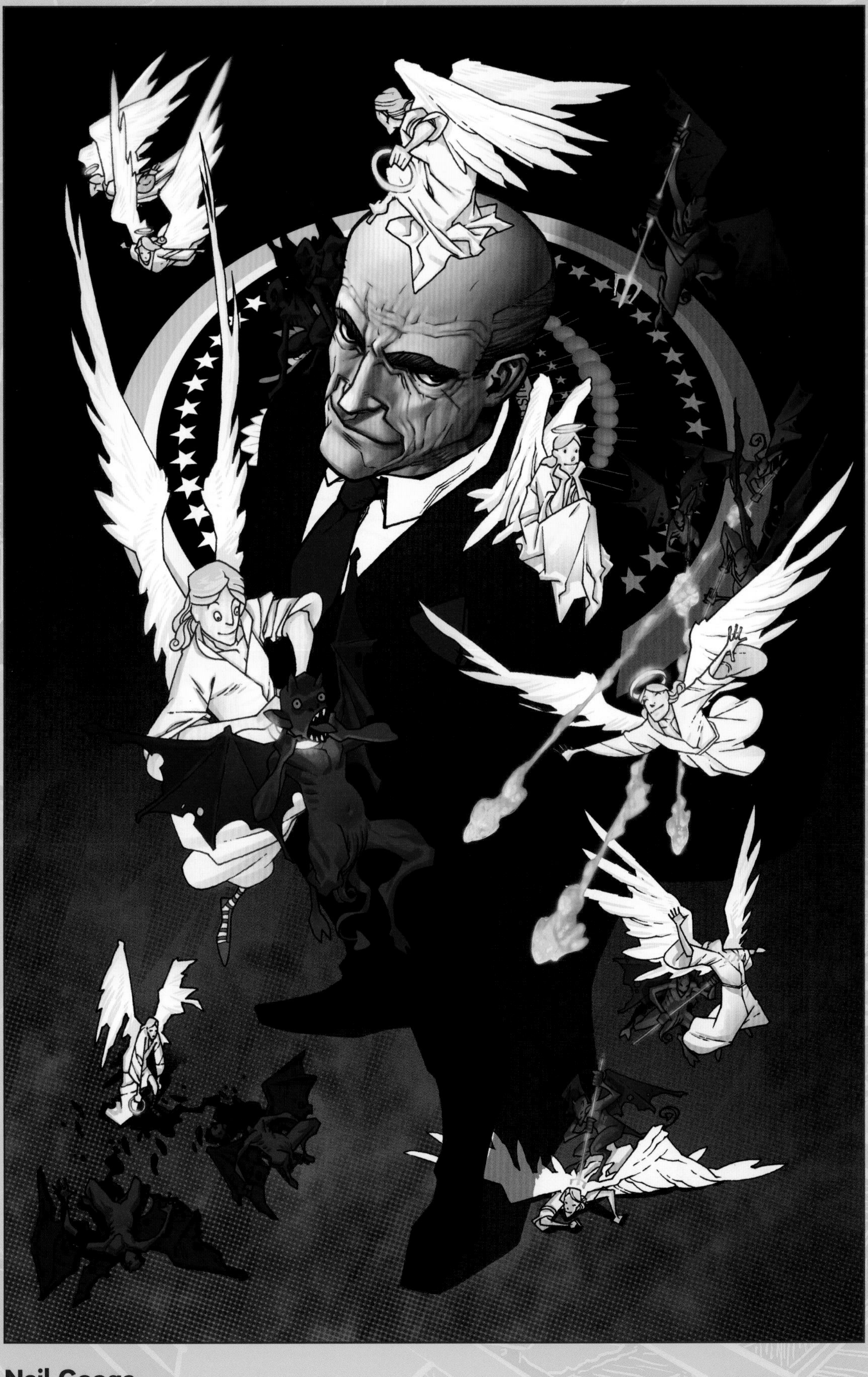

Neil Googe

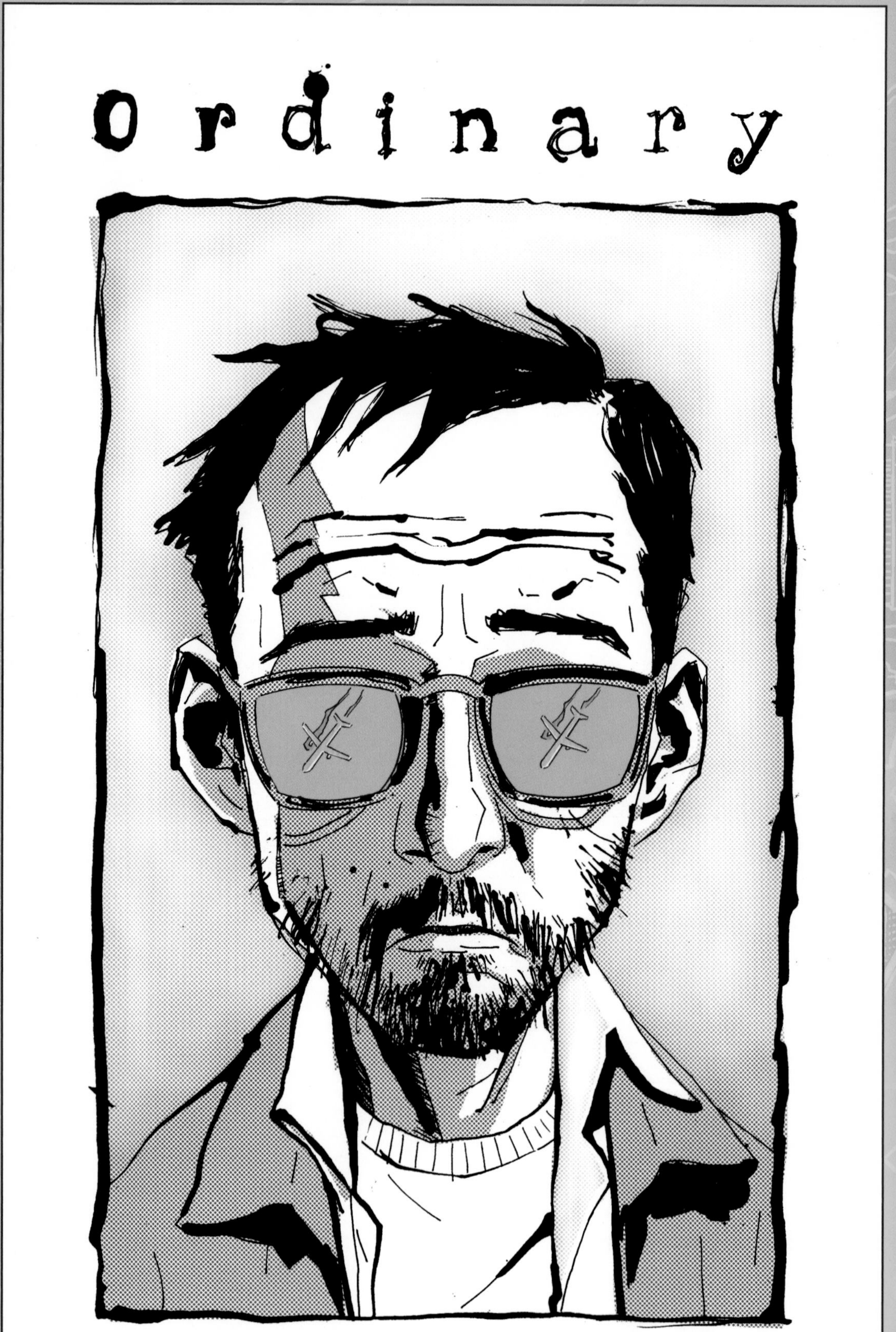
Ordinary

Dom Reardon

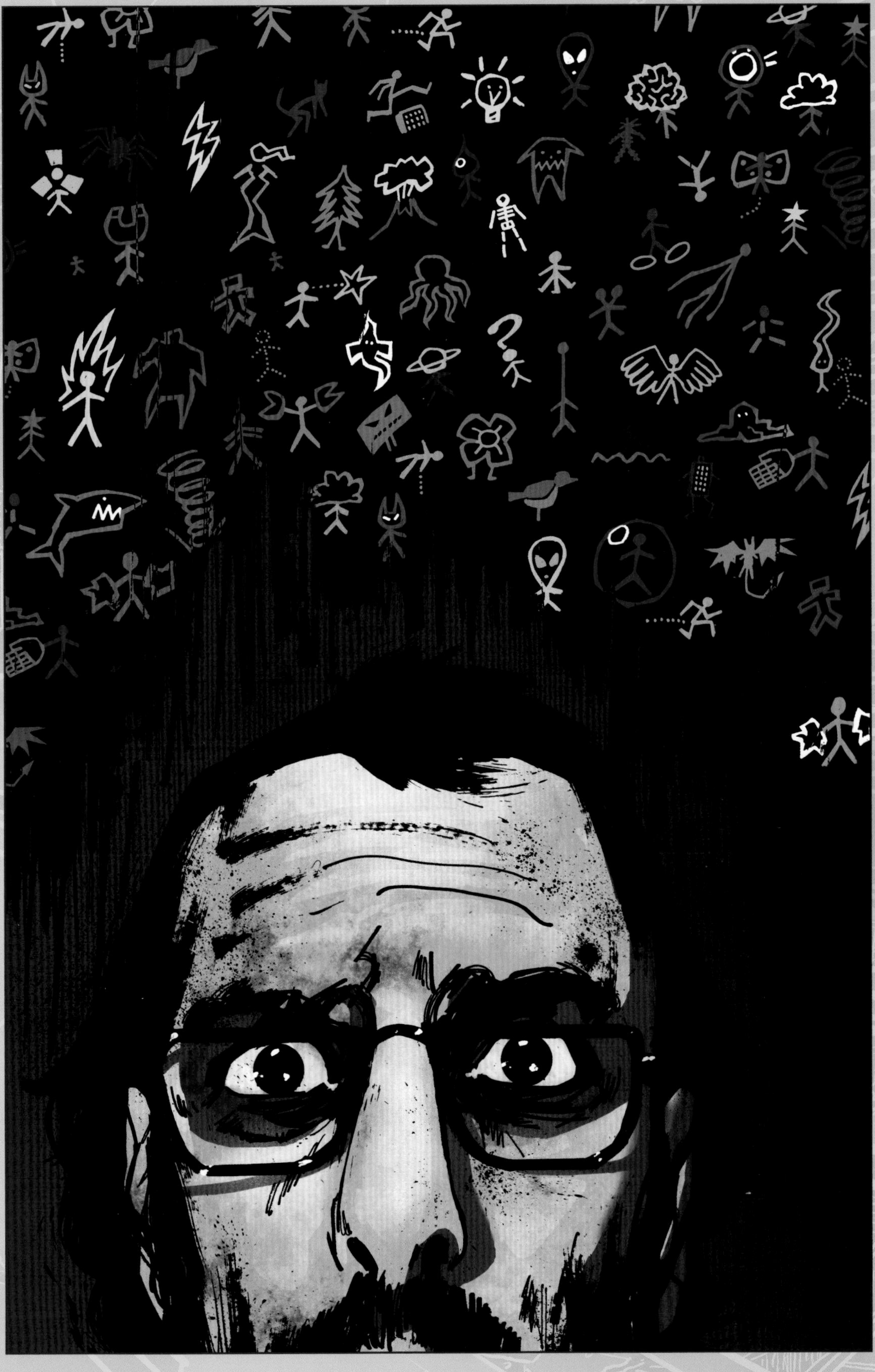

Henry Flint

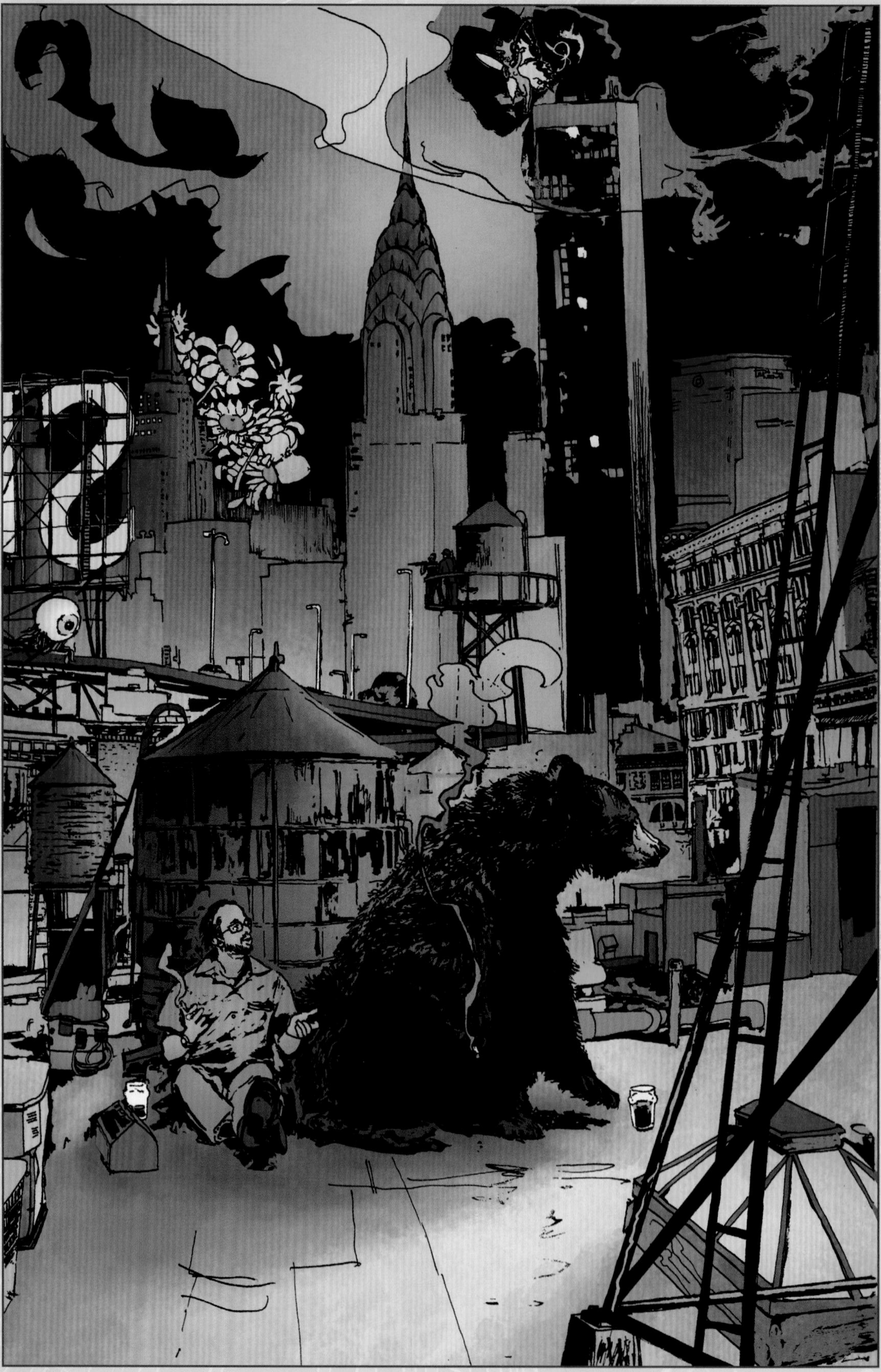

Alison Sampson & Ruth Redmond

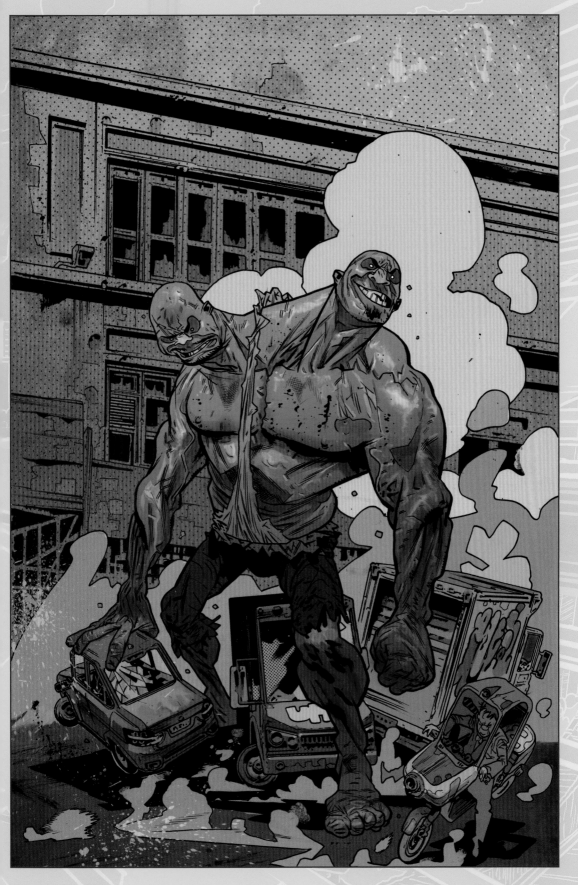

James Harren

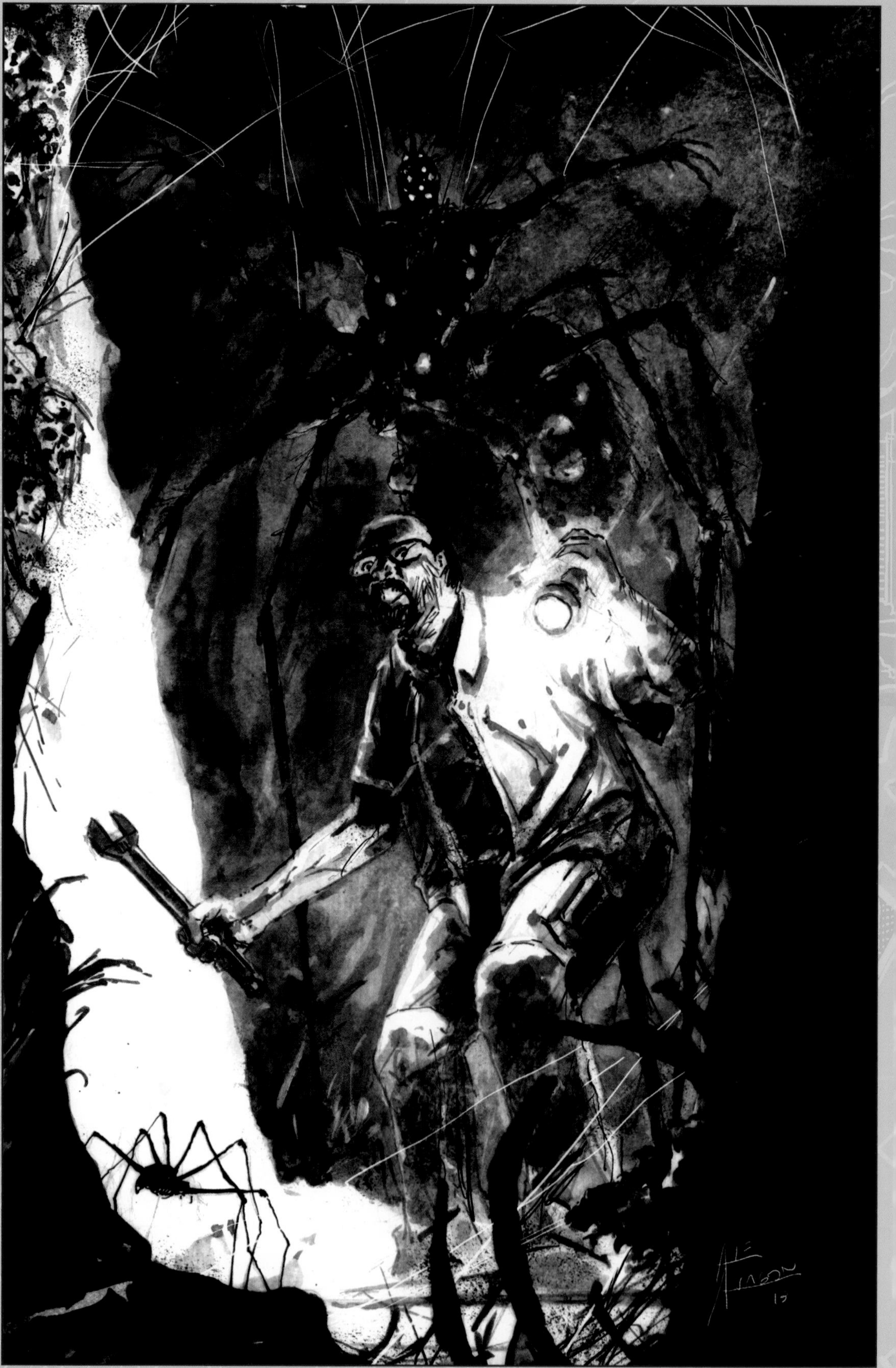

Ale Aragon

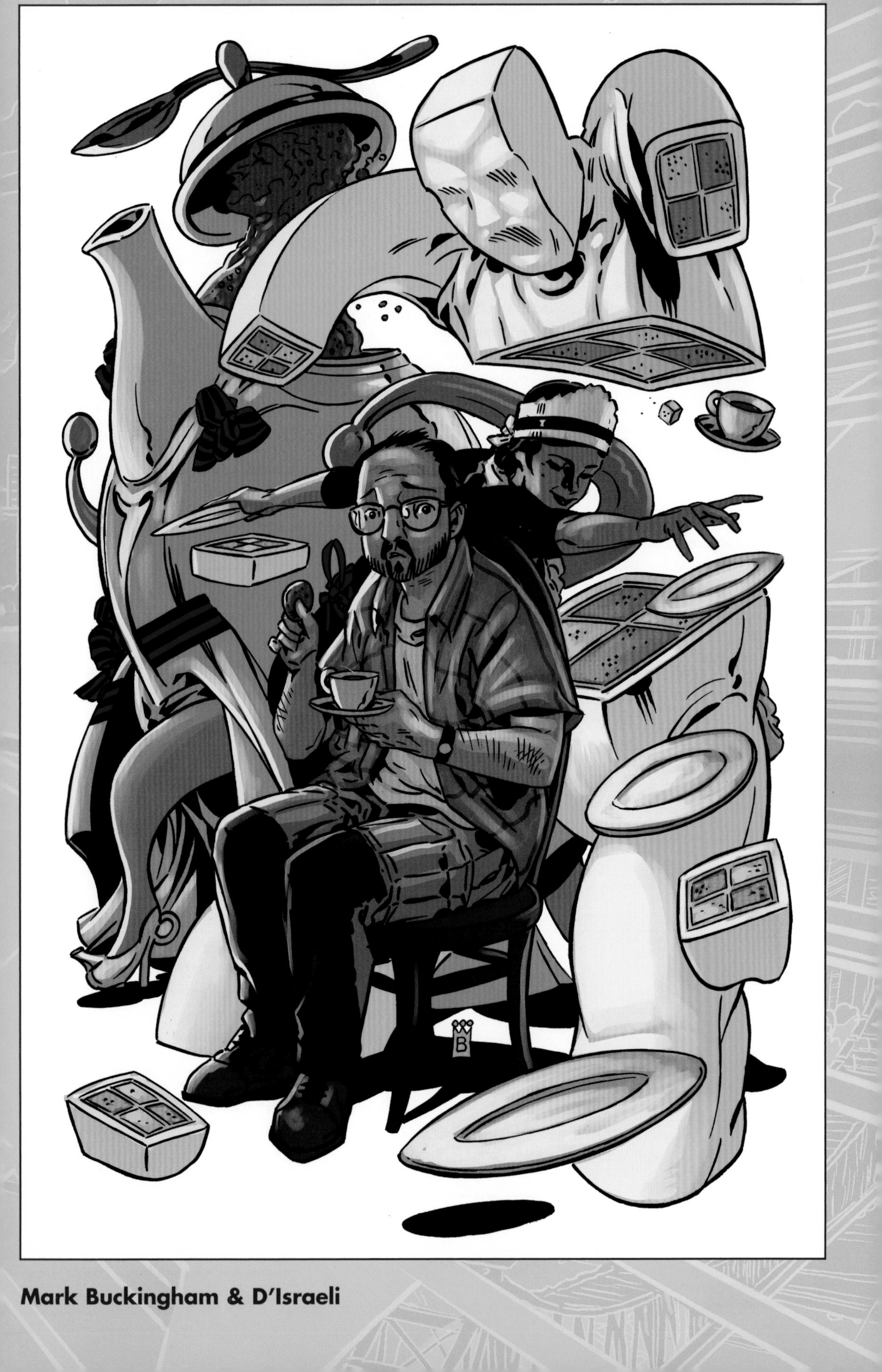

Mark Buckingham & D'Israeli

ORDINARY SCIENCE

By JV Chamary

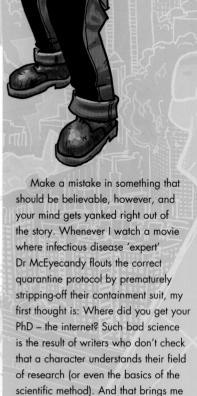

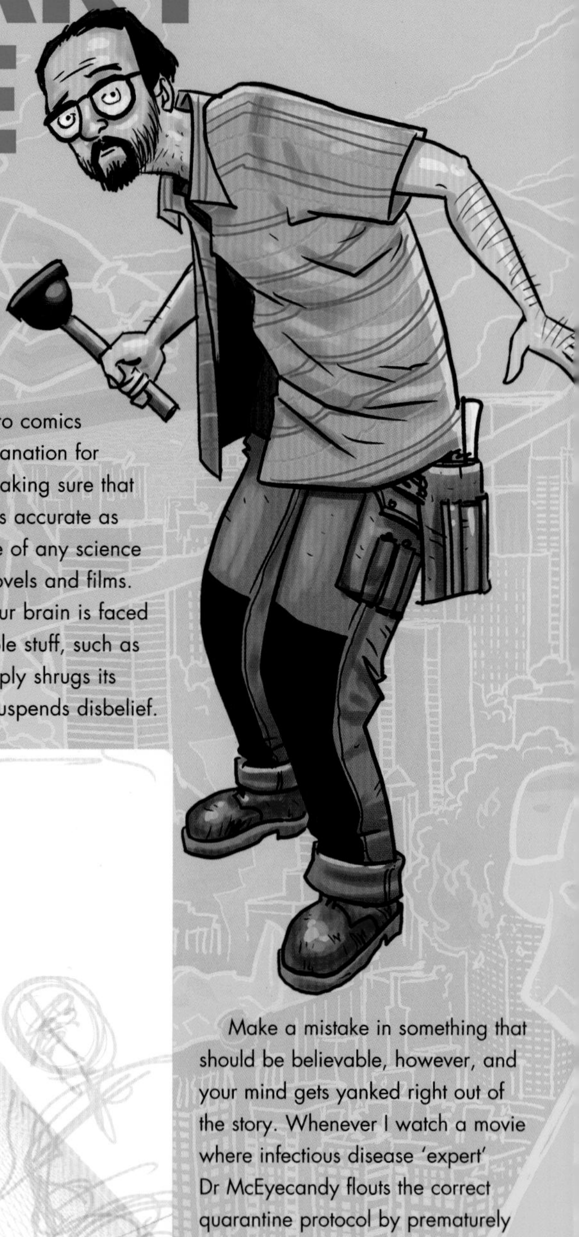

Before I get to the science of *Ordinary*, let's talk about the elephant in the lab: Are superpowers really possible? The short answer is No. During my career as a science writer, I've interviewed a guy who can fly using jet-powered wings and met a blind man with sonar sense - the real Superman, the real Daredevil. And yet as cool as that sounds, gaining amazing abilities through technology or brain-training still feels like cheating to me. They're the closest we'll get to real powers, but they'll never match the stuff we see in comic books.

The secret to believable superhero comics isn't a realistic explanation for superpowers, it's making sure that everything else is as accurate as possible. That's true of any science fiction, including novels and films. That way, when your brain is faced with the unbelievable stuff, such as superpowers, it simply shrugs its logical lobes and suspends disbelief.

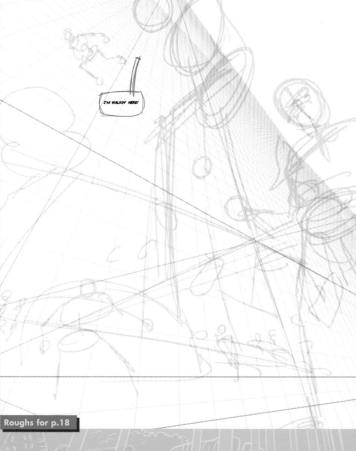

I'M WALKIN' HERE!

Roughs for p.18

Make a mistake in something that should be believable, however, and your mind gets yanked right out of the story. Whenever I watch a movie where infectious disease 'expert' Dr McEyecandy flouts the correct quarantine protocol by prematurely stripping-off their containment suit, my first thought is: Where did you get your PhD – the internet? Such bad science is the result of writers who don't check that a character understands their field of research (or even the basics of the scientific method). And that brings me to *Ordinary*.

When my friend Rob Williams emailed me to say he was writing a comic about a plague that gives everyone superpowers, asking if I'd do some science consulting, I couldn't reply fast enough. Rob knew I'd trained as an

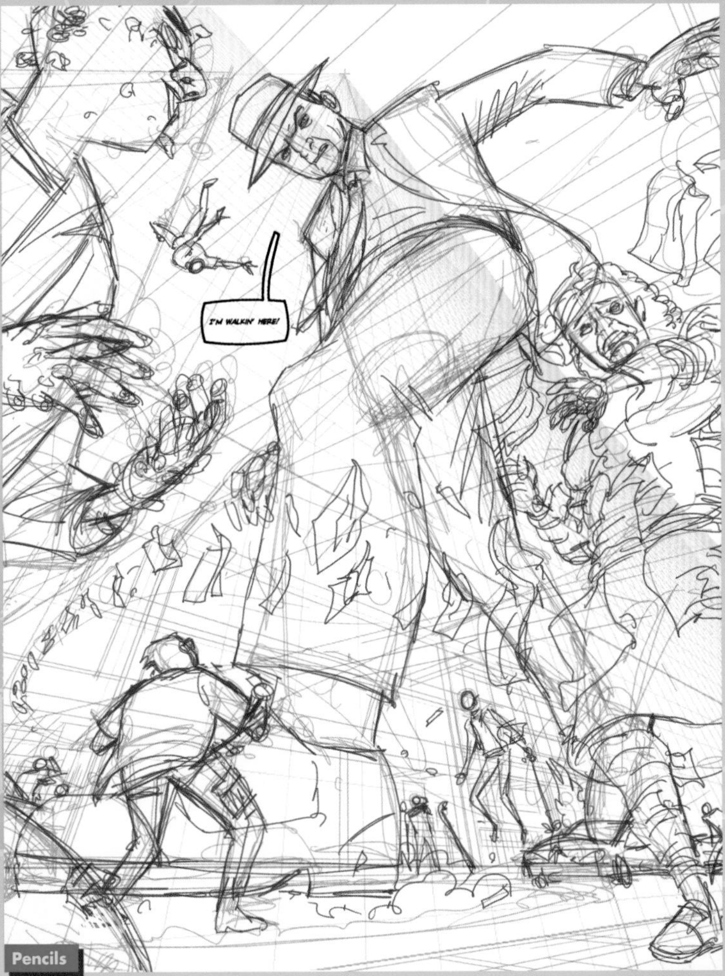
I'M WALKIN' HERE!
Pencils

evolutionary biologist and said that he wanted the science of *Ordinary* to be a "teeny, tiny bit credible".

In *Ordinary*, superpowers are a kind of contagious disease that reaches pandemic proportions almost overnight. To make that story credible, you need to ask the questions a scientist would ask, starting with: What is the infectious agent? In Rob's original script, the disease is caused by a bacterium. However, most bacteria spread slowly as they're dispersed by water or via mobile hosts like the rats that carried the Black Death. So I suggested viruses because they can occur in aerosol droplets, which is how the common cold is able to quickly pass from person to person through sneezing and even breathing.

How would a superpowers disease spread? The speed at which an infectious agent is transmitted through a population is its 'basic reproduction number' or R0, the number of people that an infected person should infect (on average) in a population of susceptible individuals. If R0 equals 1, the spread will be sustained - while someone's infectious, the agent will be transmitted

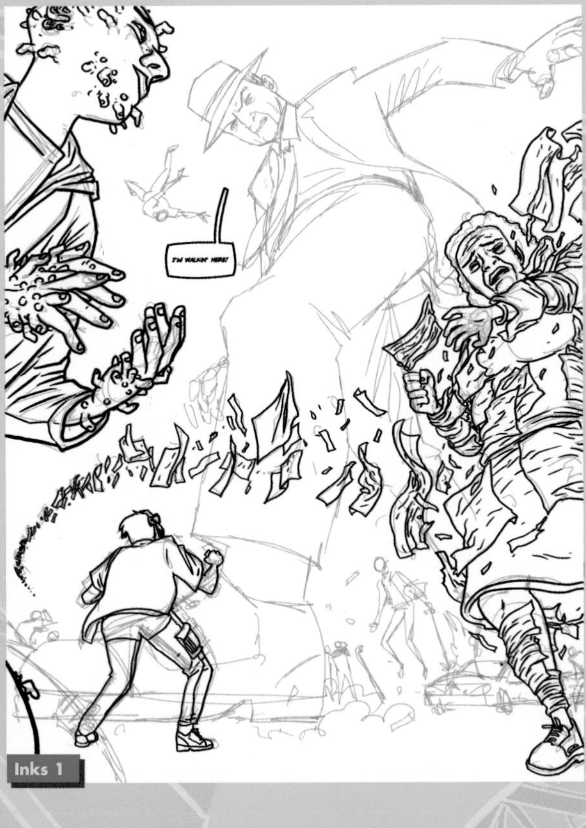
I'M WALKIN' HERE!
Inks 1

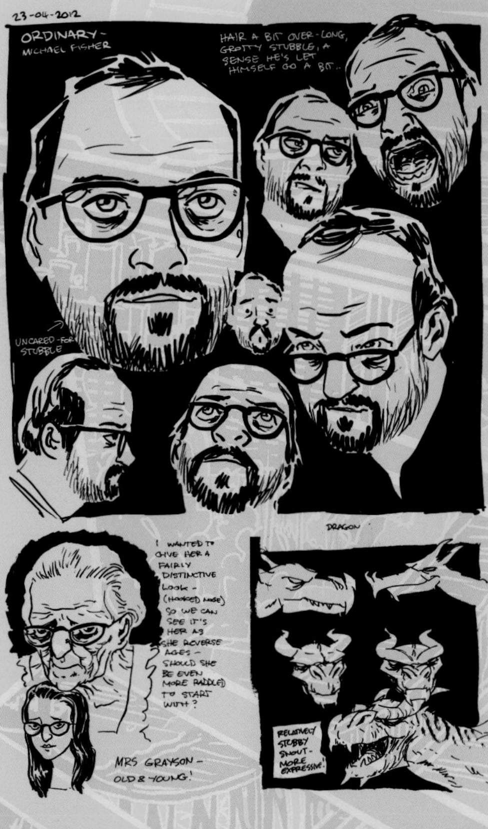
23-04-2012
ORDINARY - MICHAEL FISHER
HAIR A BIT OVER-LONG, GROTTY STUBBLE, A SENSE HE'S LET HIMSELF GO A BIT...
UNCARED-FOR STUBBLE
DRAGON
I WANTED TO GIVE HER A FAIRLY DISTINCTIVE LOOK - (HOOKED NOSE) SO WE CAN SEE IT'S HER AS SHE REVERSE AGES - SHOULD SHE BE EVEN MORE RADDLED TO START WITH?
MRS GRAYSON - OLD & YOUNG!
RELATIVELY STUBBY SNOUT - MORE EXPRESSIVE!

to one other person, and the disease will become endemic in the population. If R0 is less than 1, each person doesn't infect at least one other, and outbreaks will go extinct. Virtually everyone in *Ordinary* is infected by the superpowers virus, so its basic reproduction number must be more than 1.

When R0 is greater than 1, an infectious agent will continue to spread because every infected person creates multiple new cases. The outbreak becomes an epidemic. If a disease spreads further afield, it becomes a global pandemic. The deadliest pandemic in recorded history, the 1918 Spanish influenza, killed 50-100 million people even though the flu virus only had an R0 of 2. The ongoing AIDS pandemic caused by HIV has an R0 of 5 at most. Bacteria tend to replicate slower than viruses, so their R0 is generally low. About 3.3 billion people – half the world's population – is at risk from malaria, a blood parasite that probably has an R0 over 100 because it's carried by mosquitoes that bite multiple hosts.

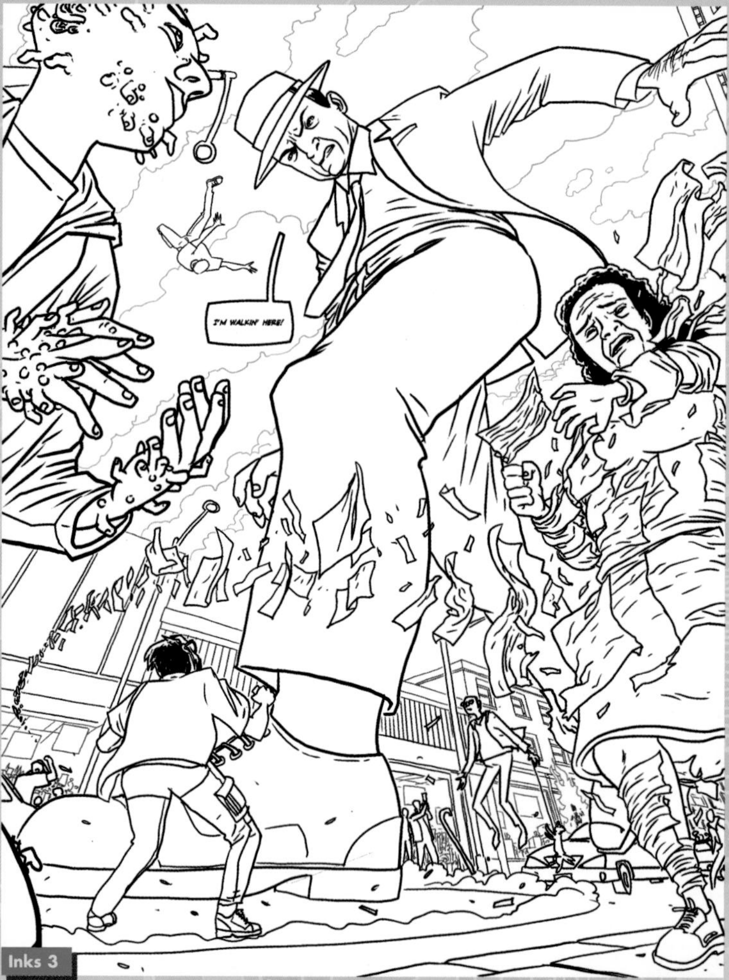
I'M WALKIN' HERE!
Inks 3

So what's the R0 of *Ordinary*'s superpowers virus? The simplest equation for calculating the basic reproduction number is '$R0 = C \times P \times D$'. C is for Contacts, the number of people that an infected person encounters; P is the Probability they'll transmit the disease; D is the Duration that they're infectious. The maths is pretty easy. D has a maximum value of 1 and the superpowers disease is permanent, so assuming that

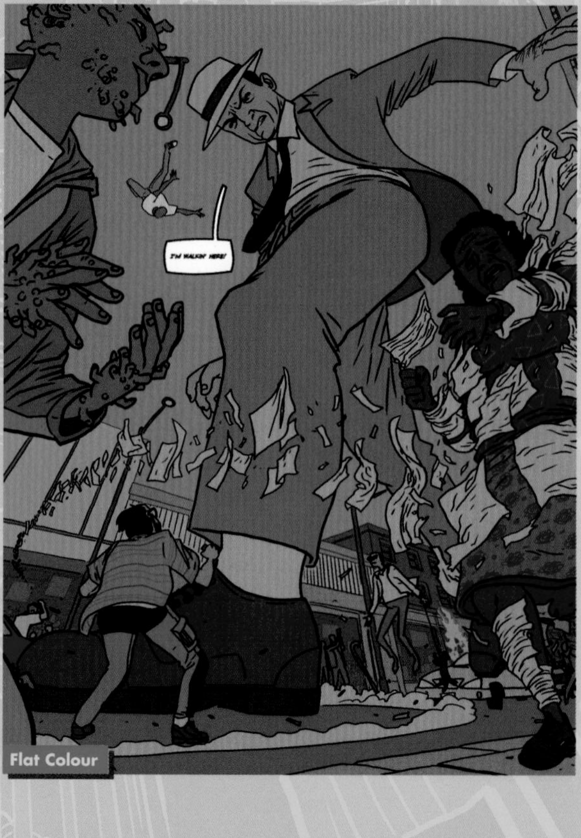
I'M WALKIN' HERE!
Flat Colour

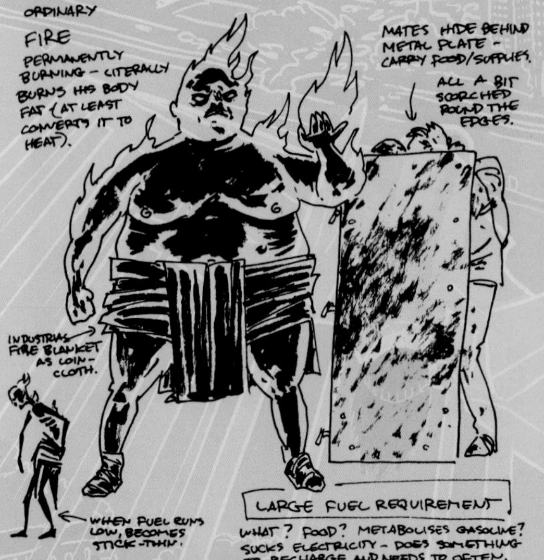
ORDINARY
FIRE
PERMANENTLY BURNING – LITERALLY BURNS HIS BODY FAT (AT LEAST CONVERTS IT TO HEAT).
MATES HIDE BEHIND METAL PLATE – CARRY FOOD/SUPPLIES.
ALL A BIT SCORCHED ROUND THE EDGES.
INDUSTRIAL FIRE BLANKET AS LOIN-CLOTH.
WHEN FUEL RUNS LOW, BECOMES STICK-THIN.
LARGE FUEL REQUIREMENT
WHAT? FOOD? METABOLISES GASOLINE? SUCKS ELECTRICITY – DOES SOMETHING TO RECHARGE AND NEEDS TO OFTEN.

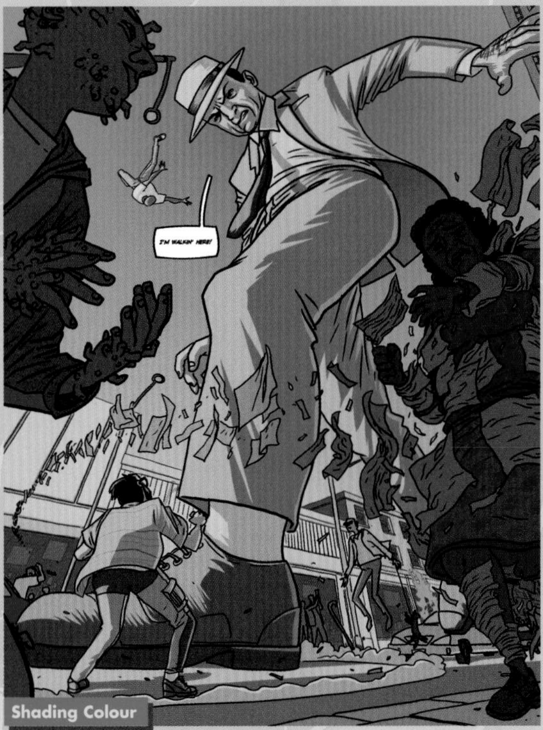
I'M WALKIN' HERE!

Shading Colour

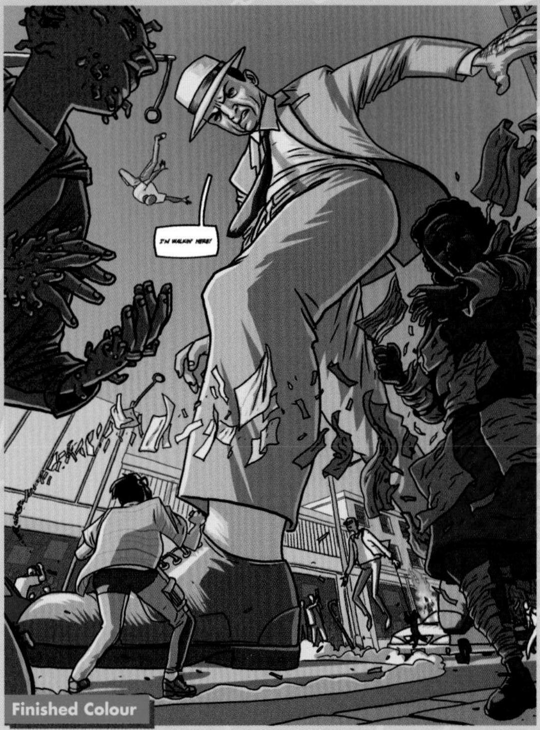
I'M WALKIN' HERE!

Finished Colour

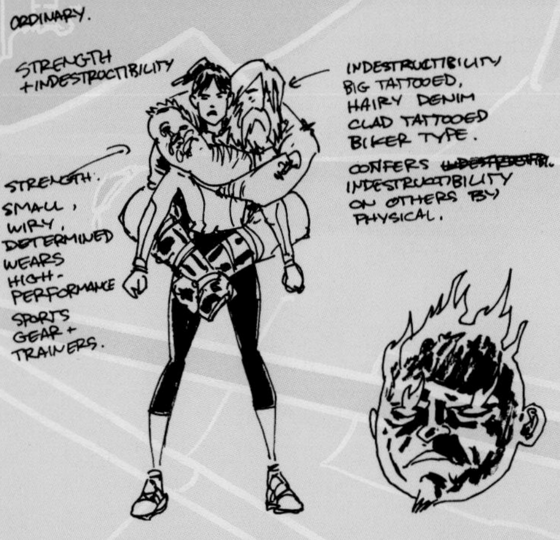
ORDINARY.
STRENGTH +INDESTRUCTIBILITY
INDESTRUCTIBILITY BIG TATTOOED, HAIRY DENIM CLAD TATTOOED BIKER TYPE.
CONFERS INDESTRUCTIBILITY ON OTHERS BY PHYSICAL.
STRENGTH.
SMALL, WIRY, DETERMINED WEARS HIGH-PERFORMANCE SPORTS GEAR + TRAINERS.

the infectious period lasts the duration of infection, D equals 1 (for any time period). P also has a maximum of 1, when 100% of individuals are susceptible, and *Ordinary*'s hero, Michael, is the only person immune to the virus. So P is 1 divided by the global population (7 billion), multiplied by everyone except Michael (7 billion minus 1). That's so close to 1 we can say P equals 1. C is the number of encounters. Most of us come into contact with tens of new people each day, hundreds in a month, thousands in a year. Overnight then, the R0 of a superpowers virus is 10 x 1 x 1 = 10. After a month, it's 100. Within a year, R0 would be well over 1000. And if the virus didn't need close contact, somehow surviving as an aerosol, that number would be even higher. *Ordinary*'s superpowers pandemic would be the most infectious disease in human history.

Obviously I didn't tell Rob about the 'basic reproduction number' or any other eye-glazing maths. Disease epidemiology is interesting enough for an essay on the science of *Ordinary*, but even 'R0 = C x P x D' is too technical for a few word balloons. Luckily, Rob had other questions, such as: If a scientist wanted to stop the superpowers plague, how would they distribute the cure? In the real world, injecting a medicine into the body via vaccination would be the only sure-fire way to eradicate that disease in every infected person. But for the sake of the story, Rob wanted the cure to be airborne. Would that work? Yes, I said, although carrying it on the wind and rain means it would be at the mercy of the elements, so cross your fingers that the cure would eventually reach everyone. Distributing an airborne cure might not be 100% effective, but it is plausible.

Comic-book science is a balance of fact and fiction, weighted by how adding believability improves the story. Fictional scientists should understand science, whereas superpowers don't need to be possible. In fact, I'd go as far as to say they *shouldn't* be possible. Because if superpowers were real, they would no longer be 'super' - they would just be ordinary.

JV Chamary is a writer with a real PhD in evolutionary biology

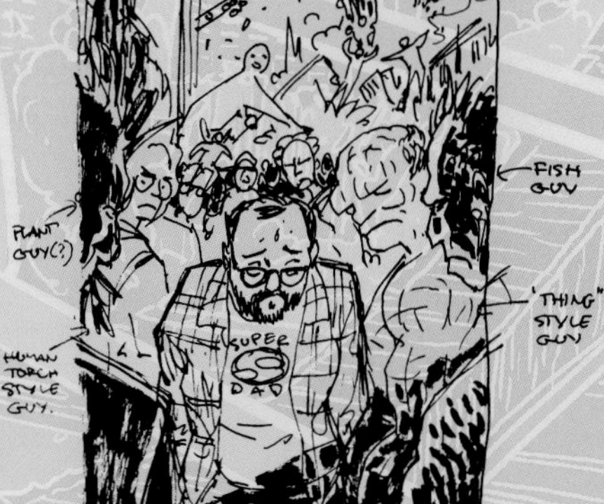
30-04-12.
FISH GUY
PLANT GUY(?)
'THING" STYLE GUY
SUPER DAD
HUMAN TORCH STYLE GUY.

BIOS

Rob Williams

Rob Williams' comic credits include *The Royals: Masters of War* for Vertigo Comics, *Ghost Rider* and *Daken: Dark Wolverine* for Marvel Comics; *Low Life* and *Judge Dredd* for *2000AD* and *Doctor Who* for Titan Comics. His *Ordinary* superpower would probably involve an ironic uncontrollable hair growth. His work can be found at **robwilliamscomics.co.uk**

D'Israeli

Under the pen name D'Israeli, Matt Brooker has been a comic artist since 1988. An early adopter of digital media, he has produced all his work on computer since 1999.

He is perhaps best known for his inking work on the groundbreaking *Sandman* series, and for his collaborations with writer Ian Edginton, including Titan's *Kingdom of the Wicked, The War of the Worlds, Scarlet Traces, Leviathan* and *Stickleback.*

Other career highlights include *Lazarus Churchyard* (with Warren Ellis), *Judge Dredd, Batman* and *Timulo* (for Deadline magazine). He is a regular contributor to the UK's *2000AD* comic.

When not globe-trotting, he lives in Nottingham, UK, and wishes he had a cat.

disraeli-demon.blogspot.com
disraeli-demon.tumblr.com

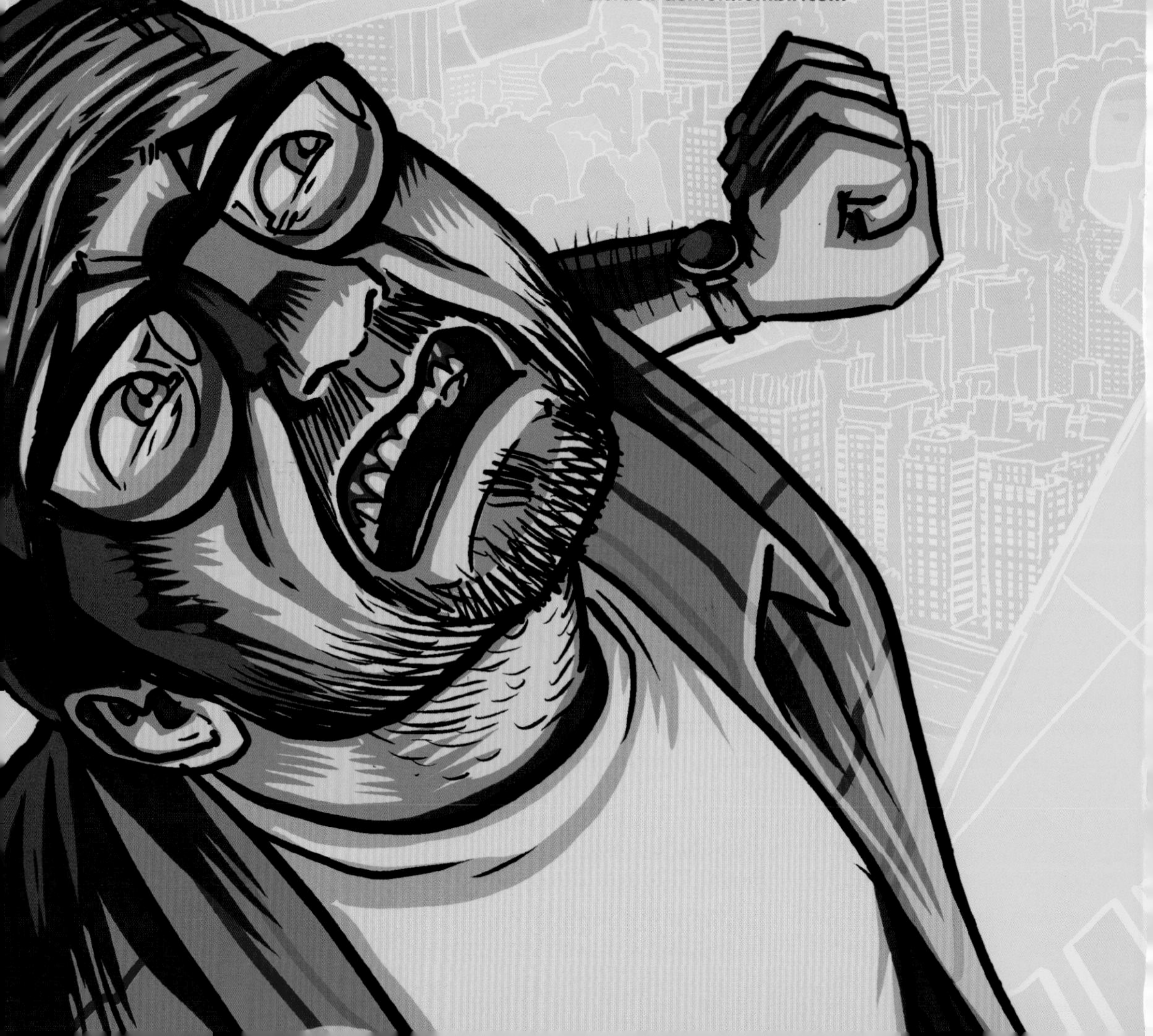